What does Thorvald Hansen say?

Selected articles and Post Scripts excerpted from Church and Life

THORVALD HANSEN

Compiled and edited by Sheri Muller

ACKNOWLEDGEMENTS

The publication of this volume has been made possible through the generosity of the Albert Ravenholt Trust.

Thank you to Thorvald and Johanne for assisting in the selection of materials for inclusion in this book.

A special thank you to Aleta Johansen, the author's niece, who assisted in the editing process, and Austin Bittner, a History student at Grand View University, who assisted with the compilation of this book.

Contents

Church and Life: A Brief History

Church and Life (originally, *Kirke og Folk*) was begun by the Danish Evangelical Lutheran Church in 1952 as an exclusively Danish publication in line with its original purpose which was to serve the Danish readership of the church. Until the 1930s the official church paper had been *Kirkelig Samler*, but when this had been replaced by the English language publication, *Lutheran Tidings*, the Danish readers were served by a page called *Kirkelig Samler* in the Danish language *Dannevirke*, a privately owned weekly which was unofficially related to the church. When this publication ceased in 1951, Danish news of the church was no longer available and this was missed, particularly by older readers. It was to fill this vacuum that the new Danish publication was begun.

The first issues were distributed gratis to some 750 individuals who might be interested, but within a short time it became a subscription paper with some 1,000 subscribers. It was a 16 page paper issued twice monthly. When the Lutheran Church in America was born in 1963 and *Lutheran Tidings* ceased publication, some of the readers of that paper became subscribers to *Church and Life*. Today it has become an exclusively English language publication of 12 to 16 pages (depending on the material available) and is issued monthly. The subscription price is $20 per year. Gifts and memorials make up the shortfall, and the paper continues to function in the black. For its content the paper depends upon the voluntary contributions of a significant number of writers. The December issue is at least twice the normal size for Christmas.

In 1983 the name was changed to *Church and Life*. This is not, nor was it intended to be, a translation of the Danish, but rather an indication that the church body out of which it grew was concerned also with this earthly life.

Throughout its long history the paper has had six full time editors: Holger Strandskov, Paul Wikman, Michael Mikkelsen, Johannes Knudsen, and Thorvald Hansen. The present editor, Joy Ibsen, is the daughter of a former pastor in the Danish Evangelical Lutheran Church.

Throughout its publication history, Thorvald Hansen has been one of *Church and Life's* most prolific contributors. He served as editor from 1982-2005 and has contributed approximately 250 articles over the years. This work is a compilation of some of Thorvald's favorite articles, along with a selection of his Post Scripts.

Thorvald Hansen: A Brief Biography

Thorvald Hansen was born on January 22, 1917 in Troy, New York to Peter T. and Jenny (Gary) Hansen. He married Johanne (Johansen) on June 19, 1948. They have three daughters. Thorvald and Johanne currently live in Des Moines, Iowa.

Thorvald attended Grand View College and Seminary from 1942-1946. He continued his undergraduate education at the University of Minnesota in 1947. He received his baccalaureate degree from Drake University in 1951. He then went on to earn a Master of Arts from the University of South Dakota.

He was ordained in Des Moines, Iowa in June 1946. He served parishes in Alden, Minnesota (1946-1950); Brayton and Exira, Iowa (1950-1953); Cozad, Nebraska (1954-1961); and Gayville and Viborg, South Dakota (1962-1965). After the completion of his Master of Arts degree, Thorvald returned to Grand View College where he taught Political Science from 1965-1973, served as Recorder from 1973-1978, and was the College Archivist from 1979-1987.

Thorvald began his authorial and editorial work while he was a student at Grand View. In the years since, he has written numerous articles for various publications, written and edited several books, and served as editor of *Church and Life* (1982-2005) and *Lutheran Tidings* (1960-1962). His works include: *An examination of the school prayer controversy* (1965); *We laid foundation here: the early history of Grand View College* (1972); *Reflections: the story of Luther Memorial, Des Moines* (1974); *School in the woods: the story of an immigrant seminary* (1977); translated *Pioneer days on the prairie* by K. C. Bodholdt (1980); *Story of the Danish immigrant* (1981); translated *Peaceful grove: sketches of pioneer days* by Frederikke Johansen (1982); *Danish immigrant archival listing: a guide to source materials related to the Danish immigrant in America to be found in repositories in the United States, Canada, and Denmark* (1988); *Church divided: Lutheranism among the Danish immigrants* (1992); *That all good seed strike root: a centennial history of Grand View College* (1996); and contributed the article "N.F.S. Grundtvig's view of education" to the *Grand View College Reader* (2006).

Articles

The Church and the Pioneers

Volume 29 number 5, March 1980

I have recently had the opportunity of reading, *The Diary of Elisabeth Keren*. She was the wife of an immigrant Norwegian pastor in Iowa in the 1850's. I have also given attention of late to the little book by the Danish immigrant pastor, K. C. Bodholdt, *På Prairien I Nybyggertiden* (*Pioneer Days on the Prairie*). These two books have many differences but they also have much in common. Through both of them one may gain a fuller picture of the pioneer pastor at work among his countrymen in the new world. One of the things that impressed this reader was the vast amount of traveling those men did in the interest of preaching the Gospel

The story of the Danish Church, with which I am most familiar, and especially the statistics of that body, to which I have ready access, tell the story more concretely. The figures for the year 1889, for example, are quite instructive. Chosen somewhat at random, they nevertheless represent a period during which the church was growing and had not yet been rent by schism. A seminary had been established, men were being added to the ministerial roll and congregations were being organized in many places.

There were eight districts in the church at that time but the district lines did not correspond to those of a later era. Thus, for example. District Seven included not only Nebraska but also parts of Kansas, southwest Iowa, and a congregation in Salt Lake City. In that district there were 10 pastors, 24 congregations, and an additional 20 preaching places. It was the largest district in the church, at least in terms of the number of pastors, congregations and preaching places. For the Danish Church as a whole the comparable figures were: 48 pastors, 100 congregations, and an additional 84 preaching places. It should be noted that these figures may not be exact because some few pastors failed to submit a report and also because it is not always possible to determine whether a particular location was a congregation or a preaching place. In any case, the relevant fact is that a small number of pastors sought to serve a large number of locations. Some congregations received no more than monthly service and some preaching places were served only occasionally but, however infrequent the services and the visits, it is obvious that the pioneer pastors did yeoman service.

To accomplish this a great deal of traveling was necessary. Pastor Koren, the Norwegian, was away from home a large part of the time. Pastor Bodholdt was typical of the Danish immigrant pastors trying to reach their countrymen. Bodholdt accepted the call from Kronborg and made his home there but he only served that congregation two Sundays of each month. His call provided that he was to travel to other places in Nebraska on the other

Sundays. Thus, he went to what is now Cozad, he organized the congregation at Looking Glass (Rosenborg), he preached at Wood River and Grand Island and, during a vacancy there, served the congregation at Nysted. He was usually away from home for several days at a time and, like Pastor Koren, he hardly traveled in style.

In a time when most journeys were made by rail, by lumber wagon or on horseback, countless hours were spent on the road in all kinds of weather. Mrs. Koren was constantly concerned about her husband's health. Bodholdt was so cold on most of his winter journeys that he almost always came home with a cold and would just recover from it in time to set out again. Not only did the transportation leave much to be desired but the funds with which to travel were very scarce. The pioneers had little or no cash, with the results that the collection taken at the services, which was generally the only salary for a visiting pastor, was not always large enough to cover the railroad fare to say nothing of meals and lodging enroute. Accordingly these latter were, if at all possible, avoided.

Nor were these the only problems. The wives of such pastors led lonely lives indeed. Mrs. Koren writes often of how she longed to see her husband return and of how quickly the time passed before he must leave again. Bodholdt's wife died at Kronborg the day before their first wedding anniversary but she left him with an infant son. Later he remarried. Therefore, he knew a constant concern for loved ones at home.

It might well be asked, "What was the use of it all, at least as far as the Danish Church is concerned?" The American Evangelical Lutheran Church went into the merger with only 76 congregations. What happened to all the others and to the great potential exhibited in the eighties? Did the church fail somewhere along the line by putting forth less than valiant efforts? The answer depends upon how one looks at it. If one thinks of the church in terms of constantly seeking to increase membership and the number of congregations, then surely the church failed.

Before one makes such a judgment, however, certain realities must be taken into account. The first of these is that both the pastors and those whom they served were Danish. With the best of intentions those pastors could not have preached in the English language in such a way as to gather the non-Danish-speaking people in a community. A second factor is that the Danish-speaking settlers needed a worship experience in the only tongue that they could really understand. A third important factor is the lack of manpower. Other factors enter in also. There was a lack of interest on the part of many Danes. Intermarriages account for much of the attrition. Bodholdt writes, for example, that though there were Danes in one community, the younger people, presumably through intermarriage, had gone over to Roman Catholicism while the older people were not much interested. Then, too, there were numerous Norwegian congregations as well as some English speaking Lutheran congregations. In one community in which Bodholdt preached, the few Danes there were persuaded to join an English language congregation. Finally, it must be recalled that among many, if not most, Lutherans, Grundtvigianism was suspect. That it split the Danish Church is well known but what may not be so well known is that a fundamental cause of that split was the attitude of other Lutheran groups toward the Danish Church. Certainly it would have been fine if the Danish Church could have grown and prospered. The fact that it did not, however, does not justify the conclusion that it failed. To come to such a conclusion is to ignore what was accomplished.

It is difficult for those of us who have grown up in this country to appreciate how important it was to the immigrants to receive spiritual nourishment in their own tongue. A fact that is so easily overlooked in a concern for the future is that the church served in a particular time and place. The record of the ministerial acts reported for 1889 give some insight into how well the immigrant church served. No less than 440 burials were conducted an average of nine per pastor. There were 399 marriages and 321 baptisms. It is true that these ministerial acts could have been performed by an available pastor. The danger is, however, that these would then have come to be viewed simply as official or professional acts and thus lacked the personal dimension expected of the church at such times.

Neither must the social dimension be minimized. The lonely immigrant, struggling on the prairie or isolated in the city, sought the church on Sundays to worship but also to meet those of a similar background and culture in order that his loneliness might be eased for a little while. One such immigrant, reporting the death of another said of him, "The years during which Pastor Bodholdt came to us. . .were the happiest times the old man experienced in America."

For an ordination in Greenville, Michigan, in 1875, Pastor Adam Dan wrote a hymn which came to be well known in the Danish Church. The title, in translation, is: "We Publish the Greatest of Tidings Abroad." This does not quite capture the sentiment expressed by the original, "Vi Rejse Omkring Med Det Dejligste Bud," which, literally, means we travel around with the most delightful news. This is exactly what those valiant pioneer pastors did and in so doing they filled a vital need in their time.

Did the immigrant church fail? Yes, perhaps, to the extent that it did not direct more attention and energy to the future in the hope of becoming a strong and viable organization. However, to have done so would have been to neglect the present and that would have been a greater failure.

D.S.U. - A Study in the Unique

Volume 30 number 18, November 1981

D.S.U. – Dansk Sammensluttet Ungdom – was, without question, unique. It was unique in structure, in activities, and in accomplishments. It played a significant role in shaping the lives of both individuals and communities. For at least two generations Danish young people's societies helped to bring joy and meaning into the lives of countless immigrants and their descendants. Many who read these lines may find old memories freshened and look back on an earlier day with nostalgia. More than that, however, there will be gratitude – gratitude for what D.S.U. was, and gratitude for having had the opportunity to be a part of it.

Prior to the turn of the century there was little organized youth work among the Danes and none within the Danish Church. The reasons for this are not far to seek. The immigrant church was, generally speaking, composed of younger people and the need for a separate youth group did not exist. As the average age of church members slowly rose, some thought was given to youth groups but many pastors were lukewarm to the idea while others were if not openly opposed, at least skeptical. Not only were they unfamiliar with auxiliaries directly connected to the church but their doubts as to the wisdom of such were strengthened by the fact that even some American churches had reservations. One American church paper is reported to have said, "All of these fashionable clubs are clubbing the church to death."

However, by the turn of the century things began to change. In more and more communities, organizations of young people existed. These local groups were referred to as young people's societies, and each group often took for itself a specific name. Thus, the group at Tyler, Minnesota, was called "Nordstjernen" (the North Star); that at Nysted, Nebraska, was known as "Prairierosen" (the Prairie Rose); and the one at San Francisco was called "Baunen" (the Beacon). Such organizations were often centered on gymnastics. Some were, or had been, rifle or target shooting clubs. Similar organizations, incidentally, are still very much a part of the social scene in Denmark.

As organizations they were not directly tied to the church but many of the members of such a group were active in the church and the local pastor was often a leader or speaker for the young people's society. Meetings were usually held twice each month either in a home or in a building owned by the society or the congregation. The meetings featured lectures on a wide variety of topics, gymnastics for both men and women, singing, round games, and other wholesome and enlightening activities. Visiting speakers were sponsored regularly and there is much evidence to indicate that pastors were often on the young people's "lecture circuit." From time to time a local group might present a dramatic production or sponsor a dance. Some pastors frowned on public dances but had no objection to the young people having one of their own.

The average age of such a group was well beyond that which is typical in today's youth group. Most of them had reached maturity and it would, therefore, be inaccurate to refer to them as youth groups. The society founded at Minneapolis in 1905, for example, adopted a rule providing that anyone over the age of fifteen might be a member but it set no upper limit. The only other statement about age was a requirement that the president of the organization be between twenty-five and forty, thus indicating a desire for mature leadership. Like most others this society was not an integral part of the congregation but the rules did provide that one board member must be a member of the congregation.

In 1902 the young people's society at Omaha invited six other societies in Nebraska and Iowa to send delegates to a meeting to discuss closer cooperation with the possibility of forming a regional fellowship. Five societies responded to this call for a meeting and sent delegates to Omaha. Here, on December 28, 1902, a common organization was formed consisting of the five local groups and providing for the addition of others. The common organization was to have the following purposes:

1. To promote cooperation among the various local groups,
2. To aid in the development of activities in the various local societies;
3. To hasten the formation of young people's societies in those Danish communities in which there were no such.

A digression is in order at this point to say a word about the chairman of that meeting, O. C. Olsen, an Omaha businessman. Olsen was some 32 years old at the time. He had long held an interest in both the church and young people's work. In 1898 he had written an article in *Kirkelig Samler* (Church Gatherer) the official church paper, in behalf of some kind of young people's work but he had not met any response. It was he, more than any other, who prompted the call for the meeting in 1902. It was natural that he should preside at the meeting. For many years Olsen remained active in young people's work. When the organization began a paper in 1907 it was he who was chosen as the first editor, a position which he held, without pay, for almost 20 years. O. C. Olsen was also active in church affairs, both locally and nationally. For a number of years he served on the national church board. It was he, also who wrote a little book called, *Early Days in our Church*, the first English language history of the Danish Church in America.

At an annual meeting in 1905 the name, "Dansk Sammensluttet Ungdom

– Mellemstaterne" was adopted. The translation of that name poses somewhat of a problem. Literally, one could translate it, "United Danish Youth in the Central States." However, "United Danish" carries with it the connotation of the United Danish Church, and in this instance that would be incorrect. "Youth" also gives a problem in that, generally, one thinks of teen-agers in connection with this word. Therefore, it is best to translate the name somewhat less literally, albeit correctly enough, by calling it the Danish Young People's League in the Central States. Later, as other regional leagues were organized, "in the Central States" was dropped and a district number being substituted. Before long the organization was known far and wide as DSU and it shall be referred to as such in what follows.

By 1915 there were seven districts in DSU but there was no structural link between them. That did not come until 1920 but even then it was on the district level that DSU found its greatest support. Travel to an event within the district was not the formidable undertaking a larger journey would be. Even within the larger districts seldom would any society be located more than a day's journey away. By 1921 there were a total of 53 local societies, located from the Atlantic to the Pacific coast and comprising seven districts. Though the bulk of the membership was in the Midwest the two coasts were well represented.

If DSU was unique in structure it was no less unique in activities. Each district had an annual meeting or convention to which the local societies sent delegates to participate in the business meetings. Many others also attended, however, and, as the years passed these annual meetings drew an even greater number of participants. Attendance was spurred by the fact that the railroads often gave group rates. So, too, did the fact that the host society provided lodging and breakfast in the homes without charge. A nominal registration fee permitted delegate and visitors to share in the meetings and in the common meal at noon and in the evening. If there was no suitable building for that purpose, a large tent often served as a dining area.

The programs on such occasions always featured lectures, usually by pastors and folk-school leaders. Discussion centered on current problems, singing, round games, folk dancing, perhaps a play or a dance, worship services, and a gymnastics exhibition were other common features. The gymnastics exhibition was by teams from one or more local societies. Both men and women were generally represented by teams. Gymnastics was an important part of the activity of almost all of the societies. In this connection it should be noted that it was through the financial efforts of DSU that the original gymnasium at Grand View College was replaced by an improved structure in 1910.

In addition to the annual meetings in the districts, great national gatherings were held from time to time. The first of these was held at Tyler,

Minnesota, in July of 1908 with the local young people acting as both sponsors and hosts. For this event the list of guest speakers reads like a "who's who" in the Danish Church. The meeting was open to all, whether members of DSU or not. Some 250 were registered in advance and at least 50 came without being registered. From the neighboring towns of Ruthton and Lake Benton another hundred participants came. A thousand persons are reported to have attended the events on Sunday.

The first such gathering held under the sponsorship of a national board met in Des Moines in 1921. A booklet printed for that occasion contained the program and other facts about DSU. One page contains some interesting statistics which were presented "...for consideration during an idle hour." These figures, representing the replies from 31 societies in the seven districts, gave a good insight into the state of DSU at that time. They show that slightly more than half of the local groups had a library with the average number of books being 158. Two thirds of the societies had gym halls and the necessary equipment for gymnastics. Of the 1461 members, 12 percent were graduates of public high schools, and 3 percent were college graduates. Some 28 percent had attended a Danish-American folk school, and 5 percent had been students at such a school in Denmark. Fourteen percent, or slightly over 200, had attended Grand View College. Finally, 41 percent of the members of DSU were also contributing members of the Danish Church.

DSU was also unique in its accomplishments. One of its most fruitful accomplishments, and one that served to bind the far-flung societies together was the establishing of a paper. As early as 1903 there had been discussion of such a paper and limited steps in that direction were taken shortly thereafter. The semimonthly, *Dagen* (The Day), which was published in Minneapolis, granted to DSU a small section in that magazine. Headed The League of Young People's Societies (Ungdomsforeningernes Forbund) the section, usually a page or two, was edited by Pastor H. C. Strandskov. It contained announcements, news items from the societies and some articles. It was entirely in the Danish language.

When *Dagen* was discontinued at the end of 1904, the columns of *Dannevirke* (Breastwork of the Danes) were used. However, this was not a regular feature, there was no separate heading, and there was no editor. The result was a kind of hit-and-miss arrangement which was entirely dependent upon editorial contributions. Renewed attempts to begin a young people's publication still did not meet with success. Finally, at the annual meeting of the First District, held in Omaha in 1906, it was decided to issue a paper twice each month. A committee was named to set the operation in motion.

After considerable delay the first issue of *Ungdom* (Young People) appeared on April 15, 1907. Subscribers paid one dollar per year for the eight page paper. That the paper was begun at all was largely due to the efforts of the previously named O. C. Olsen, who consented to be editor, and Pastor V. S. Jensen, who traveled widely in the interest of securing subscribers. He was able to secure 800 subscribers. By 1920, which may be considered a peak period for both the paper and the DSU, there were some 1800 subscribers. The number of pages had rather quickly risen to 16 and the subscription price had risen to $1.25. During the course of its 37 year history *Ungdom* had only three other editors, namely, Pastors C. A. Stub, Johannes Knudsen, and Harris Jespersen. The paper almost exclusively Danish for many years but by the 1930's English was the dominant language. By the time of the paper's demise at the end of 1944 it had become completely English.

Ungdom served as a link binding the various districts and local societies together. News items, announcements, reports of meetings, and itineraries of traveling speakers are but a few of the things that might be found regularly in its pages. Beyond this there were articles on a wide variety of subjects that were of interest to young and old alike. Such articles often issued in polemics but these were conducted on an intellectual level that indicated the maturity of both the writers and the readers.

Another of the unique fruits of the DSU was the establishment of young people's homes in some of the larger urban centers where Danes were located. Chicago, Des Moines, Omaha and Minneapolis were sites for such homes, though it must be added that the home in Omaha was rather short-lived. In these homes young people of both sexes might find a home away from home where they could gather or live among young people of a similar background. This meant that young people of Danish descent who found work in the cities might live in a familiar atmosphere at a reasonable cost. Those who did not actually live there, notably girls who found employment as domestics, would find such homes a pleasant gathering place on the days when they were free. For many years these homes served an excellent purpose. During the earlier period they were generally owned and operated by a young people's district but toward the end of the operation and sometimes even the actual ownership developed upon the local group. The last of these homes to function was that in Minneapolis which finally closed its doors in 1966. One of the most important and lasting contributions of DSU was the publication of *A World of Song* in 1941. This publication resulted from the need for an English language songbook for use at young people's meetings. The first edition of the book contained ten sections, each in itself a small songbook, gathered in a ring binder. Two more sections were added soon after. Though the book did contain many American songs, as well as songs from other lands, perhaps the bulk of its contents represented translations of Danish songs that had been used in the societies for many years. In 1958 the book was revised and a hard cover edition resulted. *A World of Song* has long been out of print but it has been and continues to be used widely both in Danish-American circles and other groups.

Meanwhile changes were taking place. After 1934 the name DSU gave way to the Danish American Young People's League indicating that by that time English had become the leading language. But there were other changes as well. Immigration could no longer be counted upon to swell the ranks and the average age of membership was declining. Further, American practices and customs were having an impact upon both the young people and the church. The result was agitation in both the church and the societies for closer ties.

This came about in 1946 when a large young people's convention meeting at Tyler, Minnesota, voted that the young people's league "...shall endeavor to serve as an integral part of the . . . . Church." This brought to an end a unique phase in the history of Danish young people's work in America.

A song written by the poet and author, Pastor Kristian Ostergaard, around the turn of the century for the young people's group at Ringsted, Iowa, expresses well the spirit of the Danish young people as they banded together in societies and in leagues of societies. In the translation by Pastor S. D. Rodholm, the first stanza of that song states:

> We march not as rebels to fight for our cause.
> With weapons that tyrants employ.
> We carry no eagle, we follow the cross,
> And our aim is to build, not destroy.
> We pledge all our skill, a palace to build.
> For beauty, for truth, and good will.

The Impact of Grundtvigianism on America, 1850-1875: Part 1

Volume 36 number 7, July 1987

Let me begin by saying that I have long been fascinated by the schism that took place within the Danish Evangelical Lutheran Church in America in 1894 and that I am interested in making a thorough study of the matter. Others have dealt with the schism but it has always been within the context of a larger subject. It is my intention to deal exclusively with the split and its theological and sociological origins. The study which I shall present today will deal only with the climate in which the split grew. What follows, therefore, represents a bird's eye view of anti-Grundtvigianism as it developed in this country long before it issued in the schism in 1894.

Prior to the mid-nineteenth century there were few Danes in America. The number of foreign born who listed Denmark as their country of origin was fewer than 2,000 in 1850. At that point a combination of push and pull factors operated to dramatically increase immigration to this country to the extent that by 1870 there were more than 30,000 Danes in America. By the end of the century there were more than 150,000. Among the push factors, or forces impelling them to leave their homeland, were the war with Prussia in 1864 and poor economic opportunities. Prominent among the pull factors, forces drawing them to America, were the Homestead Act of 1862, the hope for greater social and economic opportunity, and the persistent activity of travel and immigration agents. Despite the increase, however, the percentage of Danes in America never approached that of the Norwegians and the Swedes.

The settlement pattern of the early Danish immigrants was decidedly different from that of those who came later. They tended to be widely scattered and there were no Danish communities in the sense that we have come to know them. The characteristics of these early immigrants were also different. Quite a number were seamen who, for one reason or another, were attracted to put down roots in this country. Many others came from among the upper classes. Speaking of these early immigrants, Kristian Hvidt says, "In many instances they were the children of the more wealthy who had turned sour on Denmark and therefore, more or less of their own free will, emigrated to America."

Because the Danish immigrants were relatively few and because they were so scattered a specifically Danish church work was out of the question. Some of the more prominent Danes were members of the Episcopal Church. Others were attracted by the leading preachers of the day such as Henry Ward Beecher. Still others joined Baptist, Methodist, and other reformed congregations. Indeed, P. S. Vig writes: "It would perhaps be difficult to find any church body in America that did not have some Danes among its members." Vig added, "however...the vast majority of Danes who became immigrants to America before 1860 stood outside of any church relationship, even if we include the Mormons."

By the latter part of the 1860s changes were taking place. The Danes did not suddenly become interested in the church but their numbers did increase and some Danish settlements began to dot the American landscape. It was there that, in 1867, when he was appointed by the Iowa governor to represent the state at the World's Fair in Paris, the Danish-born pastor. C. L. Clausen went from there to Denmark. His purpose was to try to interest Danish churchmen in a mission in America. The upshot of his visit was the formation of a "Commission for the Propagation of the Gospel Among the Danes in North America." This Commission was organized by churchmen on the island of Funen in 1869. Things still moved slowly but by 1871 three men were sent to America to investigate conditions there.

Grove-Rasmussen's Findings

The majority of the members of the Commission were either avowed Grundtvigians or leaned in that direction. The Commission was not without Inner Mission representation, however. Indeed, one of the most influential members, and the one who maintained close contact with Clausen, had helped found the Inner Mission Society in Denmark in 1863. He continued as a member of the Inner Mission Board until 1874 at which time he resigned because he was not in agreement ".. . with the rest of the Board especially with respect to its relationship to the Grundtvigians." He favored a greater degree of cooperation.

If the majority of the Commission members were Grundtvigians, the men whom they sent to America were not. This is especially true of A.L.C. Grove-Rasmussen who, quite by chance, was chosen to head the group. This North Slesvig pastor had headed the Inner Mission in the area since 1867. His report was certainly sympathetic toward Grundtvigianism but he was definitely an Inner Mission man. The men who accompanied him were also, if not completely Inner Mission, at least strongly oriented in that direction. Andreas Sixtus Nielsen had been a lay preacher for Inner Mission in Jutland and, though he later broke with that movement, much of the early influence remained. Rasmus Andersen had been associated with the so-called "Godly Assemblies" on the island of Funen. Both later were ordained in America and remained in the service of the Danish Church for many years. Nielsen died at Withee, Wisconsin in 1909 and Andersen in New York City in 1930.

It is significant to note that while there was theological disagreement between the Inner Mission Society and the followers of Grundtvig in

Denmark, there was a mutual respect. The Grundtvigians were by no means considered to be heretics or even non-Lutherans. This continued to be true and even the long-time leader of the Inner Mission, Vilhelm Beck was later to deplore the fact that his statements were used against Grundtvigians in America.

Grove-Rasmussen traveled as far west as Grand Island, Nebraska and he had an opportunity to visit with many people regarding his mission. His observations are presented in a report which he wrote after his return to Denmark. He learned that there were decided differences among Lutherans in America and, in the words of one German pastor whom he met, there was among them "... a great itch to fight." His findings concerning Grundtvigianism are perhaps best summed up in this one sentence in which he states: "At times one could both laugh and cry concerning the Grundtvig-phobia that one could run up against there."

Numerous examples of this Grundtvig-phobia, or fear of Grundtvigians, are cited by Grove-Rasmussen. He tells of one pastor who said it would be painful to him if a Grundtvigian pastor should come. Upon being asked what was wrong with the Grundtvigians, the man replied that Grove-Rasmussen knew them better than he did. Of this Grove-Rasmussen wrote "Without question that was the truth because it was obvious that he knew about as much concerning Grundtvigians as residents of the moon." He concludes this portion of his report by saying:

On the whole, I believe it is desirable that the Danish pastors in America come to stand in a friendly but independent relationship to the various Lutheran Synods, and they keep themselves completely out of the burning controversies that are to be found among these.

Grove-Rasmussen noted that a Norwegian-Danish Conference had recently been formed among the Lutherans but he did not feel it would be advisable for pastors coming from Denmark to join that group. He pointed out that the first article in the doctrinal statement of the Conference declared the Bible to be the only source of Christian faith, life, and doctrine. Concerning this he writes, "Scarcely any pastor in the Danish Church would be able to subscribe to such a statement in all honesty due to the understanding that has arisen among us as to the relationship between the Word and the written scriptures." Then he goes on to say, "To get that article changed would be difficult precisely because the light which shines in our church glares in the eyes of many..."

This fifty-five page report, in addition to comments about the Grundtvigians, contains a number of other incisive observations but time will not permit discussion of these. Suffice it to say, therefore, that this report established the need for a church work among the Danes in the new world. Not only was Grove-Rasmussen's report followed in this respect but the pastors who began to work among their countrymen in America established an organization that was completely independent of the Norwegian-Danish Conference and all other Lutheran groups. In September of 1872 those pastors founded the Church Mission Society out of which the Danish Evangelical Lutheran Church was to grow. As Enok Mortensen has written:

> It is not without significance that the small group called itself a mission society, not a church; for even though they wished to do mission work among their compatriots in the new land, they were still bound with strong ties to the mother church of Denmark, of which they considered themselves to be an integral part.

They looked upon the State Church in Denmark as being not only the mother church but as embodying a spirit of freedom and roominess which they hoped to emulate in their mission among the immigrant Danes. The Society which they established soon became the Danish Lutheran Church in America and they did seek to maintain this freedom and roominess for over 20 years. But, in the end it could not be maintained and in 1894 the break came. The story of those 20 odd years is beyond the scope of this paper. It is enough to say that the seeds of schism which began to germinate during that period had been sown long before there was any organized church work among the Danish Lutherans in America. Therefore, I want to go back to about 1850 to establish the context in which the Church Mission Society was later to appear and to take a look at the source of the attitude that Grove-Rasmussen referred to as a Grundtvig-phobia. It will also be necessary to take a brief look at Grundtvigianism in Norway.

Grundtvigianism in Norway

Any definitive account of the schism in the Danish Lutheran Church in America must necessarily give attention to the reaction to Grundtvigianism in Norway. Indeed, it is not too much to say that the consequences of the Norwegian reaction were greater in America than in Norway. An established, state supported, church could take theological differences in stride. Among the immigrant pioneers it was another matter. I do not pretend this to be a thorough study of the Norwegian scene but a brief glimpse is important to an understanding of the American reaction.

For many years Grundtvig was looked upon with much favor in Norway. His Nordic studies and especially his attack on rationalism were widely and favorably recognized. Later, his so-called "matchless discovery" — the view that the authority of the Church derives from the baptismal covenant and that the scriptures must be understood in the light of the Apostle's Creed — found much support in Norway.

The foremost exponent of this view in Norway was Wilhelm Andreas

Wexels. Though he had numerous opportunities to advance, Wexels remained by choice an assistant pastor in Oslo where, for more than a generation he influenced Norwegian religious thought. He never worked out a theology, nor did any other Grundtvigian in Norway, but their views found much support, even on the Theological faculty at the University of Oslo. Grundtvigianism thus became a stimulus to religious life in Norway.

During the 1840s Wexels was appointed to a commission for the revision of the explanation to the catechism. That revision came to reflect Grundtvigianism, a fact which brought about a good deal of criticism. This may be said to mark the beginning of the end of Grundtvigianism in Norway. Much of the strength of the movement lay in the clergy and after 1850 that strength began to wane. One historian writes:

Despite the strength of Grundtvigianism in clerical circles about 1850 and a few years thereafter, it was doomed to final insignificance as a theological movement in Norway. It met defeat at the hands of Lutheran Confessionalism… Increasingly, especially after Wexels' death in 1866, it became identified with religious and political liberalism and exerted its influence chiefly in the educational and cultural realms.

The rise and fall of Grundtvigianism in Norway was clearly reflected among the Norwegian immigrants in America, where it was known, incidentally, as "Wexels teaching." It was ultimately to influence not only the Danish immigrants but the Danish Church.

Clausen, Grundtvigianism, and the Norwegians

The appearance of Grundtvigianism on the American religious scene antedates the establishment of the Danish Lutheran Church in America by at least a quarter of a century. It is well known that the first Lutheran pastor to work among the Norwegians in America was the Dane, Claus L. Clausen. What is perhaps not so well known is that he was greatly influenced by Grundtvig.

The detailed story of how Clausen became a leader among the Norwegians need not be retold here. It is enough to say that he went to Norway for his health one summer and while there made some contacts who urged him to go to America as a teacher and preacher among the Norwegian immigrants. To make a long story short, he and his wife arrived in Wisconsin in 1843. He was examined in theology by a German Lutheran pastor who then ordained him. The ordination took place in Evan Heg's hayloft sanctuary at Muskego, Wisconsin on October 8, 1843.

Though Clausen had a pietistic bend and was much influenced by what later came to be called Inner Mission, he was also greatly influenced by Grundtvig. During the spring of 1843 he had heard Grundtvig preach several times. Of this he writes: "It was food for the development of a true

Christian life, which in truth could be called healthful; unerring milk for newborn babes but also solid food for adults." This was hardly his first contact with Grundtvigianism. His diary gives ample evidence that he was well acquainted with Grundtvig's views. Rasmus Andersen, states flatly that: "Few Danish-American pastors knew as much about Grundtvig." Clausen was not alone in his admiration for Grundtvigianism. Some of the other pastors who came to America were also impressed by the churchly view even though they, in some respects, were champions of tradition. One such was J. W. C. Dietrichson, the first Norwegian in America to have been ordained by a bishop in Norway.

At that time there were a few scattered Norwegian preaching places but Dietrichson was a believer in organization and formality. He prepared a constitution for his group at Spring Valley, in eastern Wisconsin, which expressly referred to doctrine as revealed "…in God's holy word through our baptismal covenant as well as in the canonical books of the Old and New Testaments." This was an unmistakable Grundtvigian statement. An abortive attempt was made by the same Dietrichson to form a synodical organization in 1849. A similar, but more successful attempt was made in January of 1851. It was then that a constitution launching the Norwegian Lutheran Church in America was adopted. Only the second paragraph of that constitution need concern us here. That paragraph defined church doctrine as "… revealed through God's holy word in our baptismal covenant as well as in the canonical books of the Old and New Testaments." The constitution was adopted in January and the congregations were to act on it by May. They appear to have failed to do so. There is nothing to indicate opposition to the doctrinal basis of the new church but the laity were wary of what they considered elements of clericalism in the constitution. Meanwhile, Clausen served as superintendent of the Church. In effect, he was Bishop but without the title.

As already noted, the theological climate was beginning to change in Norway and three new pastors who arrived in 1851 had been under the tutelage of professors whose teachings were shaped by Lutheran confessionalism. At least one of the three who came was determined to eliminate the Grundtvigian influence in America. This result was that at the very next convention, in February of 1852 the offending phrase "in our baptismal covenant" was eliminated. All but Clausen voted for this elimination. Then Clausen, who wanted to step down anyway, was replaced by one of the new men who was given the title of president.

The point of all this is that the Norwegian Lutheran Church in America came within a hair's breadth of embracing Grundtvigianism as its doctrinal basis. The action in 1852, however, meant a definite rejection of Grundtvig and the acceptance of a more orthodox stance. And, during the next twenty years, opposition to Grundtvig grew to such an extent that in 1871 Grove-Rasmussen could speak of a Grundtvig-phobia in America.

The Impact of Grundtvigianism on America, 1850-1875: Part 2

Volume 36 number 8, August 1987

The Theological Climate in America

It does not appear that there were any further overt conflicts regarding Grundtvigianism among the Scandinavian immigrants until the establishment of the Church Mission Society by the Danes in 1872. Clausen had, in the view of some, seen the error of his ways and there were few Danish pastors and no Danish organization. However, the theological climate that existed was definitely anti-Grundtvigian. This is seen in two letters, both written by laymen.

In reply to a widely published request by C. L. Clausen for information about Danish settlements, F. L. Mathiesen, of Milwaukee, wrote expressing a desire for the services of a Danish pastor. Then he added:

> I am, as you will probably have discovered from the foregoing, a Grundtvigian, and though for my own sake I could wish that pastors of the Grundtvigian persuasion would come, I can nevertheless see that they would have many special difficulties to fight against. This is partly because so few of the Danes here have had their eyes and their hearts opened to the magnificence of that view, but it is primarily because the already organized Scandinavian synods are so definitely anti-Grundtvigian. Despite the fact that they are mutually antagonistic they would certainly be united in condemning the Grundtvigian pastors as heretics and would place all possible obstacles in their way and that, considering the conditions here, they could most emphatically do.

Clausen comments on this by saying that he knows the Grundtvigian pastors are among the most competent, zealous, and gifted in Denmark, but he goes on to say, "'I do believe that, all things considered, they will do better to remain in Denmark than to come here."

Another layman, who identifies himself as J. C. Paulsen, of Luck, Wisconsin wrote to Adam Dan in 1873, when Dan was already coming under the fire of the Norwegians. He wrote that he had observed the strife among the Norwegian pastors for nine years. Significantly, he added: "I had a suspicion that it would be a bitter struggle when the friends of the 'churchly view' (i.e. Grundtvigians) stepped forth openly . . .amid the many confused voices with their great scriptural principle, crying to high heaven regarding their monopoly on Lutheranism."

It was into this already charged atmosphere that the Danish pastors came and the sparks began to fly soon after their arrival. It was those sparks which eventually touched off the conflagration in the Danish Church.

The Conference and Muller-Eggen

The Norwegians and the Danes had been associated with the Swedes in the Illinois based Scandinavian Augustana Synod. In 1870 an amicable separation from the Swedes took place. The Norwegians, however, could not agree among themselves and, as a result, two groups were formed. One, which became known as the Norwegian Augustana Synod, need not concern us here. The other, the Norwegian-Danish Conference, came to figure prominently in Danish immigrant Lutheranism. The Danish Evangelical Lutheran Church Society, or the Blair group, was founded by Danes who amicably withdrew from the Conference in 1884. When the Conference was founded, C. L. Clausen was named president and J. Muller-Eggen was elected secretary. Within a short time the latter was to be in the forefront of opposition to those whom he considered to be Grundtvigians.

Johannes Muller-Eggen was born in Norway in 1841 and came to America in 1866. He attended the Augustana Seminary, which was then located at Paxton, Illinois, for one year following which he became pastor of the Scandinavian congregation at Racine. The Conference, including Muller-Eggen, appears to have been on a friendly terms with the Danes who arrived in 1871. It was Clausen who ordained A.S. Nielsen and, due to a quirk of fate, Muller-Eggen who ordained Adam Dan to succeed him at Racine.

The friendly relationship was soon broken, however. The Conference, and particularly Muller-Eggen, began to feel that the Danish newcomers did not measure up to Lutheran standards. He says that he examined Adam Dan on his theology before he ordained him and, while he was not completely satisfied, he saw no reason to deny him ordination. Nevertheless, for one reason or another, Muller-Eggen began to feel he had been deceived by Dan and others. Thus, within months Muller-Eggen became the spearhead of a movement to make things difficult for the Church Mission Society, organized by the Danes in 1872.

The formation of this body, which became the forerunner of the Danish Church, may have been one reason for the opposition. Certainly the motive for the formation of that group would hardly have pleased the pastors of the Conference. You will recall that Grove-Rasmussen, in this report, advised the Danes to be friendly toward but independent of all other groups, and he specifically named the Conference. His point was that no Danish pastor could in good conscience subscribe to a doctrinal statement which proclaimed the Bible to be the only source of faith, life, and teaching. In any event, Muller-Eggen became a determined opponent of the Danish pastors, all of whom he tarred with the brush of Grundtvigianism. That only one of them could, by any stretch of the imagination, be called a Grundtvigian did not seem to matter. Anyone who could not accept the Bible as the only source of faith and life was considered to be a Grundtvigian and, therefore, nothing less than a heretic.

In a letter to Rasmus Andersen, whom he had also come to feel was a Grundtvigian, Muller-Eggen wrote: "Alas, that I should be deceived time and again by the hypocrisy and the dissimulations of the Danes." In a later letter, written in reply to Andersen's suggestion that they could still work together for a common purpose, he pointed out that in view of the theological position taken by Andersen, this was impossible. Never one to mince words, he wrote, "When you speak of working together Andersen, I regret that you could ever dream of such a thing..."

It was against Adam Dan that Muller-Eggen took the most direct action. Shortly after Dan succeeded him at Racine four members of that parish declared Dan to be a heretic and instituted court proceedings to obtain the property. They were led in that fight by Muller-Eggen. In connection with this matter the Conference appealed to the professors at Concordia Seminary in St. Louis for an opinion on Dan's Lutheranism. This is somewhat ironic because the Conference had little use for the Missouri Synod — though the Norwegian Synod had a good deal in common with Missouri. The five Missouri professors, including C. F. W. Walther responded at great length to seven questions posed by an attorney in behalf of the plaintiffs. The burden of their response was that Adam Dan was unLutheran and a heretic. Their reply concluded with these words: "May such gross heresy and apostasy from our pure Lutheran doctrine never attain circulation among our Scandinavian brothers, but by all lawful and scriptural means be driven out and exterminated."

The case was finally decided on December 12, 1874. "Adam Dan was found guilty of preaching false doctrine but the party adhering to him being in the majority, the court gave them the property and the original name of the congregation."

This was not Muller-Eggen's only attempt to interfere with the Danish mission. In October of 1873 he visited the Danish pastor, J. A. Hieberg, in Chicago. He offered Hieberg the supervision of the Danish congregations in the Conference on the condition that he first be examined and approved by the Conference as a true believer. Hieberg declined, saying that he was too busy serving his own parish and then added: "It makes no difference to me whether you or your group approves of me as a true Lutheran believer because I have been examined, recognized, and sent out as such by our mother church in Denmark."

By that time Muller-Eggen had moved to Ludington, Michigan. While there he sought to get a number of Norwegians in nearby Manistee to join the congregation there in order that they might gain control of it. That effort apparently came to naught. He also wrote to leaders in the Church of Denmark seeking to show that Grundtvigianism was not a part of the doctrine of that church. Their replies supported his stand. However, what he either failed to understand or neglected to say was that while Grundtvig's views were not a part of the official church doctrine, they were held by many pastors and bishops in the Church of Denmark. He also sought to enlist the aid of Vilhelm Beck, the Inner Mission leader in Denmark. Beck advised that the Conference should retain control of the Danish congregations for a variety of reasons, among them being the fact that the new men were young and inexperienced. This reply by Beck led to the use of his support by Conference pastors in their strife against the Danes. When this came to Beck's attention he deplored the fact and wrote at once clarifying his position. He made it very plain that while he could not accept the views of the Grundtvigians he certainly would not condemn them. He wrote that it was not possible to condemn another group without "... falling into the error of the papacy which declares itself the one perfect church and proclaims other churches to be heretics."

Muller-Eggen then, emerges as the leading opponent of the Danish pastors who sought to work among their countrymen. One cannot but admire his zeal and tenacity. His actions really are not strange for one who was convinced of the heresy of Grundtvigianism which he conceived to be, as he once wrote, "... the most dangerous and soul-corrupting of all of the false teachings in the Christian Church."

This was not a personal vendetta on the part of Muller-Eggen. With the possible exception of Clausen, the Conference was squarely behind him. Those who had predicted difficulties for the Danish pastors, and particularly for the Grundtvigians, had not exaggerated. Norwegian pastors in numerous communities placed whatever barriers they could in the way of the Danes. Even from as far off as Perth Amboy, New Jersey the newly ordained Danish pastor Soholm could write in 1873 that he had to put up with a great deal from a pastor of the Norwegian Synod.

Sociological Factors

I have developed at some length the basic theological problem that was peculiar to the Scandinavian Lutheran churches in America. I t would, however, be a mistake to conclude that the split of 1894 grew primarily out of theological differences. There were other differences; differences that I would characterize as sociological and that I would contend were more basic. While I have no question but that the theological differences were sincerely held, I would maintain that they were unwitting rationalizations growing out of a particular sociological environment.

I expect to be able to develop this view more fully in the future. For the present it will have to suffice to briefly state some of the social problems that obtained among the immigrant churches during the nineteenth century.

The first is what the eminent immigration historian, Marcus Lee Hansen, has called, "'spontaneous immigrant Puritanism." Even Grove-Rasmussen, during the brief time he spent in America, noted that Americans tended to go to extremes, and not least in matters of religion. American churches, therefore, tended to judge immigrant churches on a puritanical basis. Further, because American churches were proselytizing among the immigrants, the latter were forced to adopt the standards which prevailed. Numerous examples could be cited but one will suffice to make this clear.

An immigrant church in a particular community was seen as being too lax in the matter of discipline. Very soon the pastor seized upon an opportunity to bodily remove an unrepentant drunkard from the worship service. The pastor was found guilty of assault and battery but, and this is the important thing, never again was the Lutheran church in that community looked upon as lax. "Thus," to quote Marcus Lee Hansen, "the immigrant church was started on a career of puritanism, which had absolutely no connection with the saints at Boston. . ."

Another problem, especially acute in the immigrant church, was that of leaders who felt their authority threatened by changes and developments, both internal and external. Of this one writer has said: "It was the peculiar plight of the immigrant church to possess a threatened leadership, which lay at the heart of the pervasive church turmoil. Threatened leaders labored feverishly to centralize authority, revitalize faith, and maintain the loyalty of their flocks. . ."

Finally, differences within and among the immigrant churches were very common. The Danish case was by no means an exception. By 1875, for example, there were five different Norwegian church bodies. John Bodnar, writing in 1985, has said: "No institution in immigrant America has exhibited more discord and division than the church."

Conclusion

One could go into much detail in showing the impact of Grundtvigianism upon religion in America. Incidentally, as I worked with this subject I came to the conclusion that a more precise title for these remarks would have been "The Impact of America on Grundtvigianism." At any rate, there can be little question but that what happened during the early period had a profound bearing upon the life of the Danish Church. That, however, is another and a longer story. It is enough to say that the early problems continued and that they were later compounded by internal dissensions. The result was that a schism was inevitable the only real question was when it would occur.

That schism, deplorable as it was, did nevertheless have some positive benefits. It brought to the resulting bodies an internal harmony that made is possible for them to give a greater degree of attention to propagating the Gospel among their countrymen. And that, after all, was their avowed purpose.

Six Years in a Woolen Mill

Volume 46 number 2, February 1997

In 1935 we were, some two years into the New Deal. The great depression was by no means over. Poverty, compounded by the passage of the years since 1929, was very real. Jobs were, to say the very least, scarce. It was in such an environment that I graduated from high school on June 25, 1935.

The summer of 1935 passed uneventfully. It was passed between looking for work and trips to the swimming pool. Here we were, a group of able and reasonably well educated young men, for whom society had no use. Then, suddenly, out of the blue, came a job opportunity. I seized upon it at once without even inquiring as to its nature or the financial reward. It came about because my stepmother worked as a winder in a woolen mill. She learned of a vacancy. By the next day, I was on the job.

It wasn't much of a job, but I was glad to get it and stuck with it for some six years. It was the Aetna Mill, of Wright's Health Underwear Company, an old established knitting mill in Troy. The principal product was long underwear which, at that time, most men wore during the colder months. I was to work in the "winding room" as a "bobbin boy." In that particular room 12 to 15 women, depending upon the season and economic conditions, were employed to operate machines which wound yarn from small bobbins, as they came from spinning machines, onto large bobbins to be used in the knitting department. As one small bobbin was emptied a new one would be added and the loose end on it would be attached to the loose end on the larger bobbin with a square knot, or flat knot, as they called it. Each machine could wind 20 bobbins at the same time. It was my job to keep the women supplied with yarn as it came down on the elevator from the spinning room. From time to time, I also had to bag the woolen waste, move, open and empty cases of yarn not spun locally, and sweep the floor every day. Actually, it was not so demanding a job as it may seem. I always found ample time to visit with the knitters and to eat my lunch on company time. All the men did that and no one cared as long as the work continued. Knitting, by the way, is one of those jobs where if you are not busy it means the machines are running well and the work is going forward. But, busy times can come often, and in a twinkling of an eye. Eating lunch before noon meant we had the whole noon hour to smoke, either out of doors or in the front hallway, and "shoot the breeze." Incidentally, while I was never in the army, I doubt that any veteran can teach me any new earthy expressions that I have not already heard during my six years in the mill. The men there, for the most part, were veterans from the first world war.

The women who worked in the winding department were paid on a piece work basis. The yarn which they wound was weighed and they were paid by the pound. This meant that there were no idle moments for the women. It was up to the "bobbin boy" to see to it that they were always provided with the yarn and the bobbins they needed. They would hardly be happy should they be forced to lose a minute because of his failure. Fortunately, I always got along well enough with them. Unfortunately, they did not always get along with each other. Though they all spoke civilly to one another other, there was no love lost between them and, at times, one felt they almost hated each other. Ever since then, I have been opposed to the piece work method of employment. I know very well that from the employers viewpoint it is efficient and, in some respects it is a quite equitable method of reward, but what it does to the human spirit is another matter. Those women were jealous of one another. The amount of yarn they could wind would vary with its quality. If one got a better quality yarn than another, jealousies could easily erupt into words. The foreman, among other things, had to try to keep peace.

Troy, in upstate New York, is only some 175 miles from the province of Quebec in Canada. A large number of the workers in the mill were therefore, French Canadians, and lived across the river in the city of Cohoes. I had studied some French in high school, but quickly learned that there was not much similarity between their French and mine.

After I had been employed there for some three years, the foreman in that department, who was already a quite old man, quit. He had a dispute with the management regarding an efficiency expert who had been hired. The dispute also marked the end of the efficiency experts employment. The mill was a non-union shop, but complaints did have an effect. I later learned that at that time promoting me to the foreman's position was under consideration. However, for a number of reasons, including my youth and the fact that both my stepmother and aunt were employed there, I was not given the job. How fortunate I was! If I had advanced to a better paying job, I might not have gotten out of there until it was too late. The company did go out of business in the 1950's and the mill has since burned down.

The new foreman, or boss, was a younger man, a French Canadian, who had previously been a part of the millwright crew. The millwright crew, which consisted of a man and his three sons, was responsible for operating the boiler, keeping the building in repair, installing new machines, and similar things. We generally referred to the millwright crew as the "wrecking crew." I recall my new boss, whose breath was always heavy with the smell of garlic, telling me one day that he had not gone to high school and yet he had a better job than me. It did not occur to him that I had something that could not be taken from me by the vagaries of time.

I mentioned as one of the tasks of the millwrights the installation of new machinery. Only one time in those six years did a new machine come to our department. This was a more modern winding machine and I recall that the floors had to be reinforced to carry it. Most of the machines in the Aetna Mill were old — if not ancient. Aside from the sewing machines used in other parts of the building, I can think of no machines that did not date prior to the turn of the century.

Visiting in the knitting room in odd moments was not entirely a waste of time. This gave an opportunity to become familiar with the knitting machines and to learn how to operate them. This paid off in 1937. A short lived boom in the economy that year, largely due to the fact that Congress had voted a bonus for the soldiers of the first world war, meant increased activity at the mill. So it was that, for a few months, I was employed as a knitter. The cloth that was knitted was cut and sewn into long underwear.

There were three kinds of knitting machines in the mill. There were Tompkins machines which had only one set of needles. There were a few latch needle machines, which had two cylinders, or sets of needles, with knitted cloth coming out at the bottom. Cooper frames, which were the most numerous, had two cylinders of needles, with the knitted cloth coming out the top. In each case the movement of the machines was circular and the finished cloth was tubular until it was cut and sewed into garments. The different kinds of machines had differing purposes. My work was with the Cooper frames.

A knitter had to operate five knitting frames. It was his job to keep them supplied with yarn, replace broken needles, put the cloth back on the needles when it came off, as it did when the yarn broke or ran out. The machines were supposed to stop when a needle was broken, but this was not always the case. Sometimes the operator would neglect to activate the "stop motion" and, if he did not pay attention could soon find himself knitting "rags" — cloth with too many holes in it to be useful.

The knitting experience was good while it lasted. I have always liked machinery and enjoyed that kind of work. Perhaps more important, the pay was much better. There I earned $25 per week as opposed to $15 as "bobbin boy." However, the prosperity was temporary and by fall I was once again a "bobbin boy."

I look upon my six years in the mill as an important part of my education. I had some first-hand contact with the industrial world, I came in close contact with factory workers and I became acquainted with persons who were completely different from those I was to encounter later. Some I remember because of humorous incidents, some because of their endless stories, and others because of what I would call their homespun philosophy.

I remember one older man in particular who fell into the latter category.

He was probably no more formally educated than the others, but he was more widely read and was not much given to small talk. I used to enjoy talking with him and can still recall some of his sage comments. When, for instance, I would mention my friends he would look at me, raise an eyebrow and ask, "Friends, or acquaintances?" Or, if my ego was showing he would say, "Step back, take a good look at yourself, and laugh."

I recall another man who was given to weekend bouts with the bottle. From the time we got paid on Friday noon until, on many occasions, Tuesday morning, he would be absent. This occurred on a regular basis. Why was he not fired? My guess is that it was because he was the only person who could operate old machines that did a particular kind of knitting for the collars and cuffs of the underwear.

Then there was Joe, the French Canadian. Joe was illiterate, but he knew how to make an extra dollar. If Joe had the slightest intimation that someone was in the market for a car or an appliance he would tip off the appropriate salesman and get a reward for his information. Another French Canadian, Barney, used to bring a hard boiled egg for his lunch every day and when he was ready to eat, crack it against his bald head. One day some practical joker substituted a raw egg and you can imagine the results.

Smoking was not permitted. It would have been dangerous in an atmosphere that was filled with dust from the wool and cotton yarn. Presumably because of the dust, most of the men chewed tobacco. I tried it once and that was enough of that. Spittoons were not provided so, over the years, piles of tobacco juice gradually built up in every convenient corner. In some places I recall corners were painted white but this did not always deter a man with a mouthful. In this connection I recall one man who liked to talk, but was one of those persons who wanted to look you right in the eye at close range when he talked. He was a chewer and when he talked there was generally a spray. I soon learned to avoid talking with him unless there could be some obstacle between us.

I was fortunate to have a job during those years, but the work was routine and boring. My experience certainly has helped me to understand the factory worker who gets tired of doing the same thing day after day and who has no hope of improving the situation. Work in the mill convinced me that this was the sort of thing I did not want to do.

Note from the author: The previous is taken from Footprints, a small volume written largely for the benefit of my family.

I Remember When: Part 1

Volume 51 number 6, June 2002

Unlike many of the readers of these pages who grew up in small towns or rural areas and who lived their formative years working and playing amid other Danes, I grew up in the city, where except for a few, the Danish language was unknown. Because my mother had died in the great flu epidemic of 1918 I was raised largely by my grandmother. She had been an immigrant and her first language was Danish. She could speak English, but not too well and she preferred Danish. The result was that until she died at 82 and I was almost 18, our common language was Danish.

It was quite another matter on the street and in the schoolyard. Some of my playmates were of Danish background and had picked up a word or two of Danish, but could neither speak nor understand it. A favorite saying was, "Gaa hjem til din mor of spise pandkager." (Go home to your mother and eat pancakes.) That was about the extent of what could be called "street Danish." Where the expression came from and why and how it was used eludes me. In any case, I lived in two worlds, so to speak, the world of Danish at home and the world of English in the school and on the street.

My Danish world was supplemented by Danish in the Sunday School and church. Our church conducted a "Lørdagskole" (Saturday School) and my grandmother saw to it that I attended regularly. I was hardly happy about that since it was a day off from the Public School and my playmates would not be there. The thing I remember most about that school is the endless copying in longhand of Balslev's Bible History. Though we did do other things, copying is the thing I recall most from Vacation School. Rehearsing for a Danish play is also something I recall from Vacation School. In retrospect I can look upon those schools as a good thing, but at the time I cannot say that I enjoyed them. To further lessen my enjoyment was the fact that the Public School did not close for the summer until late June and opened again the day after Labor Day.

The fact that the church schools were conducted only for a half-day did compensate to some extent for what seemed to be lost hours.

Incidentally, though I had seen his name beneath many a song and hymn in our books, I knew nothing and heard nothing about N.F.S. Grundtvig until I came to Grand View College.

There are other memories of an entirely different nature that growing up in the eastern city of Troy, New York that seem to be unlike anything I have met since.

Riding the bus downtown which I often did, first with my grandmother and then after I was about ten years old on various errands, was always an interesting experience. Enroute downtown the bus passed by several Roman Catholic Churches and all the men and boys of that faith, tipped their hats. Protestants were careful not to make any move that could be interpreted as honoring the church. I have often thought about this since then and have come to feel that maybe the Roman Catholics had something there.

A custom that I have not seen in the Midwest is the vegetable peddler. In the days when most housewives were at home, a man with a horse and wagon, and later a truck, and a load of vegetables would travel the streets. Some had regular routes and steady customers. Generally, the housewife would come to the wagon, select the vegetables she wanted and, after paying for them, return to her house. Some peddlers, and I remember one in particular, in addition to vegetables sold fish on Fridays. They must have been cleaned by the peddler right on the spot because I can recall cats eating the fish head that had fallen in the gutter.

Also on the street during the summer months was the iceman. In the earliest days I can recall him coming with a wagon. Later he came with a truck until refrigerators eliminated the ice and ice boxes. We boys would flock around the ice wagon saying "Mister, can I have a piece of ice." Inevitably, as the ice was cut into 25 or 50 pound pieces, there were chips that small boys would eagerly grab and suck on.

Our street had been paved in about 1924 and we boys took full advantage of it. There was not too much traffic in those days and especially so in a residential area. That, and daylight saving time which meant an extra hour of play, made the evenings doubly enjoyable. So, with our homemade scooters and homemade race cars we would make use of the street. Meanwhile, parents would be sitting on porches visiting with similarly occupied neighbors. Then we would hear, off in the distance, the familiar toot, toot of the popcorn man, as we called him. At last he would round the comer and be on our street with his horse drawn fancy wagon, from which he sold popcorn, ice cream, candy bars, etc. Meanwhile, children would run to their parents begging for a nickel to buy an ice cream cone. Sometimes the money would be forthcoming, but more often it would not. Somehow we understood that in those days even nickels were very scarce and we made the best of it, as we went back to our play.

As the summer faded into fall and as we became a bit older, roller skating on a paved street became the in-thing to do. I recall one newly paved street which one year attracted hundreds of boys and girls, and even some adults to a three block area for roller skating. Of course there were many tumbles, but injuries were generally no more serious than wounded pride.

During the winter months there were coal deliveries, first from wagons and later from trucks. The coal would be in canvas bags of 100 pounds each.

The man would then set up his portable chute in the proper basement window and begin to carry the bags in. First he would set the bags at the proper height on a board in the wagon, after which he would put a bag on his shoulder, walk to the chute and dump the bag into it. There were 20 bags to a ton and we could always know how many tons of coal he delivered. Incidentally, that was anthracite, or hard coal. Soft coal was not permitted for home use, a fact of which I was deeply appreciative after coming to Des Moines which was then shrouded in soft coal smoke.

Street comers were often the scene of huge election night fires. For several weeks prior to election day groups of boys would range up and down alleys looking for things that would bum. They would also collect wooden boxes from stores. That was before the cardboard box became dominant. They would hide these items in vacant areas. It was necessary to hide them because rival groups would lay hold of them if possible. On election night these items would be piled high on a street comer and then lighted. The resulting fire was to be in honor of the winner of the election, but to we boys the fun was in the fire. I'm not sure the police always appreciated this, but there were so many fires they could not begin to police them. Then, too, it was rather harmless.

Each block was bisected by an alley. Barns, and later garages, ash cans and garbage cans lined the sides of the alley. This was the site of operations for the garbage men. Generally, each resident had two cans, one for garbage and one for ashes from stoves and furnaces. I can barely recall when they came with a wagon, but I well recall the big Walther four wheel drive trucks which replaced the wagons.

The alley was also the place where the "rag man" traveled. The "rag men" had a wagon drawn by horse that often looked like it was about to fall over. They would travel up and down the alleys shouting "rags, rags" and hoping for some response. This was before recycling was general and we would often bundle up old newspapers and sell them to the rag man. Several bundles of papers, perhaps 100 pounds, would bring only five or ten cents. For other items the rag man would often say, "I can't give you anything for it, but I'll take it off your hands." Little wonder that there were stories about the rag man being quite wealthy — but I doubt that he was.

The winter months brought a different form of recreation. Sledding and skiing on a hill that was not too far away was an after-school pursuit. Of course it did not last long because darkness comes early in the winter months. But it was long enough for me to get wet feet even though I wore what were her own way of dealing with wet feet which was not then called overshoes. I usually could not long conceal my wet feet from my grandmother.

Winter also gave us access to an area known as the swamp. We could walk on the ice and explore. There were a number of young willow trees growing there. We discovered that it could be great fun to climb one of those trees to as near the top as we could. Then we would cause the tree to bend to the extent that the top would almost touch the ground while we rode it down.

Within a mile or so of our homes there was a large park with a sledding hill and an ice rink. We seldom went there, partly because time was often too short for the long walk to the park and because it was not always open. Perhaps more importantly, it was because we preferred unstructured activities. In another direction there was a playground, complete with swings, slides and other equipment, but we seldom went there either.

The term "crepehanger," used for someone who is unduly pessimistic, is quite common. However, I have not met the actual practice of crepe hanging in the Midwest. The term derives from the fact that when an undertaker was called to a home because of a death he brought with him a floral piece with a suitable ribbon. This he then hung near the front door to indicate there had been death in that family. When passing such a home, everyone was careful to not make much noise and to show respect.

More another time!

I Remember When: Part 2

Volume 51 number 8, August 2002

I remember when the motor car was just beginning to come into its own; a time when they were not yet widespread and two cars was completely unheard of except for the very wealthy. They were still called pleasure cars, and for the most part that is what they were. Though parking had not yet become a problem, most who had a car still rode the street car or the bus to work. In those days it was still important to clear sidewalks because many walked, if not to a street car stop, then to work or to the store. There were not nearly as many cars to see in the wintertime as in the summer. Most of them were in sheds or garages, up on blocks for the winter, with batteries being removed and out of the way of the frost.

One of the problems for those who did do winter driving was keeping the radiator from freezing. This could have disastrous and costly results. As I recall, anti-freeze was available, but it was rather expensive. Of course there were a few cars, like the Franklin, which had an air cooled engine and therefore, need not worry about a radiator freeze-up. But, on the whole, air cooled engines were not too successful though they did make a brief comeback in the post-war era with the Volkswagen Beetle.

One reads a good deal these days about electric cars. There is nothing new about such. I can recall that there were a very few in town, usually owned and operated by wealthy ladies of rather ancient vintage. The cars did not look like the average sedan, with two or four doors. They were more square and boxy and with, as I recall, only one door, but plenty of window space. There was no steering wheel, but simply a lever that could be moved for turning. I never did see one with more than one person, the woman passenger and operator in it.

In the early age of the motor car there was a multiplicity of makes. Today one can easily count the number of American car companies, each with several models. Not so when I was a child. Aside from the Ford and the Chevrolet, I can remember others that have long ceased to exist, but in their day were an important part of the scene. Names like Star, Durant, Whippet, Nash, Chandler, Hupmobile, Hudson, Essex, Studebaker, Packard, Auburn and many others were part of the American scene. Names that are familiar today, like Plymouth and Pontiac, did not make their appearance until the early '30s.

Flat tires were a major irritant for the early motorist. If one could travel 50 miles without a flat he was doing well. Many even carried two spare tires. Fixing a flat was for many motorists a "do-it-yourself" project. It involved taking the tire and the rim off the wheel, getting the tires and the inner tube off the rim, patching the inner tube and remounting the tire and the rim.

Today if I run into trouble with my computer I call on one of my grandsons. In those days of the distant past, it was we younger people who knew about cars. We knew what made them go; we often knew what was wrong. We could talk about pistons, connecting rods, oil rings, transmissions and differentials as readily as today's youth can discuss modems, computer speed and the merits of this or that software.

There were not many women drivers in those days. One of the factors mitigated against women drivers in the early years of the automobile was the need to crank the engine to start it. Using a hand crank to start the motor could be a very dangerous business and many a broken arm attested to that fact. Therefore, until advent of the self-starter, the number of women drivers was quite limited.

Today mechanical sweepers clean the streets from time to time. There was a time when the street sweeper was a fixture of city life and he cleaned paved streets every day. This was made necessary by the fact that there were still a good many horse drawn vehicles in the days, and the horses were not street-trained. The street sweeper was equipped with a garbage can on a cart, a broom and a shovel. He could thus easily pick up the droppings, deposit them in the garbage can, and move on to the next pile. Of course, from time to time an enterprising gardener would beat him to it and thus have fertilizer for his garden.

There were others besides peddlers who used horses. Our milkman, who was a Dane, by the way, used a horse and wagon to service his route. There were also regular deliveries of bread, rolls and cake to those who desired such service. A horse and wagon was used for this until about the 30's.

Speaking of milk deliveries, the milk was not pasteurized and carefully bottled. Our milkman had the milk in a large cream can. The customer brought a container and the milkman, using a large dipper, would transfer milk from the cream can to the customer's container. Payment would be made with tickets previously purchased for that purpose. Each ticket was for one pint.

A bit later I recall some large milk companies who not only pasteurized and bottled their milk, but made it possible for the customer to pour off the cream. The bottle was so designed that the area at the top, where the cream was, could be separated from the rest of the milk by a special spoon made for that purpose. One simply inserted the spoon until it reached the narrow part of the bottle. Then one could safely pour off the top and "voile," you had cream. This practice did not last long. Homogenized milk put an end to that.

When I was a boy, the supermarket had not yet become a part of the city scene. Neither had its predecessor, the self-serve grocery. I well remember of the first self-serve store and what an innovation it was. Instead, the clerk or the proprietor would get what you wanted from a shelf somewhere in the store. If the shelf was high, he would use a pincer device with a long handle to retrieve the item. The customer was generally separated from the shelves by a counter which became the focal point for his purchases. There were many of these small grocery stores and/or meat markets in every city and town. The owner generally knew his customers and could chat with them while he served them. It was not the impersonal relationship of today's supermarket. Regular customers usually had an account and their purchases were added to that account. They settled weekly or monthly. If they were unemployed, and many were, they could pay only occasionally and the merchant trusted them. Unfortunately, as supermarkets became more common, many of these same customers went to the larger store where things might be a bit cheaper, thus deserting the man who had carried them through hard times. This was certainly one factor in the decline and fall of the comer grocery or meat market.

Most stores were independently owned and the proprietor was always knowledgeable about his stock. A hardware store, for example, was a store devoted exclusively to items that would fall within the general category of hardware. If you wanted an "easy out" you simply told the clerk. He knew what it was and where it was. The drug store was somewhat of an exception to this in that the druggist carried a number of items that could not be called drugs. And, in addition, he almost always sold ice cream and had a soda fountain.

Everyone did a great deal of walking in those days. While the distances to the Public School were not excessive, almost the only way to get there was to walk. Being driven to school was unthinkable, if not impossible, and school busses, in the city, were still far off in the future.

Those were the days when doctors still made house calls. Their schedule usually provided for hospital and house calls during the morning hours with afternoons being reserved for office visits. Medical science had not advanced to the extent it has today and there were relatively few complaints for which the doctor's knowledge was called upon.

Household pets were not nearly as numerous as they are today. A boy might have a dog which had once been a stray. Though dog food was available not very many people bought it.

Money was scarce and the family has to be fed first. The dog existed on scraps and, unfortunately such things as he could find by tipping garbage cans. There was no such thing as a dog tie-up or fenced in areas for dogs.

The entertainment world was quite limited. The limitation was two-fold. The technology behind the moving picture and the radio had not advanced far. The other limitation was the cost. If we were lucky we could get the ten cents needed for a Saturday afternoon matinee at the local theatre. There was as yet no sound and one had to follow along by means of captions — which really was good reading practice. An important part of the show, and probably the most important, was a weekly installment of serial story. One had to see what happened to the heroine after last week's cliffhanger ending. Because there was not sound in the movie, a pianist would play for the whole two hours. She usually did a remarkable job of coordinating the music with the action on the screen.

The earliest development in the field of home radio was the crystal set. These were quite inexpensive and could even be made at home. A set of earphones, a piece of galena for a crystal, and a coil wound around an old oatmeal box were the chief components. Then one was ready to tune in nearby, and sometimes relatively far off stations. I recall that the topic of conversation among some men the next day revolved around the most far away station they had been able to receive.

Well, as Archie Bunker would say, 'Those were the days."

I Remember When: Part 3

Volume 52 number 8, August 2003

Since my mother died in the flu epidemic of 1918, when I was 21 months old, I grew up in the home of my paternal grandparents. They lived in that part of Troy which, prior to 1901, was the city of Lansingburgh and was now referred to as simply "the burgh." It was here, too, that the Danish Church was located.

Though I grew up in a city, my playmates and I were not crowded for room. We had ample place to play, to explore and to exercise our imagination. The reason lies in the fact that a very large amusement park, complete with a track for horse racing, had existed in the area. The park ultimately failed and was abandoned after the horse barns had burned for the third or fourth time. The large vacant area was then laid out in building lots, but, in those years development was slow. The result was acres and acres of play area with no streets or roads. Other neighborhood boys and I took full advantage of this. There was a public playground just a few blocks away, but we hardly ever went there.

As we grew older and could wander farther from home, there was a Boston and Maine railroad track and a steep wooded hillside, topped by a large cemetery, to be explored. Troy is situated in the Hudson River Valley and, especially to the east, the valley was bordered by a large hill of some 300 feet or more. In our part of the city this hillside was impossible for any kind of development. To make it even more appealing to growing boys was the fact that a brook, or the creek, as we called it, ran from the lakes in the cemetery to the valley below and ultimately to the river.

In the undeveloped field we often chose sides and played ball. There were not enough of us to make up two full teams but we made our own games. We also played "cops and robbers" and "cowboys and Indians." On the hillside we followed the path to the cemetery, climbed the rocks which were a part of the hill, or simply sat at the top and looked out over the city.

In the summer evenings we played on the street. Our street had been paved in 1924 so we could roller skate, race our pushcarts, ride our bikes, or, play various games until dark. The games we played I later learned, were more or less universal and of the "run, sheep run" type. New York state has had daylight saving time for as long as I can remember so our evenings were always quite long.

Of course life was not all play. There were things to be done at home. I can recall helping with the cleaning by dusting the lower parts of the furniture which my grandmother could not easily reach. It was also my job to take out and sweep the throw rugs. I was taught that in the winter time it was good to sweep a little snow on them and then sweep it off. This was supposed to make them cleaner. Whether it did or not is another matter. I was also expected to help with housecleaning in the spring and fall, when the whole house was given a thorough cleaning. This meant taking out and beating the mattresses and hanging out in the sunshine all the clothes in the closets.

And then there was school! I can't recall much about starting school. I do know that I attended kindergarten and that the next school year that building became a junior high school. This meant attending another elementary school from the first through the sixth grades. Neither was very far from home and there was only one busy street to cross. This was really no problem because there was relatively little traffic.

The school buildings had separate entrances on opposite sides of building for girls and boys and within the building there were separate stairways. However, girls and boys were not segregated in the classrooms. This practice was followed all the way through school, from elementary through High School, though I am unable to say if it is still being practiced. The last time I saw the High School building, which is no longer used as such, the words "Boys" and "Girls" was still set in stone above each door.

School in that time and place was marked by discipline. Teachers and students today would be surprised at the discipline school children knew in those days. It never occurred to us to complain and it would have been useless in any case. Parents would have supported the school in those days. Food and drink were not permitted; neither was candy nor gum chewing. This may seem like a stringent rule, but actually it was a rule against rudeness. It is rude to eat or chew gum in front of others in a closed environment. There were other limitations as well. We were not permitted to speak to our neighbors and even whispering was not allowed — though often attempted. If we wanted to speak or leave the room we simply had to raise a hand and ask permission, which was generally granted. Were we in rebellion against such rules did we feel like prisoners in a classroom? Of course not! We accepted them as a necessary part of the school day.

While school occupied a major part of my life during the years when I was growing up, I have no unpleasant memories of the Public School. The things I learned there gave a good foundation for later learning and responsible living.

Christmas Holidays Among the Danes in Troy

Volume 52 number 12, December 2004

In the above title, Lansingburgh could as well have been used as Troy since the Danes settled in Lansingburgh and not in Troy. The Danish Church at Lansingburgh, founded in 1874, was, one of the earliest Danish Lutheran Churches in America. Even after Lansingburgh became a part of Troy in 1901, regular news items from that congregation continued to be reported as news from Lansingburgh in the Danish language weekly, *Dannevirke*.

Just when and why the first Danes settled in Lansingburgh is not known to me. Efforts to find out have, to date, failed and my speculations on the matter have led me to the Dutch. It is well known that Danish architecture was influenced by Dutch architecture and other Dutch influences may have made themselves felt. In any case, Lansingburgh was founded by the Dutch as indeed were many communities in a good deal of the Hudson River Valley. There are other possible explanations such as the fact that this was the eastern terminus of the Eire Canal. Immigrants could have stopped off here and remained rather than continuing their journey westward. Be that as it may, there was a sizeable Danish colony in Lansingburgh.

Immanuel congregation was founded by Danish immigrants under the guidance of Pastor A. L. J. Søholm, who was then serving the congregation at Perth Amboy, New Jersey. During the years of my childhood, which were representative of the latter years of the 32 year pastorale of Ole Jacobsen, the English language was just beginning to be used in the church. In 1925, for example, there were seven English language services. There were 20 children listed as being in the English language Sunday School, but 44 in the Danish. It was still, therefore, a very Danish oriented congregation.

Aside from the language, the Danish background of the congregation was not reflected to any great extent in the Sunday School. This was largely because, in the matter of the Sunday School, there was no Danish tradition upon which to draw. In one case, however, existing tradition did prevail and this was the time that the Sunday School program was held. Danes generally observed the week between Christmas and New Year's Day as a time for relaxation and visiting. The Christmas season did not come to an abrupt end the day after Christmas. Accordingly, the Christmas program of the Sunday School was usually held on the Sunday evening after Christmas. This was long a practice in many congregations of the Danish Church in America. The bulk of program was presented in the Danish language. While there may have been some English language participation, I am unable to recall such.

A large tree, appropriately trimmed, was set up in the front of the sanctuary. The front pews were removed to make room for the tree. The tree was positioned in such a way that the Sunday School children could march around it.

As the sanctuary was filling with proud parents and grandparents, the Sunday School children were being lined up in the basement. Then, at the proper time, the children marched up the stairs and into the sanctuary singing *Her kommer Jesus dine Sma* (Thy Little Ones, O Savior Dear). I rather doubt that Hans Adolph Brorson wrote this as a children's hymn, but certainly the first line lent itself well to the entry of the children. So, too, did the first line of the last verse, *Her står vi nu 1 flok og rad* (Here we stand as a group in rows) which was sung as the children gathered before the Christmas tree. One stanza of this hymn, incidentally, was universally used in the Danish Lutheran Church in America as a response to the Apostle's Creed. It begins, *Lad verden ej med al sin magt* (Let not the world lead us astray).

The program as I recall it some 75 years later did not feature shepherds in gunnysacks or wise men in bathrobes. Neither was there a manger with a doll representing the baby Jesus. There was some singing by the children and numerous recitations, most of them in Danish, centered on the Christmas theme. This meant that a great deal of memorizing had gone on prior to the program. Memorizing was never my problem, but reciting before a filled church was something else and I was always vastly relieved when my turn was over. I do recall one time when I was an embarrassment to my parents. Oh, I knew my piece well enough, but right in the middle of it, I stopped to scratch my nose. You may be sure that I later heard about that.

When the program was over and all the children were seated on the front pews, the pastor read a story. Whether this was always Danish I can't say. I would guess that in the early 1920's it was Danish and later changed to English. As the years progressed there would be fewer who could understand a Danish story. This being completed, the time had arrived for the eagerly awaited gifts. Each child was given some Christmas candy and a book, suited to the proper age level. Books were very cheap in those bygone days. Most children's books sold for fifty cents (about $10 today). Boys of elementary school age generally received a Tom Swift book. Tom Swift was an inventor of whom many boys, including myself, were fans. There was a whole series of books each related to his adventures centered on a particular invention. We were hopeful that we would get one of the series we had not already read. If we did, there would be some trading going on. The girls, who generally received copies of the Bobbsey Twin series, were in a similar position.

The program in the church was concluded with a hymn, after which everyone adjourned to the basement. Here coffee and cake was served along with plenty of visiting. In the absence of memory on this point, I presume that cocoa was served to the children. So ended the Christmas observance in that congregation. Now, once again New Year, with its annual banquet, hosted by the Danish Brotherhood, took center stage on New Year's Eve in Dania Hall.

In those years the Brotherhood always sponsored a banquet and dance on New Year's Eve. The Danish Brotherhood had its own hall, but it was too small and not equipped to serve a banquet. They, therefore, used Dania Hall. I am unable to say just who was responsible for the building of Dania Hall, but I suspect it was built be the local chapter of the Danish People's Society (Dansk Folkesamfund). The building has long since burned down. Most events that involved the entire Danish community were held here. So, for instance, there were plays, dances, guest speakers, and larger meetings. Those who attended the church convention in Troy in 1941 will recall that the meals were served in Dania Hall. It was a rather large building at the corner of two busy streets, some three blocks from the church. On the ground level there were stores and the hall was upstairs. At one end of a hall, and down a few steps, was the bar. This was always a busy place and not least on New Year's Eve - even though prohibition was in effect.

I would guess that there were 175 to 200 people present. The banquet was the first order of business and it got under way with a prayer by the Danish minister who had been invited. Generally there were no speeches and when the meal was ended the tables were cleared and taken away to make room for dancing. Meanwhile some of the men headed for the bar and the minister, his duties having been fulfilled, usually headed home. The dancing went on until quite late and I can still recall seeing small children asleep amid coats on the pool tables in another room. Those of us who were a bit older wandered around becoming increasingly bored and anxious to go home.

This brought to a close the public events of the Christmas season for the Danes in Troy. After New Year's Day, it was back to work or back to school, as the case might be, and another year had begun.

They Turn Fifty
Volume 56 number 12, December 2006

The Interstate highways, which some see as a blessing while others are less than enthused, are now fifty years old. Of course the highways were not suddenly born in that year, but legislation creating them was a highlight of the 1956 congressional session. Many obstacles intervened, but as the years passed, motor travel increased and defense needs became more obvious. In the years before 1956 the desirability of a highway network occupied the minds of many a traffic engineer, defense specialist, economist and highway traveler until work on the network was finally begun .

The Motor Convoy

Shortly after the close of the First World War, during the summer of 1919, a convoy set out from Washington, D. C. headed for San Francisco. Sponsored by the War Department and officially called the "First Transcontinental Motor Convoy" the expedition consisted of some 78 vehicles, ranging from large trucks, to travel kitchens, machine shops, pleasure cars and motorcycles. The whole enterprise was to be operated by almost three hundred men. The majority of these were enlisted men, but there were also officers and observers from the War Department. One of these was a young Lt. Col. named Dwight D. Eisenhower.

The motor car was relatively new at that time and most of what passed for roads were at best fair and at worst non-existent. Some of the bridges along the route of the convoy had been constructed for horse and buggy traffic and could not withstand the loads imposed by trucks and other vehicles of the motorized convoy. In many areas axle-deep mud was a major impediment. Two months later, after traveling over 3200 miles, the convoy reached its goal. Though on a good day they had covered as much as 80 miles, they averaged 58 miles per day and the average speed was computed at slightly over six miles per hour.

But the entire expedition did not arrive in San Francisco. Nine vehicles had been damaged beyond repair and left behind. Twenty-one men had been injured to the point where they were not able to continue. However, no fatal injuries were reported and the entire operation was a success in many ways. Nevertheless, it did serve to reveal the sad state of the transportation system in America. In the course of the journey the convoy had damaged some 88 bridges and culverts; it had been involved in over 200 instances in which the roads were such that the vehicles became mired in mud, ran off the roads, tipped over or suffered other mishaps.

Between the Wars

The period between the two world wars, roughly 1919 to 1939, was marked by a modicum of prosperity during the 1920s and a great depression, following the stock market crash in 1929, lasting throughout the 1930s. Despite the financial condition of the country, more and more families acquired motor cars and industries purchased trucks, large and small. The result was that vehicular traffic grew, and streets, roads and highways grew in number and in status during those years. Americans could now take shorter or longer pleasure drives and it was possible to drive from coast to coast though not without some difficulties on many roads. The so-called Lincoln Highway, through the Midwest was not as glamorous as its name implied. Road maps became available and the roads were numbered. The East-West roads were, generally speaking, even numbered while the North-South routes were given odd numbers. That numbering system has been continued to this day.

World War II

The Second World War, in which America became involved December of 1941, had an eventual impact on the highways in this country. Dwight D. Eisenhower had by this time risen to the rank of general and it was he who was given the responsibility for the European theatre of operations. From his headquarters in England he directed the movement of the Allied troops and the supplies necessary to sustain them. It had been determined that the movement toward Germany and the destruction of the Nazi war machine should proceed directly through France and indirectly through Italy and the underbelly of Europe. In both instances roads were to play a major role in the logistics of the moves. The hedgerows of Normandy slowed the advance of the allies to a crawl. The French roads proved to be somewhat better, though even there the difficulties were far from over.

Ironically, it was in Germany that the Allied forces met the best roads. This was because during the early 1930's the German government had planned a network of four-lane, high speed roads to be called "Autobahn" (literally, auto trails or auto tracks). During the war, the Nazi war machine made good use of these superhighways, as they shifted their forces from one front to another. When the Allied forces entered Germany they found these roads to be far superior to any they had previously encountered. The logistics of the campaign were much simplified by the existence of these superhighways. This fact was not lost on the military and not least on General Dwight Eisenhower.

The Post-war Period

During the war automobiles and tires were scarce items, but when the war ended these slowly became more and more available. By late 1947 the huge backlog of orders was gradually filled and once again America was on wheels. Many states were busily improving and building roads and bridges as rapidly as funds allowed.

It was during this period that three states, Pennsylvania, New York and Kansas, undertook the construction of four-lane roads, to be paid for by tolls based on their use. Ground was broken for the first of these, the Pennsylvania Turnpike, in October of 1938. The Turnpike was envisioned as a 532 mile, four-lane highway running from East to West and linking some of the state's major cities including Philadelphia, the capital Harrisburg, and Pittsburgh. The route chosen necessarily went through mountainous Allegheny territory, thus requiring the construction of numerous tunnels. The first segment of the Turnpike, a 110-mile stretch between Carlisle and Irwin was opened in October of 1940. The entire project was completed by 1956.

The Kansas Turnpike was opened for traffic October 25, 1956. It had been under construction for the prior twenty-two months. The route was westward from Kansas City to the capital Topeka, and then southwestward, through Wichita to the Oklahoma border.

The state legislature created The New York State Thruway in 1950 and in the years that followed the 496 mile system was built. Beginning in New York City, it ran northward via the Hudson River valley to the state capital at Albany. At that point it turned westward via the Mohawk River valley to Buffalo after which it then turned south and west to the Pennsylvania border. A Thruway going north from Albany to the Canadian Border, called the Northway, was also a part of the system. A personal note may serve to indicate how much difference a four-lane, controlled access highway can make. In 1949, prior to the construction of the Thruway, we had occasion to travel the route from Buffalo to Albany. Traffic was heavy and the cities and towns through which we had to pass were numerous with the result that that trip took 12 hours. A few years later we traveled the same route on the Thruway in six hours.

The National Scene

Not surprisingly, Dwight Eisenhower, the General who had successfully prosecuted the war in Europe, was elected as the 34th president of the United States and took office in January of 1953. Mindful of his experience with the First Transcontinental Motor Convoy in 1919 and of the difficulties he experienced in North Africa and Europe and of the value of the German Autobahn, he lost no time in urging upon the Congress a defense highway system for the United States. The Congress had previously, in 1944, authorized a national highway system, but it had not been fully funded and nothing much came of it. In his message to the Congress the president said:

"Together, the uniting forces of our communication and transportation systems are dynamic elements in the very name we bear - United States. Without them, we would be a mere alliance of many separate parts."

Finally, on June 29, 1956, Eisenhower was able to sign a law which assured funding for a National Highway Defense System, as the project was originally called. This included the non-contiguous states of Alaska and Hawaii as well as the territory of Puerto Rico. Eisenhower saw this highway system as a highlight of his presidency and it was not inappropriate, therefore, that in 1990, by an act of Congress the highway system should be renamed. It is now officially known as the Dwight David Eisenhower National System of Interstate and Defense Highways. The system, as it has gradually come into use over the years, is truly national. It has linked together all of the contiguous states, east and west, north and south. No state, not even the smallest or the least populous has been left without its interstate and has become a part of the network. The mileage of the entire system is somewhat over 48,000.

The system of Interstate Highways has become an asset beyond expectations to America. Now in the fiftieth year since its creation brought the boon of safety to motor travel, it has made it possible to travel long distances in much less time and it has made even the most remote areas more accessible. Quite apart from this, it has been a stimulus to commerce and industry. Through new construction and manufacturing it has been responsible for the creation of greater employment and for the increase in service industries.

The defense aspect of these highways has been stressed time and again. Indeed, it played a large, if not essential, role in their creation. Had the defense card not been played it is doubtful that a national system would have come into being at that time. There is no question but that the existence of these highways makes it easier and faster to move the military from place to place. But, as the Americans found in their experience with the German Autobahn, an invading force can also make good use of such roads.

The Interstates Today

Prominently as the Interstates figure in the highway systems of the United States, it should be noted that they constitute only about one percent of the total highway structure. However they carry some 25 percent of the nation's passenger traffic and account for some 45 percent of the nation's highway freight movement. This heavy use, plus the fact that many of them are aging, accounts for the fact that many of them have already been repaired while others are in the process or stand in need of major repair. Then, too, the traffic is much heavier than it was fifty years ago.

On some Interstates it can be a pleasure to travel today. This is the case with 1-90, as it runs through southern Minnesota and South Dakota. Both passenger and truck traffic are relatively light and the rest stops are plentiful and good. I-35, which runs from Canada to Mexico, is more widely used and the truck traffic is on the increase. I-80 is one of the main routes between the east and the west coast. Here in the Midwest, it connects Chicago, Des Moines, Omaha and Denver. To drive on it is to feel that one has become a part of a dangerous, high speed race and we avoid it like a plague. Part of the problem is that there are almost as many large trucks as there are passenger cars. One cannot but wonder at the standards of those who apparently think that this is an efficient way to move non-perishable freight. Sooner or later something will have to be done about I-80 and similar situations. Perhaps an extra lane for trucks only could be the answer, but that is a problem that only traffic engineers can solve.

Conclusion

We, who are old enough to know what travel was like before the days of the Interstate highways, can only be glad that there were those who saw a serious problem coming and who took steps to meet it. These days one often sees signs at construction sites that read "Your Tax Dollars at Work." In my view the tax dollars that went into the Interstate system was money well spent.

In the preparation of the above article I have consulted numerous articles on the Internet and elsewhere. I am especially indebted to an article on the Internet by Logan Thomas Snyder, which first appeared in the AMERICAN HISTORY magazine for June of 2006.

An Uncommon Library

Volume 57 number 5, May 2007

Sunday School libraries are rather common today, and they may have even existed eighty years ago. But, past or present, one would expect the contents to be somewhat similar, with books of Bible stories, adventures of missionaries, and children's books related to the Christian faith. I do know of a library related to a Sunday School that did exist some eighty years ago, but it was a most uncommon library in that it held no explicitly religious books, and really the only relationship that the library had to the Sunday School was the fact that they were in the same church building, indeed in the same room.

The Danish Evangelical Lutheran Church had been established in Lansingburgh, (now Troy) New York in 1873. For several years it was located on Fourth Avenue, but in 1914 it was moved several blocks north and east to a new church and parsonage which the congregation had just completed on Seventh Avenue. This was only three blocks from where I lived with my father and his parents. It was here that I received my first taste of Sunday School and its uncommon library.

The library could be called uncommon because all of the books were written in the English language, whereas everything else in that building, and that includes the Sunday School, was conducted in Danish. Further, there were relatively few children's books. The Tom Swift series would appeal to the boys and the Bobbsey Twins to the girls. One can account for the presence of these children's books by recalling that at Christmas time every child was given a 50 cent book from one of these two series and any extras (books) would go to the Sunday School library.

It is much more difficult to account for the presence of what are best called adult books. Had they been the remnants of a reading circle, such as existed in many Danish congregations, they would almost certainly have been in the Danish language. In any case, regardless of their origin, they constituted a major part of the collection. I would guess that there were some 800 books in the total collection. It was the general practice to come early for Sunday School so we could make our two selections for the week and have them recorded by a teacher who acted as a librarian.

But if memory is dim and subject to error on the details of that library, the benefits and value to a growing child of that long-ago book collection remain to this day. To be sure, I learned to read in the public school, but there is no question in my mind but that my long-time interest in the printed word came through that uncommon library. It was through it I learned what so many others, before and since, have discovered - that reading opens a door to the world.

Tom Swift was an inventor and through his fantastic inventions he was always able to defeat his enemies and win the day. Though I knew such a character was fictional I did learn something about the physical world and the science which helps explain it. Then there were stories of travel and adventure. I was with Richard Halliburton as he climbed the Matterhorn in the Swiss Alps. I laughed with him when, after reaching the top, he looked down and said, "At last, I can spit a mile." It was also there that I first learned of Perry Mason, the indomitable lawyer. Mason was the literary creation of Earle Stanley Gardner, who was himself a lawyer. There were several Perry Mason books in the uncommon library and I enjoyed reading them. Recently, I discovered a TV channel that quite regularly runs programs based on Perry Mason cases. Of course, with the many intervening decades, these programs are not based on the original stories nor are they written by Gardner. What have been preserved are the characters of Perry Mason and his faithful secretary, Della Street.

There were a large number of adult books in that collection and we children were free to check out any that appealed to us. In this connection I recall one such book. It was called "Merchants of Death." Published shortly after the First World War, it presented a picture of some of the behind-the-scenes activity in that war. It was not a pretty picture. It focused on the Krupp Iron Works in Germany plus similar suppliers of arms for the allied forces. It made me aware that the soldiers and others who do the fighting and dying may be guided by ideals, while others seek only profit and are guided by the bottom line. It was not an introduction to an ideal world but to a world in which profit rules.

Though many might look askance at this uncommon library I am grateful that it existed and that I had an opportunity to share in it. Undoubtedly it affected my life then and in the many years since. It did much to shape my thinking on children's libraries and the accessibility of children to more than the fantasies of childhood. It has also helped to shape my thinking on collections of so-called religious books.

The Johnstown Flood: A Book Review
Volume 57 number 7, July 2007

Though far removed in time and space from the flood which destroyed Johnstown, Pennsylvania in 1889, time and again, over the course of many years, I have heard and read references to that tragedy to the extent that I became curious about it. Thus, when I recently came across a book called *The Johnstown Flood*, written by no less a writer than David McCullough, the author of such masterful and thorough books as *Truman*, *John Adams*, and *1776*, I determined that this was a book I must read.

As anyone who has traveled the Pennsylvania Turnpike will know, much of that state is hilly, if not mountainous, and where there are mountains there are valleys between. It is in just such a valley that Johnstown lies, some 65 miles east of Pittsburgh. The principal, stream is the Little Conemaugh, which is filled by many tributaries as it flows eastward down the mountains. Though Johnstown was the largest city in the valley there were a number of other smaller towns and settlements surrounding it. It is estimated that there were some 30,000 people living in the valley at the time of the flood.

Johnstown was an up and coming city in 1889. Arc lamps lighted its streets at night. There was a horse drawn street railway, a telephone exchange with 70 phones, a new hospital and a modern hotel with an elevator and steam heat. Many of the homes had bathrooms and in many offices there were typewriters. Two new business blocks had been readied on Main Street. The town also had an opera house, a library, a number of churches; and, in the greater Johnstown area there were 123 saloons.

In the hills, high above and to the west of Johnstown, stood the relatively new buildings and grounds of the South Fork Fishing and Hunting Club. The patrons of this exclusive club were men associated with the iron and steel production for which Pittsburgh was noted, men like Andrew Carnegie; Henry Clay Frick, the coke magnet; Andrew Mellon; and Philander C. Knox, both of whom were later to hold cabinet positions in the American government. The club, with its main lodge and many cottages was situated on the shore of a mountain lake that had been created by damming the waters of the South Fork, one of the many tributaries of the Little Conemaugh.

The dam had been built some 50 years before by the state to ensure a constant supply of water to a system of canals. With the coming of the Pennsylvania Railroad the dam was no longer needed. The dam was then sold to the railroad, which really had no need of it but could use the right-of-way. The dam was unattended and finally came into the possession of a man named Ruff. He made some changes at the dam which did nothing to improve it. The most serious change he made was to remove the discharge pipes at the base of the dam and sell them for scrap. It was Ruff who finally sold the dam to the South Fork group.

The dam, as planned in 1839, was to be an earthen structure, some 850 feet across and 62 feet high. There was to be a spillway at each end and discharge pipes at the base to relieve the pressure in times of excess rains. An earth dam was perfectly acceptable and at that time most often used. One condition was stipulated: the water must never be allowed to go over the top of the dam. Prior to 1889 there had been concerns about the dam when the spring freshets had caused the tributary streams to overflow their banks, but the dam had held on such occasions. Under the new owners, the South Fork Fishing Hunting Club, little had been done to maintain the dam except to add a little soil to the top and to add some heavy screen as fish barriers to the spillway which, incidentally decreased the efficiency of the spillway. Meanwhile the lake provided good fishing, especially since it was well stocked with fish. Members of the exclusive club could also enjoy various kinds of boating from canoes to sailboats and even a steam launch.

In the closing days of May in 1889, severe thunderstorms struck the Great Plains states. Beginning in Kansas and Nebraska, the storms moved east. When the storms reached western Pennsylvania a couple of days later, an estimated six or more inches of rain were falling every 24 hours. The ground was water soaked and could hold no more. From the surrounding hills and the tributaries of the South Fork, the water poured into the lake. The spillways could not take the excess and the water began to cascade over the top of the dam. The pressure on the dam was too great and in a relatively short time it gave way. It was the bursting of this dam that turned what would have been an ordinary spring flood in Johnstown into what has been called, "One of the most devastating disasters America has ever known.'"

There were efforts to warn the citizens of Johnstown some 20 miles away, but for the most part, these were not too successful and unfortunately, those messages that did get through were not taken seriously. There had often been rumors of the dam breaking and some dismissed this as just another rumor. It was not long before they heard the thirty foot wall of water rushing toward them, but then it was too late for most to escape. The power of the water was so great that houses and large masonry structures were swept away. A railroad roundhouse was destroyed and fifty ton locomotives were scattered about like match sticks. The lucky people sailed by on roofs of ruined houses from which a few were able to jump to nearby higher ground as they passed. A large portion of the wreckage, debris and many bodies came to be lodged against a stone railroad bridge. This massive pileup could not be dislodged until it was finally dynamited. Meanwhile fire had broken out in the mass of rubble. The fire may have helped avert a feared epidemic of typhoid. As much as six months later bodies were found many miles from Johnstown; some bodies were never found. The official list of victims from Johnstown and the surrounding communities as published in 1890 contains the names of 2,290.

In the wake of the flood there was some talk of bringing lawsuits against the South Fork Club. But since the Club was capitalized for only $35,000, such suits were deemed useless and individual members could not be held responsible.

The arrival of Clara Barton from Washington, D.C. with a contingent of 50 doctors and nurses signaled that the American Red Cross was on the scene. Clara Barton was now 67. She had served in the Civil War and in other places where help was needed. Since 1881, following a long struggle, she finally succeeded in establishing an American branch of the International Red Cross. This was the first major disaster in which the American Red Cross was involved. She set up an office in an old railroad car using a packing case as her desk. The Red Cross workers brought and erected several large tents. Some were used for hospitals and it quickly became evident that the tents provided the quickest, cleanest and best housing. Clara Barton stayed for five months and when she finally left it was with many tokens of gratitude for the great work she had done. When she returned to Washington, a dinner held in her honor, was attended by President and Mrs. Benjamin Harrison.

A copious bibliography which evidences thorough research, and a complete index round out this scholarly but eminently readable work. A couple of maps and a section of pictures leave much to be desired and are the weak spots in what is otherwise a very fine and informative book.

Immigrant Utopias

Volume 57 number 12, December 2007

Europe was in ferment during the nineteenth century. The American revolution and the French revolution, both of which had taken place during the last quarter of the eighteenth century, had brought to the fore new questions as to the status of the individual in society. The emphasis in the one on the equality of all men, and in the other on "Liberty, equality and fraternity," had inspired and given hope to some, but had struck fear into the hearts of others. It was inevitable that this should give rise to reformers, particularly in England and France, reformers who were concerned with the social and economic welfare of the working class. Beginning in 1814, Count Saint Simon, a Frenchman, who was an insistent reformer, wrote a number of books with a socialistic bias. This was before the word "socialism", which did not come into general use until after 1830, and long before the days of Karl Marx. Meanwhile the Scottish factory owner and philanthropist, Robert Owen, was attracting much interest in Britain by setting an example in using his own plan for a more just social organization of society. In other European countries there were also reformers who were aware of the inequities in the social and economic order under which society was organized. Reform was definitely in the air in early nineteenth century Europe.

Yet given the social and economic conditions of the time and the need for reform, and given the plethora of reformers, strangely enough no serious and lasting change took place during those years. A part of the problem was that there was no consistency in the proposed reforms. There were as many suggestions for reform as there were reformers. The word socialism, for example, covered a number of different reforms though they did have certain things in common. Then, too, some of the reformers were eccentrics. Saint Simon was a poor and humble man who was nevertheless often seen as a crank, yet his thoughts represent some of the best views of the modern age. Though Charles Fourier was a kind and good man, his views were often laughed at. It is interesting to note, incidentally, that none of the plans for reform included democracy. Generally, they looked toward a kind of social engineering and dismissed the masses as being unable to govern. Another factor which may help to explain the failure of reform in Europe at that time is the inertia of established governments. The social and economic climate of a place and time are not lightly or easily changed. It was this resistance to change on the European scene that led the reformers to more and more look to the new world as a proving ground for their theories.

New World Utopias

Those who sought to reform society and place its social and economic structure on a more equitable base should not be lightly dismissed as crackpots or those who sought to escape from the pressures of the real world. They were determined to establish reform without violence and this was one reason for turning to America. They saw an embryonic community as being more amenable to new ideas than an old established society.

The aforementioned Robert Owen was the first to bring his scheme to the new world. In 1825 he purchased an old German settlement at New Harmony, Indiana. Here he sought to organize the settlement in a kind of communistic society. His son, Robert Dale Owen, was to be the leader of the community. However, within two years, New Harmony, begun with high hopes, exhibited more discord than harmony. While Owen was personally likeable, his anti-religious views worked against the harmony he sought. Charles Fourier, the Frenchman, who shared Robert Owen's socialistic views, was seen as less of a threat and was more readily tolerated. Fourier feared capitalism and saw it as ultimately destructive. He sought to have the members of society gather in what he called phalanxes, or associated groups which could then transform society. Some 40 of these were formed in the ten years after 1830. They all failed except for Brook Farm which provided the inspiration for a novel, *The Blithdale Romance*, by Nathaniel Hawthorne. Brook Farm became definitely socialistic in 1843 but by 1847 a fire put an end to the already poverty-stricken community.

Scandinavian Utopias

Unlike some of the utopian societies founded in America, the colony established by the Swedes at Bishop Hill, Illinois, did not have its beginnings in economic reform. It was founded by a sect called the Janssonists in the interests of religious freedom, though as a practical matter to aid the emigrants and to foster the settlement, communistic practices were quickly adopted.

Erik Jansson, who was also known as the prophet, was a flour salesman and a lay preacher. In his travels as a salesman he came in contact with many lay readers of the Bible. From 1842 and onward he met often with them to discuss the Bible and other religious writings and to pray together. Before long they formed a sect whose belief was that the believer could immediately lead a sinless life. They often engaged in book burnings of Lutheran works and devotional material that was contrary to their beliefs. Inevitably, these beliefs and actions put them in conflict with the authorities in Lutheran Sweden. Jansson spent most the two years prior to 1846 in prison.

Meanwhile, two of Jansson's followers, the brothers Olof and Jonas

Olsson decided the group should emigrate. The fall of 1845 found Olof consulting in New York with Olof Gustav Hedstrom and making preparations for the arrival of the Janssonites and selecting a site for their settlement. Olof Hedstrom was a lay preacher associated with the Methodist Church and his "Bethel Ship" lay permanently anchored off lower Manhattan. Here he preached the Methodist doctrine to new arrivals, gave practical information as to the travel routes, and suggested the best places for them to settle. In this case, Hedstrom directed Olsson to his brother Jonas Hedstrom in Illinois. Jonas, who was also a lay preacher, aided Olsson in selecting a site in Henry County, some 140 miles west and slightly south of Chicago.

The prophet, Erik Jansson, was still in Sweden where he had been arrested for the sixth time. There, while being transported to a prison, he somehow managed to escape and by the summer of 1846 he had found his way to the Henry county site. With Olof Olsson and a few who had already arrived, he purchased land for the settlement. Two years later the settlement had a population of 800 people it also had a name; Bishop Hill, a name taken from a location near Jansson's birthplace in Sweden. Some engaged in farming, but they also established several industries, some of which proved to be profitable. They built substantial buildings of brick which they had molded themselves. One large building, completed in 1851, was four stories high, with a kitchen and dining hall on the first floor while the three floors above were divided into seventy family dwellings.

Bishop Hill continued for some years as a communal enterprise, in fulfillment of its ideal, but also of necessity. The dictatorial Erik Jansson was murdered, in May of 1850 in a dispute over a marriage plan. His successors governed the community more democratically and still maintained a collective stance, but there began to be speculation in capitalistic enterprises. The colony eventually lost faith in the leaders and the collective principle was given up. The property was divided among those settlers remaining. Today only a few substantial buildings remain to remind the visitor of their collective origin.

There is nothing in the experience of the Norwegian immigrants comparable to the Bishop Hill colony of the Swedes. Economic reasons were secondary for the Norwegian emigrants; religious freedom was a prime factor in the early migration. There was a Quaker colony in Stavanger in the southern part of Norway, where the Quakers were constantly at odds with the Lutheran state church. Their fellow Norwegians were sympathetic with and much influenced by the Quakers. By 1824 two men were sent to investigate conditions in America. One of them died, but the other, Cleng Peerson, was able to report favorably and received promises of help from Quakers already established in the New World.

Plans were quickly made to cross the Atlantic in a sloop, which they had named the Restauration. The sloop was small, (54ft. x 16ft) and the 52 passengers made it quite crowded. Not all of the passengers, who have since been referred to as "the sloopers" were Quakers. After three months at sea they arrived in New York on October 9, 1825. Here they were met by Cleng Peerson, and a number of Quakers who stood ready to help. They soon discovered they needed more help than they had imagined. On landing in New York the sloopers learned that they had unwittingly broken the law in that the sloop was carrying many more passengers than allowed on a ship of its size. They, therefore, faced a heavy fine, but a well-to-do Quaker put up the bond money, helped formulate a petition for the release of the ship, and sought a waiver of the fine. This was granted. The New York Quakers then directed the sloopers to Kendall, a colony in upstate New York, some 25 miles northwest of Rochester, on the shore of Lake Ontario. The New Yorkers further aided them by providing the necessary funds for their travel. The sloop had been sold but brought only $400 which would not have been enough.

The sloopers did go to Kendall and settled there for some years until they gradually accumulated enough money to move farther west. Some of them then migrated to the Fox River region, considerably west of Chicago, in Illinois where there were other Norwegian settlements.

Among immigrants from Norway prior to 1860, there were few who came with any specific plans for a utopian settlement. Nils Otto Tank was an exception. While still in Norway he was converted to the teachings of the Moravians. In 1849 he learned of a Moravian colony in northeastern Wisconsin in the Green Bay area. He had married a wealthy Dutch woman and, therefore, having the necessary means, purchased land in the northern part of the Green Bay region and sought to establish a socialistic colony, to be called "Ephriam." Settlers did come and took up the land he had made available, but they did not accept his communal ideas. Tank was descended from the nobility and the settlers simply did not trust a man of his background. Within a short time they moved farther north in what is now Door County and founded a colony in which there was to be private ownership of the property.

Another exception was the colony of "Oleana" founded under the aegis of Ole Bull, the celebrated violinist. Bull had firsthand knowledge of the 1848 revolution in Paris and had been influenced by it. There are indications that he had utopian ideas and wanted to put them into practice. He was definitely interested in the welfare of his fellow Norwegians and he sought to found a large colony for them. Therefore, in 1852 he bought a large tract of land in Pennsylvania for a Norwegian settlement. In September of 1852 the first colonist arrived. Shortly thereafter Ole Bull arrived and with him came an engineer who was to lay out lots on which the settlers could build. Bull himself selected sites for a carpentry shop, a nursery, a church and a schoolhouse. The entire enterprise appeared to be off to a good start.

Nonetheless, Bull owned the land and would sell to the settlers at a price which was considerably higher than they would have paid for government land. He did offer them work at one dollar a day, but within a short time his funds were running low and he had to cut the pay to fifty cents a day. He then set off on another concert tour to raise more money. He returned the following spring and for a time things seemed to go fairly well, but by September Bull withdrew from the project and sold the remaining land back to the original owners. Thus another immigrant utopian project failed.

Danish emigration to the new world came late. Prior to 1850 there were relatively few Danes who came to America. Thus, the period of reform in Europe that had taken its cue from the French revolution and from the developments in France in 1848, saw no reformers in Denmark with a utopian bent attracted to the land across the sea.

The labor movement was coming to the fore in Denmark during the early 1870's and the Social Democratic Party was formed largely due to the activities of the labor activist, Louis Pio. Though they had lived in Denmark for some generations, the Pio family had come from France. Partly due to adversities which he had personally experienced, Pio began to play an active role in the labor movement and he eventually became a socialist. By 1873 he had become the editor of the socialist paper, *Social Democraten*. Meanwhile, because of things he had written and said, Pio had come to the attention of the Copenhagen police. He and some others were arrested when they insisted on holding a meeting in defiance of the police. They were sentenced to prison. Two years later they were pardoned by the King, partly because there was some question as to the health of Pio. Upon his release from prison, Pio resumed the editorship of the socialist paper.

The police continued to see Pio and an associate Poul Geleff as a threat and used funds supplied by two major industries in Copenhagen, to essentially bribe Pio and Geleff to leave the country. In April of 1877, Pio, Geleff and a small group of settlers left Copenhagen bound for Kansas where they intended to establish a utopian colony. Kansas was chosen because Geleff had been there the year before and Kansas had found favor with him. At Salina, Kansas they gathered to make plans for their colony. A fund, expected to last six months, was raised by each contributing slightly less than $100, with Pio contributing the most, some $300. At Hays, Kansas they got title to the land under the terms of the Homestead Act. Here they bought supplies they felt they would need and, filled with high hopes, they set out on foot for the colony site.

The hopes and dreams did not last long. Within six weeks what had begun so enthusiastically, had failed miserably. What had happened? It was said the men worked hard and worked well together, but the women simply could not get along. Harsh words and jealousies were an everyday occurrence. Whether or not it is fair to place the blame for the failure on the women is questionable, but suffice it to say that the break-up came because human nature asserted itself. So it was that the remaining funds and goods were divided equitably and each left for his own destination.

Pio, for his part went to Chicago where he lived until his death in 1894 at the age of 52. He was engaged in a number of different occupations during those years. At one time or other he was an editor, a real estate salesman, a civil servant, a customs house clerk and a civil engineer. He also frequently met with the prominent Danes of Chicago on a Friday afternoon in Wilkins Wine Cellar for relaxation and discussion.

Shortly before his death, Pio did found a colony, albeit not a socialist or utopian colony. In collaboration with the capitalist, Henry Flagler, Pio established a Danish settlement called White City, some five miles from Ft. Pierce, on the east coast of Florida. The town of White City, about 100 miles north of Miami, still exists today.

One by one, from New Harmony and Bishop Hill to Brook Farm and Louis Pio's dream, the utopian colonies all failed and without exception, they floundered on the rock of human nature. What does this, and 2,000 years of intermittent warfare tell us of the prospects for world peace? It tells us that in spite of good intentions and the best efforts of humans, the quest for a collective peace is bound to fail it is bound to flounder on the rock of human nature. Such peace as one can know will come only to the individual. As we sing:

> "Happy is he who has peace in his heart,
> Peace with himself with his God, with his neighbor:
> He has of happiness found the best part,
> Reaps he but little reward from his labor."

Sources consulted:

Morison & Commager, "The Growth of the American Republic," Vol. I.

"Ljungmark," Lars, tr. by Kermit Westerberg, *Swedish Exodus.*

"Semmingsen," Ingrid, tr. by Einar Haugen.

"Norway to America," Hanson, Thorvald, *The Bridge*, Number eight, 1982.

Nielsen, George, *The Bridge*, Vol. 13, Number one, 1990.

Legislating From the Bench

Volume 58 number 8, August 2008

It has become increasingly common in our time to accuse judges, particularly Supreme Court justices, of "legislating from the bench." By such a charge is meant that the offending judges have usurped the power of the legislature and created a new law by their decision. If observers agree, they have nothing but praise for the decision of the Court. Both political parties, if and when they happen to disagree with a decision, are prone to using this charge. So common has this accusation become that it is heard even among the presidential hopefuls, with some proudly declaring that they would not appoint judges who would be guilty of "legislating from the bench." Certainly one may often be displeased with a court decision, but such a disagreement should find expression in fact and not on ridiculous charges. Such charges are often a substitute for the hard work of presenting a sound counter argument.

A little reflection, which is often in short supply among critics, will make it evident that most court decisions, especially those involving the constitution do, in effect, have the force of a new law. Therefore a judge cannot exercise his responsibility of interpreting the constitution without giving the appearance of legislating from the bench.

As long ago as 1907, no less a person than Charles Evans Hughes, who spent many years on the Supreme Court, and retired in 1941 as Chief Justice said, "The constitution is what the judges say it is." Oliver Wendell Holmes, Jr, who served on the Court for 30 years, described the power of the judiciary, in constitutional as well as general legal interpretation, as being legislative in nature.

The basic question in a constitutional system of government is how the individual is to be protected from questionable actions by the elected arms of the government. As early as 1803, a unanimous decision by the U.S. Supreme Court in the case of Marbury v. Madison, established the principle of judicial review. What this means is that the constitution is the supreme law of the land. Other laws enacted by legislative bodies, be they federal or state, when challenged, must be measured against the constitution. If a legislative act, when challenged, is found to be in conformity with the Constitution, it, too, becomes the law of the land. If, however, the act is found to be at variance with the constitution the latter must prevail and the act is declared unconstitutional.

Problems of interpretation arise because of the nature of the constitution. There are sections of the constitution that are vague and ambiguous. It is incumbent on the court, therefore, to choose between conflicting opinions in a particular case and interpret the constitution so as to determine the law. The Court does this through a study of the briefs presented, a study of the constitution itself and, in so far as possible, determining what the framers of that document had in mind with that section.

There is another fact involved that tends to guard against the Court's actually legislating from the bench. The Court does not issue advisory opinions. It does not make suggestions as to how a piece of legislation should be drawn to conform to the constitution. The Court will consider a case only if the appellant can show that he has suffered some sort of loss or injury because of present legislation. Thus, while the Court is not a legislature, it cannot render an opinion without appearing to create a new law and it is this fact which gives rise to the charge of "legislating from the bench."

Evolution and God

Volume 59 number 5-6, May/June 2009

I recently saw an article the heading of which said, in effect, Evolution vs. God. The article was obviously written by someone who was intent on proving that the theory of evolution has no validity. However, no matter how intent one might be in disproving something, it is grossly incorrect to pit God against it. No one can know the mind of God. What the writer should have said was Evolution vs. the Bible. There are many who pretend to know what the Bible says about evolution. The error in the heading arises out of the common error of equating the Bible with the word of God. All protestations to the contrary, the Bible is not literally the Word of God. It is true that many believe it is but that does not make it so. Many a Christian controversy could be avoided if the true nature of the Bible were understood, accepted, and appreciated.

In the world of science, and the secular world in general, the criterion is seeing, or receiving evidence of the concept through the senses before believing. "Seeing is believing," we say. In the theological world, or the world of the spirit, this statement which is so common and valid in the everyday world is, so to speak, inverted, or stood on its head, so that it becomes "Believing is seeing."

In some cases the author of several books about the Bible is known and credited with such a concept. For example, Hosea is the author of the book in the Old Testament that bears his name. So too, the apostle Paul is a prominent writer of books in the New Testament. In other cases tradition has settled on one or another person as the writer. Thus, the Pentateuch, or the first five books of the Bible are generally ascribed to Moses. Indeed, the Danish version of the Bible lists those five books as the books of Moses; thus Genesis is The First Book of Moses, Exodus, The Second Book of Moses, etc.

Of course the writer could claim to be an amanuensis, or secretary, who wrote exactly what God told him or her to write. While such an argument would be as difficult to refute as it would be to maintain, it would, to say the least, involve God in some very strange statements and contradictions. To suggest that the Bible is the word of God, based on the amanuensis theory, is to raise more questions than answers.

If, on the other hand, as many scholars believe, the books of the Bible were written independently by numerous individuals at various times and places, it is inevitable that their writing should reflect the culture, beliefs and customs of their time. Thus, through a reading or misreading of the Bible, some would conclude that God is opposed to abortion, what they really mean is that the writer of the book cited is reflecting the culture of a particular time and place. The position of God on the matter is not and cannot be known.

The Bible has a hallowed and valuable place in the Christian faith. Many of its precepts are as valid today as they were the day they were written. But make no mistake Christianity is not the religion of a book. Much as one might like to, one cannot fathom the mind of God by referring to a book. Life is not that simple.

The Triangle Fire

Volume 62 number 1, January 2012

The year 2011 marked the centennial of one of the most disastrous and dramatic industrial tragedies in the history of New York City. One hundred twenty-six persons lost their lives in this accident either by being burned alive or by leaping to their death from upper floor windows. The scene of this tragic accident was the Triangle Shirtwaist Factory which occupied the eighth, ninth and tenth floors of the Asch Building, later known as the Brown Building, in the area of Manhattan called Greenwich Village. Some 500 people worked on these three floors high above Greene Street and Washington Place. A pedestrian on one of the streets saw smoke pouring out on an eighth floor window and sounded the alarm. The time was 4:40 p.m. on March 25, 1911.

Meanwhile, on the eighth floor, workers quickly discovered they were trapped. The door leading to the stairway was locked from the stairway side. This reflected a common practice among employers. The door was locked to prevent petty theft by employees if they could leave without inspection. In any case no amount of effort could open the door. This left two alternatives – they could stay in the room and risk being burned alive or they could jump out of the eighth floor window and most certainly perish when they hit the street. The building did have a fire escape, but it had not been maintained and in some places had pulled away from the building. It could not be trusted with the weight of one person to say nothing of all of those in the workroom. The result that most took the option of jumping out the window. Of all the bodies later found on the street only one showed any signs of life.

The owners of the factory, which produced women's blouses, called shirtwaists, were Max Blanck and Isaack Harris. They had been at the factory that afternoon with their children.

The New York City fire department was not long in arriving at the scene, but there was little they could do. They had no ladders that could reach the eighth floor and, though the fire hoses were hooked to a fire hydrant, and the fire engine was operating, they could not reach high enough to extinguish the blaze with water.

In the aftermath of the disaster there were some developments related to it that should be noted. The victims were placed in coffins and buried in a common grave at one of the city cemeteries. The owners of the Triangle factory gave each of the victims' families $75.00 for the life they lost. The two men, Blanck and Harris, were indicted by a Grand Jury and charged with manslaughter. However, in spite of the evidence against them, they were acquitted. They were later, in a civil suit, found to have violated the law and were given a large fine.

In other developments legislation was eventually passed with led to improved standards for working conditions. The fire also had a positive effect on the growth of the International Ladies Garment Workers Union, an organization which has consistently fought for better working conditions for women.

Post Scripts

Volume 31 number 19, December 1982

As I write these lines a familiar feeling begins to make itself felt. I have experienced it at Nysted, Tyler, here in Des Moines, and in other places. Names like Helveg, Hoiberg, Thorvald Knudsen, Rodholm, Alfred Jensen, — one could call the roll of revered names in the Danish Church — come flooding in as one approaches a lectern or pulpit where these men have stood. Contemplation of these names and what they have meant to the church is in itself an exercise in humility. Now I must add the name of Johannes Knudsen, who edited this paper for so long. To contemplate replacing him as editor is alone enough to deflate the most pronounced ego. As I begin this work, therefore, I must ask you, the reader, to bear with me. 1 can't promise you a superior paper; I can't even promise a good paper. All that I can promise is that I will do my best to carry on in a long and noble tradition. I do not plan any drastic changes, though there will inevitably be some changes. I can say that I do not plan to edit the paper exactly as Johannes Knudsen did. Even if it were possible for me to do so I am sure it would not be the most desirable procedure. Rather than have the paper be a poor imitation of what Johannes Knudsen might do, I want it to represent the best that I can do. Then, and only then, will it be worthy of the heritage and tradition out of which it has grown.

One change in *Kirke og Folk* will be evident from the very outset. The last page has been the location for two editorials, one in English and one in Danish. I do not plan to write Danish editorials. This is in no way intended to minimize the Danish. I fully intend that the body of the paper shall reflect the best that is available to me in both Danish and English. My reason for not writing Danish editorials is two-fold. The first is that while 1 am able to speak and read Danish my writing of it leaves a great deal to be desired. Pastor Willard Garred has agreed to be editorial assistant and will proofread and write some Danish but I cannot expect him to put my thoughts into Danish words. The second reason is that I prefer that the editorial comments should be addressed to the entire readership of the paper and not any one segment of it. Therefore, this whole page will be written in English and, in the absence of any indication to the contrary, will be written by me. There may be times when the writings of others may appear here and, therefore, rather than call it the editor's page or something similar, I have chosen to call it Post Script because it will come at the end of each issue and often as a kind of related or unrelated afterthought.

From time to time I will call upon specific individuals to write for the paper. But, don't wait to be asked. If you have something or know of something that you feel should be printed I urge you to send it to me. This is especially true with regards to Danish material which becomes increasingly difficult to obtain. Naturally, I neither can nor will promise to print everything that might be sent but unless I see it there is no chance at all of its being published.

Not everyone can or wants to write but in one area each of you can help. Johannes Knudsen wanted very much to print news items. So do I. This is one reason for the existence of *Kirke og Folk*. However, I can keep others informed only to the extent that you keep me informed. So, I urge you to let me know when something interesting and significant happens to or among those of Danish background. Yes, maybe someone else will do so but it is always better to get a news item from two or three, or even ten, people than to never learn of it at all.

Letters from readers will be most welcome, and especially if they are critical. Your critical comments might lead to an improvement of the paper. If you want your letter printed this should be indicated. There is one condition, however — no anonymous letters will be printed except in the most unusual circumstance and then only if the editor knows who the writer is.

All editorial correspondence should be sent to me at my home address: 1529 Milton, Des Moines, Iowa 50316. If you lose that address, however, don't let that stop you. Send it to me at Grand View College and I will get it.

By a decision of the DIC Board, and following a suggestion of the late Dr. Knudsen, *Kirke og Folk* will become a monthly beginning in 1983. The paper will be issued on the 15th of each month. This means that the absolute deadline for materials to be in my hand must be the first of each month. This is necessary in order that there may be time for proper editing, mailing a copy to Askov, printing, and mailing of the completed paper.

Due to the nature of this issue, which carries so much material regarding Harald and Johannes Knudsen, all of which is in English and especially timely, there is very little Danish this time. This, however, emphatically does not mean that Danish will be eliminated in future issues. Readers are asked to understand that the sudden transition of the editorship and the abundance of materials about the Knudsens has made a difference this time.

Volume 32 number 6, June 1983

Over 100 people were registered for the event celebrating the bicentennial of the birth of N.F.S. Grundtvig which was held at Grand View College during the second weekend in May. It is safe to say that in most respects the event exceeded all expectations.

The featured speaker, Dr. K. E. Bugge, came from Denmark to participate in the meeting. That Dr. Bugge is one of the foremost Grundtvig scholars in Denmark, was quickly evident. Time and again listeners were impressed by the facts at his command and his addresses made the life and thought of the Danish bishop come alive for the audience. His first two lectures were more formal, with panels selected to respond to these. The last talk was more informal and Dr. Bugge showed slides related to the life of Grundtvig. In future issue we plan to bring excerpts from his talks.

Dr. Ernest Nielsen spoke to the group on Saturday afternoon and centered his thoughts on the translation of Grundtvig's writings. He stressed the need for scholars to have access to unabridged versions of Grundtvig. Another speaker, Dr. Roger Axford, came from Arizona State University at Tempe. His remarks were on the lighter side.

Participants in the meeting were unanimous in their view that it was a most worthwhile and enjoyable event. It was an event that did credit to the man who really conceived it and whose presence was missed — the late Dr. Johannes Knudsen.

A decision was made at the Danish Interest Conference Board meeting, which was held in connection with the Grundtvig celebration, that represents, in some respects, a drastic change. It was decided to give *Kirke og Folk* an English language name. It was felt that the English language articles are in a majority and that it is no longer in keeping with the times to retain a Danish title. Some might even be discouraged from subscribing to the paper on the assumption it is for Danes only. On the other hand, no one labors under the delusion that the change of name will result in a flood of new subscriptions.

The name chosen was *Church and Life*. A direct translation of *Kirke og Folk* would, of course, have been most desirable but, as every Danes knows, there is a problem with the word "folk." The problem arises in trying to find a word that embodies the concepts found in the Danish "folk." Therefore, the word "life" was settled on. This expresses some of the ideas found in the word "folk" and it is even somewhat expressive of the Grundtvigian concepts which undergird the paper. The old name will be retained in the masthead in smaller type which will say, "formerly *Kirke og Folk*." The use of the new name will begin with the July issue.

This change is really not as drastic as it may appear. The content of the paper will not be effected by the change. Neither will the spirit. For practical reasons we will call it *Church and Life*, but *Kirke og Folk* is by no means dead.

Another state has now been added to the ranks of those permitting pari-mutuel betting and, as this is being written, there is a possibility that Iowa will also have a state lottery. Arguments for and against such steps have occupied the legislators and the newspapers for months, and in some cases for years. This year, more than ever before, the bottom line is money. Through race-track gambling and a state lottery legislators see a way to easy money for the state without raising taxes. The fact that such steps might encourage crime, that those who can least afford it often become its victims, and that no matter what name one applies, it is still gambling — all of these arguments fell on deaf ears. Given the economic climate of America today, it is not too difficult to imagine that one day there will be a national lottery.

Aside from the possible increase in crime and the moral issue involved, my concern here is that we appear to have reached a point where anything goes as long as it will bring in money. The blame for this state of affairs rests squarely upon your shoulders and mine. I really can't blame our legislators. They are faced with the need for raising money. They know that you and I may be critical of them if our taxes are raised. So, they take the easy way out. They know that we would not soon forget about taxes. We would be reminded of those every year. They know also, from experience, that we will soon forget our objections to gambling and make the best of it. It is another example of the fact that we get the kind of government we are willing to pay for.

Today and every day, more than 34,000 children die, the majority from starvation and diseases made fatal by malnutrition.

Volume 32 number 10, October 1983

While there seems to be a general acceptance of, as well as some indifference to the new name for our paper I have also, to date, received a total of three letters opposed to it. Indeed, the writer of one of these letters sought to make an issue of it and circulated a petition on the question during the recent Fall meeting at Tyler. I am told that a small percentage of those present signed it.

The essence of the complaints is two-fold. It is claimed that the changing of the name represents a forsaking of our heritage. It is further claimed that the method of changing the name, which was done by a unanimous votes of the Board of the Danish Interest Conference, was undemocratic. Regarding this latter claim, two observations are in order. The first is that this represents a very narrow view of Democracy. To imagine that the business of the DIC can be conducted on the basis of Athenian Democracy or like a New England Town Meeting is to be completely unrealistic. A second observation is that a decision by the entire DIC presupposes attendance and voting rights at the meeting. Further, it must be borne in mind that the DIC publishes and heavily subsidizes the paper.

The other concern, that of forsaking our heritage, would be more serious, if true. However, I cannot accept the notion that changing the name of the paper represents turning one's back upon his heritage. If the complaints involved the content of the paper I would be much more concerned. There has been no complaint on that score.

I do not intend to become involved in endless and fruitless polemics concerning this issue. I yield to no one in my recognition of and respect for our Danish heritage. I do hope, however, that it goes a bit deeper than the name given a paper. It is one thing to maintain our roots, and this some of us are trying to do in numerous ways, but we do not want to become so entangled in them that we destroy them.

From time to time I receive requests at the archives for sources of information on Danish cooking and customs. Usually such requests come from persons planning a cookbook or some other expression of Danish customs. I think it is well that there are such expressions but I am beginning to think it is being overdone. One might easily give the notion that the Danes are a people who go about in quaint costumes eating "æbleskiver." Most of us know better. Not only is the Denmark of today one of the most advanced countries in the world but our heritage goes far beyond foods and customs. There is, for example a great body of literature, much of which has unfortunately not been translated but which has nevertheless had a great impact on the immigrants and their children. There is a way of life, a way of thinking and, acting that is decidedly Danish. There are thinkers that have greatly influenced Western Civilization. Men like Tyge Brahe, Bertil Thorvaldsen, Soren Kierkegaard, N.F. S. Grundtvig, Hans Christian Andersen, and Niels Bohr, to name a few, have left their mark. There is a heritage in song, gymnastics, and the folk schools. This is certainly not to suggest that the Danish heritage is greater or better than any other, but it is to say that it consists of much more than folk dancing and "æbleskiver."

Air pollution is taking its toll in many different ways. Human health is one area of concern and this is slowly receiving some attention. Removing lead from gasoline is one of the major steps in the direction of cleaner air. Air pollution, however, goes far beyond the effects it has on humans. It has an effect on stone buildings, for example. I saw the results of this on many of the fine old buildings in Copenhagen. To date, the effect has been, for the most part, aesthetic. Once beautiful buildings now have a drab appearance, an appearance not born of age but of an atmosphere that has discolored brick and stone to an extent that the builders would never have imagined. Before long the change will be more than aesthetic. Pollution is causing the stone and brick to deteriorate and serious structural damage will result before many years have passed. Pollution is a byproduct of an industrial society. Technology is now at hand to relieve this condition but it is often dismissed as not being "cost efficient." Be that as it may, someone is going to have to bear the astronomical costs involved in the repair or replacement of many buildings in America as well as Europe. It all adds up to the fact that, in one way or another, you and I are going to have to pay for the privilege of living in an industrialized society.

Volume 33 number 1, January 1984

It is quite common to hear those who have visited Denmark, particularly if they have some attachment to the church here, deplore the poor church attendance which they have seen. There is certainly no gainsaying the fact that church attendance is not as good in Denmark as in America. On the basis of my own limited observation, however, I would want to temper this somewhat by saying that, in my opinion, church attendance in Denmark is not really as bad as it is sometimes made out to be. Nor is it merely the older people who attend church. In America one often hears various explanations as to why the Danes do not attend church. However, most of the explanations that I have heard will not bear serious examination.

Be that as it may, the question as to why Danes do not go to church is, as far as I am concerned, the wrong question. Though it may bolster our own egos to think that others are not as faithful in church attendance as we are, that should not be our real concern. The real question is: "Why do we go to church why do I go to church?" Focusing attention on this question turns us aside from a self-righteous judgmental position and may lead to some needed self-examination. There can hardly be any question but that motives for church attendance can be quite mixed. Further, to my mind at least, many of the inducements and even gimmicks that are offered to get people to attend church are, to say the least, quite questionable. They have little to do with the purpose of the church to say nothing of how they relate to Christianity.

The primary purpose of church attendance should be worship. However, worship, ideally, should issue in service. There is a good deal of truth in the old adage, "When the worship ends, the service begins." Unfortunately, the evidence that this is the case in America is hardly overwhelming. So, though church attendance in Denmark leaves a great deal to be desired, the important question and the one that each of us can really come to grips with is, "Why do I go to church?"

The computer is one of the great inventions of our time. It has an almost unlimited variety of uses and it is gradually coming within reach of the average pocketbook. An Iowa poll recently revealed that the home computer was high on the list of the most desired Christmas gifts. Computers have long since become firmly established in the business world. They have become a common sight everywhere from reservations desks and banks to book dealers and parts departments. In the business world computers can perform a multitude of chores economically and efficiently. They are also, increasingly, being used in industry, where they can insure uniform production standards and eliminate high labor costs. The elimination of labor is, of course, one of the major criticisms leveled at the computer invasion. Nevertheless, despite protests, we may be sure that the computer will eventually be used more and more in labor intensive areas. And, in the long run, we will all be beneficiaries.

More recently the computer revolution has hit in the fields of education, the social sciences and medicine. Now it is being introduced into the home. In this latter case, no less than in the others, it is said to be able to perform a myriad of tasks. Indeed, so widespread are the uses of the computer that no child growing up in this day and age can feel that his education is complete if he does not have at least a nodding acquaintance with the computer.

Having said all this we must be aware that the computer, no matter how advanced or costly the model, has its limitations. To put it another way, no computer is smarter than the one who programmed it. Further, there is a serious question as to whether or not the expense of buying a computer is always justified by the results. I recently read an article by a computer authority who said it had been her experience that most of the tasks for which a computer might be used could be performed more quickly and more easily, to say nothing of more inexpensively, by traditional methods.

The computer can only be used for objective tasks, and, no matter how much one might try, the subjective cannot really be made objective. No matter how many facts he may feed into it, the computer cannot give the historian the answers to some of his most puzzling problems. No matter how many facts he may feed into it, the computer will not reveal the answer to the researcher's most troubling questions. And, no matter how many facts he may feed into it the computer cannot tell the young man that his love is returned.

The computer is a modern tool it is a good tool but like all tools it has its limitations and it is only as useful as the person using it is knowledgeable. However much we may tend to glorify it, the computer is no substitute for the human mind. It may be faster but it is really no smarter than you are — and that should be a consoling thought for those who may fear that the machines are taking over our society.

Volume 33 number 2, February 1984

This is certainly not intended to be a lesson in grammar or English. I am hardly competent to give such. However, there are some rather common usages which are not only incorrect but, when one stops to think about them, highly amusing. One such which has long amused me and which one sees time and again, even in serious writing, is "advance planning'" or "plan ahead." Is there really any kind of planning which must not be done in advance? Another very common expression is "hot water heater." Again, something is said to be, "very unique." The fact is that a thing is either unique or not unique. There are no degrees of uniqueness.

The use and misuse of language has other amusing facets. One of the expressions which was often used by Richard Nixon and which still finds its way into some discourse is, "at this point in time," which translated means simply, "now." Then, too, there are certain words that seem to become popular for a time, apparently because they sound very learned and seem to give the speaker more status. Sometimes, however, the result is more conducive of laughter than awe. For example, for a time the word "parameters" was very widely used. Unfortunately, the users did not always really know what the word means.

Probably the most persistent and growing trend is in the direction of making verbs out of nouns. Such expressions as "hospitalize" and "hosted" have long been with us and have worked their way into the language. More recently there has been a tendency to add "ize" to everything under the sun. So we "finalize," we "prioritize" and some are even busy "prioritizing." And, if parents are busy with "parenting" perhaps children can be described as "childing."

A final area in which language is misused is spelling. Here my concern is not mistakes in spelling. No matter how well intentioned one may be, errors are bound to occur. My concern is with deliberate changes in spelling, such as "nite" for night, "donut" for doughnut, "sno" for snow, etc., *ad nauseum*. As a mother once said to me, "How do you expect children to learn to spell when they see such things, usually on signs, all around?"

When he was editor of *The New York Times*, Theodore M. Bernstein wrote a lively and informal guide to better writing called, *Watch Your Language*. In daily conversation it may not be so important, but it is often important for us to watch our language more than we do. I am inclined to think that there may be a direct relationship between carelessness in language and carelessness in thinking.

Yes, I know, language changes, but I know, too, that this often becomes a rationalization for playing fast and loose with the language.

When I assumed the editorship of this paper I promised myself that, barring some major problem, the paper would never be late on my account. My deadlines are such as to allow time for editing and ample time for printing and mailing. I know, too, that the publishing company gets it's part of the job done on time. Likewise, I am told, the post office in Askov does not delay. Give or take a day or two. *Church and Life* is always in the mail on the 15th of each month. What happens to it after that only God and the postal service know. Complaints about the late arrival of the paper are very common but there is simply nothing that the editor or the publisher can do about it. *Church and Life* is no exception. This is the common fate of second class mail.

Postal rates have risen repeatedly in the past few years and they will undoubtedly do so again. In itself this is neither surprising nor as bad as it might seem. Given the cost of other goods and services the postal rates are really not unreasonable. However, it almost seems there is an inverse correlation between the rates and the service — i.e. as the rates go up the quality of the service goes down. Certainly I do not know all the facts and I do not understand all the problems that may be involved. But, when I consider the kind of postal service that used to exist, the present service seems to me to be nothing less than a disgrace.

So, if your *Church and Life* is overdue, and your subscription has not expired, there is not much to do but wait. Somewhere along the way the postal service is making haste, in a cloud of snail's dust, to get it to you. The only alternative is to have it sent by first class mail. However, not only would that be a costly matter (about 37¢ per copy) but it would involve much extra work for the publisher.

There is one consolation in all of this. Apparently *Church and Life* is not considered "junk mail" by the postal service. If it were, judging by the amount of such mail which I receive, ". . .neither snow, nor rain, nor heat, nor gloom of night..." would delay its arrival.

Volume 33 number 3, March 1984

It would not be difficult to document the view that, historically, it is the poor who have borne the brunt of war. In America, during the Civil War, the well-to-do could, for a price, escape military service. It was simply a matter of hiring a substitute. In later times there have been more sophisticated ways of passing the burden to the poor with the result that, generally speaking, those at the top have reaped the glory (to the extent that there is glory in war) and those at the bottom have reaped the suffering.

Times really have not changed. In an ever-deepening search for security, the real burden of a vastly overblown defense budget is being borne by those least able to bear it.

It is being borne by the aged who, in spite of ever- rising medical costs, must pay more for Medicare so there will be more money with which to build bombs. It is being borne by the destitute, those who do not know where their next meal is to come from, in order that the Pentagon may know from where its next bomber is to come.

It is being borne by hungry and undernourished children, who are a part of America's future, because it seems more important to some to nourish the military.

It is being borne by the homeless who must forego their need for shelter in the interest of sheltering more missiles.

It is being borne by those with a limited income in order that spending for the military may be unlimited.

It is being borne by youth, America's most priceless asset, because a government would rather invest in weapons than in education.

All this, and more, is being done in the interest of making our nation strong and secure. Yet, strangely enough, our insecurity seems to grow daily. Could it not be that this is because our real strength and security lie in doing precisely the opposite of what we are doing? Could it not be that a country is really strong and really secure only to the degree that it takes care of its aged, feeds its hungry, nourishes its young, shelters its homeless, has compassion on its poor, and educates its youth? If we fail in these things, weakness and insecurity will continue to plague us no matter how elaborate our defense or how huge our military budget.

One can hardly read a newspaper or a news release of any kind without running into the expression, "task force." Governments at every level, churches, schools, and organizations of all kinds have a task force for this or a task force for that. One seldom hears of a committee these days. I rather suspect that not only has the committee fallen into disrepute but that the new term, task force, sounds much more impressive. If I am not mistaken the term comes from the military and carries with it a sense of importance and urgency. In any case, the expression, task force, has really made itself felt in the language — for a while. Incidentally, the term "task farce" would be much more appropriate in many cases.

The use of that term for what is really a committee for a particular purpose, leads me to think of other euphemisms that have found their way into common usage. Webster tells us that a euphemism is "... t h e substitution of an agreeable or inoffensive expression for one that may offend or suggest something unpleasant." There is nothing new about euphemisms. Some of us are old enough to recall that the defense department was once called the war department — a not very pleasant sounding term but one of which I am increasingly reminded lately.

It does seem, though, that the use of euphemisms has increased in recent years. Most of them are harmless enough and may even, upon reflection, provoke a chuckle or two. One such recently came to my notice. A news release from one of the church bodies noted that family nights are now increasingly being called "inter-generational events." We have several associated with the unpleasant facts of death and burial. People do not die, they "pass away," and then they are "laid to rest." Consideration for the feelings of children probably accounts for the fact we say the veterinarian "puts 'Rover' to sleep."

Well, you listen, and think about it. You'll find that the proverbial spade is not always called a spade — and maybe that's just as well sometimes.

Enough of this. I must go put the trash out so the garbage collector — oops, I mean the sanitation engineer can pick it up.

CORRECTION: In the last Post Script — the one on use of language — I appeared to have my nouns and verbs mixed up. The sentence said, ". . .making nouns out of verbs." It should have said ". . .making verbs out of nouns." Grammar never was my strong suit.

Volume 33 number 6, June 1984

In his play, *A Merchant of Venice*, Shakespeare, with a profundity for which he is noted, has Portia say to Shylock, "In the course of justice none of us should see salvation." I think of this often when the issue of justice of one kind or another is raised. In the Christian perspective, at least, if we never get beyond justice we will have, as it were, missed the boat. It is mercy and not justice that we get from God it is mercy and not simply justice that we should extend to our fellow humans of whatever color, status, or ideology. Mercy is the ideal justice is but a step, albeit an important step, in that direction. Unfortunately, humanity still has not taken the decisive step demanded by justice.

In our own land, social, economic, and racial barriers have not really come down even though all kinds of lip service are given to their removal. Yes, things are a bit better than they were a generation ago but there is still much that needs to be done before anything like justice can be claimed. At the moment it seems that, at best, we are at a standstill in this respect. It may even be argued, and not without reason, that we are moving backward.

In our behavior toward the rest of the world justice is hardly in the forefront. While much of the world goes hungry, dieting has become an obsession in America and the Western World generally. Can we speak of justice in a world in which such disparity is clearly evident? Is there justice in a world in which many go to bed bloated while more go to bed hungry? Is there justice in a world where the rich get richer and the poor get poorer? Is there justice in Central America where a few own the land and that many do the work? Is there justice in the world when each of the two great powers acts as if Satan has taken up residence in the other's domain? It takes very little insight to know that the world is a long way from justice. The prophet Micah's reminder, "...to do justice, and to love kindness..." remains a remote goal.

All of this may sound a bit idealistic and so indeed it may be. But, let us not forget that justice has a pragmatic, a very pragmatic, dimension. Whatever else one may say about war and its causes, in the final analysis, it is injustice that makes war possible and probable. In a world of justice, no dictator, no warmonger, no wild-eyed adventurer, could raise much of a following. It is only when the reality of injustice can be pointed out and the perception of injustice can be made felt that revolution becomes a threat and war becomes a possibility.

In S. D. Rodholm's adaptation of "Kongernes Konge" (Lord of Creation) there is a line which expresses such an obvious truth that it should be burned into the minds of political leaders and their people everywhere.

78

"Show us," it says, "that peace dwell where justice is might." If that is true, and I firmly believe it is, then the converse is equally true. That is to say that unrest, and even war, follows where justice is ignored. We may long for peace, we may even pray for peace, but as long as there are those whose longings and prayers are for justice, the best we can hope for is an absence of open conflict — for a time. God help us if in that time we do not come to see that true and lasting peace is and must be rooted in justice.

People everywhere deserve justice. Unlike mercy it is an inherent right. When that right has been met, when justice has been extended to all, then, and only then, can we rightfully begin to speak of showing mercy.

There is a scene in Kaj Munk's play, *The Word*, in which one of the characters who is considered by the others to have lost his senses, returns and appears to be in full possession of his faculties. He is greeted with, "Well, I see you have come to your senses again." His reply is, "No, not my sense, but yours."

How often do we not judge the wisdom and even the intelligence of others by our own position. If they agree with what we say we tend to think they are bright, intelligent, and wise. Disagreement with us may lead to a questioning of these things. We do, indeed, tend to accept people by whether or not they have come to our senses. That can hardly be considered showing good sense.

Volume 33 number 9, September 1984

There are two areas in which every American seems to consider himself an authority. One is religion and the other is politics. They are areas in which ignorance is king and in which verbal diarrhea and intellectual constipation go hand in hand. Without question this accounts for the fact that we get so many odd, and even dangerous, ideas in both spheres. When the two are joined, as they are in this election year, partisan and religious rhetoric may easily subvert both the truth and the common good.

This, of course, does not mean that only those such as ministers and political scientists have all the answers or the only answers. Far from it! Generally, however, these people are at least aware of the complexity of the problems.

The recurring problem of prayer in the public school is a case in point. Regular readers of *Church and Life* will know that I have long been opposed to this. It is again being trotted out as an important issue in this election. Once again, much of what is being said about it represents a complete misconception of religion, a gross distortion of American history, and flies in the face of psychological reality.

While it certainly has social implications, religious belief is an intensely personal matter. Further, to imagine that God is pleased because children pray in a classroom borders on the naive. Finally, to think that such action by pupils in a public school will inspire faith is questionable to say the least. Many of the pupils will have no other contact with religion and will see prayer as a kind of starting gun for the day's activities. Meanwhile, religion in which God is served by more than words is lost from sight.

It is often said that we must return to the faith of the founding fathers by restoring religion to the classroom. Those we refer to as the founding fathers were, for the most part, Deists. They had little, if any, use for prayer. As for religion being a part of education, it must be recalled that early education was not public. While religion was later given the nod in some public schools this was by no means universal. The President, who favors school prayer, said recently that when he was growing up in Illinois each school day was begun with prayer. Perhaps so, but in 1910, or about the time the President was born, the state court in Illinois banned Bible reading in the schools of that state. Similar bans were imposed in Wisconsin in 1890, Louisiana in 1915, and South Dakota in 1929. Twelve states had banned Bible readings by 1963. It was banned on the ground that it is sectarian. Is prayer, no matter how innocuous, any less sectarian?

Those who favor prayer in the public school place great stress on the fact that it would be voluntary. Voluntary prayer is not now nor has it ever been under ban. No court or constitution has ever said that if Johnny wants to pray he may not do so. The question, therefore, centers on what is meant by voluntary. Is it really voluntary when the pupils, with encouragement from the teacher decide they should begin the day with prayer? And, what about those who are of another faith — or no faith? Is it psychologically realistic to assume that little children will voluntarily ostracize themselves from the classroom while others pray?

The fact is that religion, and prayer in particular, is in danger of becoming a political football, kicked about in the interests of partisan advantage. Much, much more could be said to show this. Suffice it to say here that the whole matter of the advocacy of prayer in the public school will simply not bear examination.

From time to time one sees references to something called the "real world." The implication of that statement is generally that anyone who is not involved in the most crass commercialism lives in an unreal world of fantasy and dreams. Thus, for example, college students are often told, or at least made to feel, that one day they will have to come face to face with reality. Those who speak with such familiarity of the "real world" are also those who are fond of such expressions as, "It's a jungle out there."

It is true of course that in some respects the work-a-day world presents some of the characteristics of a jungle in which only the most fit intellectually, socially, and economically survive. But it is quite another matter to call this the real world. It may in fact be anything but the real world. I could think of a host of questions, cold, hard, practical questions that could be directed to those who speak so knowingly of the real world. For starters one might ask when the real world will learn that the supply of energy is finite or that playing nuclear games is hardly conducive of any future.

The sophisticated exponents of what they call reality are quick to reject objections to their views as being naive. It may be that they are right but then again it may be that they are the most naive of all.

Volume 33 number 11, November 1984

Apparently something went wrong during the printing, with the result that the calendar which hangs in my office did not show any Sundays one month. Think of it — a month without Sundays. Think of the implications that could have if such were really the case.

As a teenager I felt Sunday was the most boring day of the week and I must confess that I still feel that way occasionally. On the other hand, I'm afraid that Sunday is a day whose worth cannot be fully appreciated until we are without it. Many of those who must be employed on Sunday would undoubtedly testify to that. It is the one day of the week that is completely different from all the others. For most it is a day of rest and recreation for others it is a day for doing that which they did not get done the rest of the week. For many it is a day of worship.

Sunday, of course, has its origins in the Christian faith. Since the resurrection took place on the first day of the week, the admonition to "Remember the Sabbath and keep it holy" was applied by the early Christians to that day rather than to the last day of the week. Like Christmas, Sunday is a religious holiday, though this is becoming less and less evident as the years go by — just as it is with Christmas. A quarter of a century ago the question as to whether or not stores should be open on Sunday was a hotly debated issue. Now Sunday shopping is taken for granted and, especially with the advent of the shopping mall, it has even become a kind of leisurely way to spend a Sunday afternoon, particularly if the weather is inclement.

Basically it is technology which has forced the change. Indeed, however much we might like to think otherwise, most often it is pragmatism, born of technological change, that is really in the vanguard of ideological, cultural, social, and even religious change. In the case of Sunday radical change has been brought about by the invention and ever more widespread use of the motor car.

When I think of what Sunday was like when I was a child I find myself wondering what changes the next fifty years will bring. Will Sunday become more like the other days of the week? Will the churches set aside some convenient evening for their services — as they have already done in the case of Thanksgiving — thus making a mockery not only of worship but of Christianity itself? Most of us will not be around to find out but if I have my "druthers" the elimination of Sunday from the calendar will never be more than a printing error and it will remain a red letter day.

While I was growing up I had occasion many times to pass a certain school building. It was a relatively new building and over one of the doors was the inscription, "Education, the security of a nation." Each time I saw those words I became more impressed by them and came to feel that education was indeed the key to many things, not least of which was the security of the nation. Now, some fifty years later, I have serious reservations about the matter.

In the years since that time high school education has become the rule rather than the exception and millions of American youth have either graduated from or at least attended college. Yet the phenomenal increase in such things as drug and alcohol abuse, divorce, psychiatric counseling, crime, and especially armaments, testify to the fact that, both individually and collectively, we are more insecure than ever.

One can speculate a great deal on the reasons for this and there are undoubtedly a number of causes. Seldom is a widespread social phenomenon caused by a single factor but rather by a combination of these. For what it is worth, however, I would suggest that one of the prime causes is education — or more correctly, the lack of it. While it is true that more and more people receive an increasing amount of schooling and are more adequately trained, it is becoming less and less evident that there is much education connected with the process. What is referred to as education is too often centered around teaching that will enable the student to earn more money and increase his standard of living. This, I would argue, is not education but training. Training is unquestionably important in this day and age but it should not be confused with nor substituted for education. It is an open secret that, for all of our emphasis on schooling, functional illiteracy is very high in this country.

Education involves more than being able to perform a delicate operation, plead a case, preach a sermon, program a computer, repair a motor, wire a house, or any of a myriad of other things that require special training. Education involves some knowledge of the rudiments of language, history, geography, mathematics, science (not technology), — in short, liberal arts. Training is certainly important and necessary but it should proceed only when an adequate groundwork has first been laid in the liberal arts.

Aside from faith there is no ultimate security of course. It would be my contention, however, that liberal arts offers a greater degree of security than obtains at present. Schooling, training alone, will lead to an ever increasing insecurity, both individual and collective. Education, in so far as major stress is placed on liberal arts, still best defines the path to security for this or any other nation.

Volume 34 number 1, January 1985

Således Blev Jeg Hjemlos is the title which Enok Mortensen chose to give his first novel, published in 1934. The hero of the story was an emigrant who had severed ties with the land of his birth but who had not yet established himself in his chosen country. In some respects it may be said that he felt like a man without a country. This was a very common feeling among the immigrants and probably no less so for Enok. He may well have felt that the transition from the old world to the new had made him homeless. Yet, however much he may have felt that way, Enok never really became homeless, at least not in the area in which he counts most — in the hearts and minds of his countless friends on both sides of the Atlantic. He was thoroughly appreciated in both America and Denmark. Indeed, we in America had to continually remind ourselves that Enok was an immigrant and I am confident that the Danes had difficulty realizing that he had emigrated. It was as if he had never left Denmark and yet had always lived in America. He was as welcome in one as the other. Few have ever so completely embodied the best of both worlds.

So, too, he contributed the best of each world to the other.

Through his teaching at Askov Folk School, Enok brought to the students a better understanding of America, just as through his latest novel he gave the Danes a new appreciation of immigrant life. Most of us, of course, are particularly mindful of his contributions to life in America, and especially through the Danish Church. His preaching probably had the most widespread influence largely because most of it was in the English language. The fictional literature that he produced delighted those who could read it in the Danish language in which it was written. Though not as well known, especially to the younger generation among us, Enok's contribution to research and understanding of the Danish immigrant to America was phenomenal. Without any reservation it can be said that no one, either in this country or in Denmark, had as comprehensive and correct a view of the Danish immigrant as did Enok.

The most important thing to be said about his writing and research is that he did it because he wanted to he felt it as his responsibility. In this respect his life is a vivid example of the fact that the best things and the most important accomplishments are not always those in which the reward can be measured in dollars and cents. The rewards of Enok's work, by and large, have accrued to all of us in that it is we who have profited by his research and his insights.

With the passing of Enok Mortensen another "giant" of the Danish Church has fallen. He lives on, however, both in the memories of all who knew him as well as in the written heritage he leaves behind.

Backpacking in the Adirondack Mountains of northern New York State was my favorite vacation experience as a young man. To backpack in the Adirondacks meant that one often had to cross roaring mountain streams on cable bridges. If you have ever had the experience of being on such a bridge you will know that they swing and sway and you come to feel that every step may be your last. Crossing such a bridge with a full pack on your back can be a hair-raising experience. With every step the bridge moves and you quickly come to feel that you, backpack and all, will surely tumble into the stream below.

I have often thought of that experience in later years, particularly when a certain hymn of Grundtvig's has been sung in Danish. In one stanza of that hymn there are lines in which faith is compared to a bridge above a raging torrent. There are two Danish versions of those lines. In one version, Grundtvig speaks of an arched bridge in the other he calls it a swaying bridge. Frankly, I do not know which of the two is the original but I do know that I prefer the image presented by the latter. The lines which I prefer read, in the Danish:

> O vidunder tro!
> Du slår over dybet din gyngende bro...
> *(Psalmebog for Kirke og Hjem, #614)*

S. D. Rodholm's translation of those lines reads:

> The highway of faith
> A footbridge o'erhanging the torrent of death...
> *(A Sheaf of Songs, #5)*

The Christian faith is like a bridge, a swaying bridge, upon which one must walk, especially during the more difficult periods of life. Like a cable footbridge, it can give much cause for concern, but the cables are firmly anchored in the rock that is Christ. However uncertain it may seem, faith can bear the heaviest load that is placed on it. The danger, and the only danger, is that somehow one may lose faith and, as it were, fall from it and tumble into the depths of gloom and despair. Faith is, as Grundtvig says, miraculous. Like a slender cable it can make possible great things and, above all, it can make possible the passage from death to life.

As we enter a new year, each of us, regardless of our age or station in life, knows full well that the days ahead are filled with uncertainties. This is true of both our collective and our individual lives. But, by walking the highway of faith, by walking on the "footbridge o'erhanging the torrent of death" we may be assured that, despite the vicissitudes of the moment, faith will carry us through this year and every year.

Volume 34 number 2, February 1985

In fulfilling my editorial duties for Church and Life I use a good number of 17¢ stamps. Many times, therefore, I am reminded of Rachel Carson, whose picture is featured on that stamp.

Her book. *Silent Spring,* which was first published almost a quarter of a century ago has made a decisive difference in the way many of us think about America and, indeed, the world. In a book published in 1970, the author ranks Rachel Carson's *Silent Spring* along with such others as Thomas Paine's *Common Sense* and Alexis de Tocqueville's *Democracy in America,* as one of twenty-five books that has changed America. When Rachel Carson died a number of years ago the *New York Times,* in a front page obituary, called her "one of the most influential women of her time."

Rachel Carson was influential. Through *Silent Spring* in particular, she began to flash a warning signal about what we were doing to our environment. It was she who called to popular attention the fact that western industrialized society cannot continue to grow and develop by simply using "more of the same" methods. She sounded an early warning against soil pollution, air pollution, and other forms of environmental damage that can eventually lead to an environmental disaster.

In the years since that time some progress has been made in these matters. Organic gardening is, for many, now a reality. Organic farming still has a long way to go but some authorities see it as a distinct possibility. The damage to lakes and streams has been reduced — though hardly eliminated. We have become very conscious of air pollution though there is still a good deal of resistance to taking steps that will insure clean air.

During recent years, however, the things of which Rachel Carson made us aware have begun to recede into the background. To be sure, such things as clean air, pure water, and environmental preservation are still given lip service, but increasingly such phrases as "cost effectiveness" get in the way of action.

It may well be that for the immediate present the necessary action to preserve the environment is not cost effective. But to act, or fail to act, on that basis is nothing less than to be short-sighted. After all, how should cost effectiveness really be measured? Who can say it really does not pay to clean the air, purify the water, or preserve the environment. I have a notion that our grandchildren will not thank us if we see fit to let cost effectiveness override the warnings of Rachel Carson. I am reminded of this every time I use a 17¢ stamp.

A bill has now been filed in the Iowa Legislature which would make it easier to break the law. Whether or not the bill will pass remains to be seen but, given the present political climate, it would not be surprising if it should become law. The bill would, in essence, provide a less severe penalty for breaking the 55 miles per hour speed limit; a penalty that is really not very severe in the first place.

There is on the part of many a constant concern with trying to eliminate the 55 mile speed limit, a limit which grew out of the oil crisis in the early 1970s. Leaving aside the fact that there is an unwillingness to face the reality that the supply of oil is finite, there is no question but that a lower speed limit saves lives. This is a truth which has not and cannot be successfully debated. Nevertheless, there is an all too common feeling, and especially among truckers, that the "interstate railroad," as I call it, is there to be used as they please and let others beware.

To be sure, I sometimes exceed the speed limit, though not intentionally. I know only too well that the combination of modern cars and good highways makes it easy to exceed the boundaries of good sense. But, I know this too, that if I do get a ticket for speeding I will have deserved it. I will have none but myself to blame for any consequences that might follow.

An obsession with speed, an excessive impatience has come to characterize our society. There is an old adage that says, "haste makes waste." It may be an old adage but it is a constant truth, as I certainly have experienced many times. All too often that which has been hastily done has little to commend it except that fact. I like that TV commercial which has an artist pointing to a picture and saying, "Would you believe I painted that in three hours?" A passing waiter replies, "Yes, I would."

Nowhere is this haste more evident, and often painfully so, than on the nation's highways. Not only so, but there are all kinds of attempts to justify it. Some of them are as elaborate as they are ludicrous. One I read a while ago was an article the purpose of which was to show that the 55 mile limit was costly in terms of dollars because of time spent behind the wheel of a car. I have no doubt but that figures can be adduced to show that but the bottom line is that excessive speed is costly in terms of lives.

Certainly there are emergency situations when speed is necessary. However, most of the reasons given for excessive speed will not bear examination. One I have not heard, but one that would not surprise me in the least, is that someone was hurrying to participate in a "right to life" demonstration — and never mind how many lives might have been threatened in the process of seeking to get there on time.

Volume 34 number 5, May 1985

I have in hand a press release indicating that the replies of a number of members polled within a certain Lutheran body in this country were, by a margin of three to two, favorable to the death penalty. Leaving aside the question of the wisdom of determining a Christian position by taking a poll, the result of this one is certainly discouraging. One wonders just what kind of impact the Church has had if a majority takes this view. Even more discouraging is the fact that a current poll of the total population of the United States indicates a six-to-one margin of support for the death penalty.

I surely do not condone murder and have no question but that those guilty of such a crime should be kept off the streets. However, to advocate capital punishment for that crime, or any crime, no matter how heinous it may have been, is to seek a very simplistic solution to a very complex problem — to say nothing of its implications for Christianity.

The argument is generally made that the threat of the death penalty is a deterrent. There is not the slightest shred of evidence to indicate this and there is much to show that it is not true. One is reminded of the fact that there was a time in the history of England when it was the custom to hang pickpockets in the public square. The practice was discontinued when it was found that such public events attracted an unusually large number of pickpockets.

Then, too, it is said that this is a sure way to make certain that such a criminal will never have another opportunity to commit a crime. There is no arguing with that. But suppose, just suppose, that a mistake is made — and there have been such. The classic mistake was made on a hill outside of Jerusalem some 2,000 years ago. Make no mistake — those who condemned Jesus to death were sincerely convinced he was a criminal who was best gotten rid of, and the sooner the better. They were unmistakably among those who were "whooping it up" for capital punishment.

Beyond these concerns, however, lies a very practical one. Just who are those who are executed for their crimes? The record is very clear! When was the last time a person of wealth, or power, or position was made to pay the ultimate price for his crime? Have such never been found guilty of a capital crime? Indeed they have but they have almost always been able to avoid execution. But those who are poor, those who are black, those who are defenseless, and those who are friendless are generally the ones who pay with their lives. One suspects that the real reason is that society would just as soon be rid of them anyway.

There is no question but that criminals must be restrained. If at all possible they should be rehabilitated but, regardless of the success or failure of such an effort, society has no right to play God with the life of a human being. In my view, capital punishment is nothing less than legalized murder and the hands of society are stained by the blood of every victim of its vindictiveness.

The Lutheran Book of Worship has been in use in most of our congregations for some years now. Most of us have had ample time to become familiar with and accustomed to it. For my part, I find that there are some things that I like about it. The order for worship is somewhat more simple than that in the *Service Book and Hymnal*. Indeed, in some ways it is not too far removed from the old order used for years in the Danish Church in America and still used in Denmark. Though that service was hardly carved in stone, long familiarity with it is not easily wiped out. Another generation may have as much difficulty changing from this order as an earlier generation had changing to it.

Those of us who are of Danish background might have liked to see more than eight of Grundtvig's hymns in the book but the fact there are no more may represent as much of a failing on our part as on the part of the committee. Perhaps the day will come when a new edition will incorporate more of what many of us consider fine hymns. While there is still a tendency on the part of many Lutherans in America to look askance at Grundtvig, that's not the whole story. In some cases the translations need to be adapted to America. For example, in that great Pentecost hymn, which has been translated under the title, 'The sun now shines in all its splendor," we sing of "nightingales" and "Whitsunday lilies." These things are not meaningful in America.

I would fault the *Lutheran Book of Worship*, however, for the alteration of some hymns. I am not here concerned so much with the frequent attempts — sometimes very crude attempts — to eliminate archaic and sexist language. In some cases this had led to some ludicrous lines but then, a silent chuckle is not out of order in church.

What I am really concerned about is alterations which appear to be a complete change of the author's intent. Two examples will suffice — and I must confess that they are hymns that held great appeal for me.

The first is a Welsh hymn, written in 1845, by William Williams. They hymn, "Guide me, O thou great Jehovah," has been translated into many languages. It is based on imagery drawn from the journey of the Israelites through the wilderness. Now the hymn is called, "Guide me ever, great redeemer" (number 343). I have no objection to being guided by a redeemer but I do have objection to altering the intent and even the theology, of the writer, to say nothing of the fact that the spirit of the metaphor has been violated.

The other example in which I believe the intent of the author has been ignored is the well-known hymn, "Blest be the tie that binds." In this hymn (number 370) there was a line that read, "the fellowship of kindred minds." It now reads "the fellowship of heart and mind." Even a nodding acquaintance with the circumstances which led John Fawcett to write this hymn makes it clear that this change does not represent what he had in mind. He was about to move to another pastorate but at the last moment could not leave those he had learned to know and love. Hence, "the fellowship of kindred minds."

Altering hymns in this fashion is, it seems to me, tantamount to slipping new thoughts into familiar forms. There is an alternative, albeit a more difficult one. If one does not like the thought of a particular hymn he can write a new one.

Volume 34 number 8, August 1985

"Lord, we are assembled in this Thy house..." (Herre, vi er kommet ind i dette dit hus). These are the familiar words that sounded as I came to attend the worship service of the West Denmark congregation shortly after the church building there was destroyed by fire. The congregation does use the new service but has retained the old opening and closing prayers. The service was held in the parish hall, as it will be for some time, and I could not help but reflect on the larger meaning those words took on at that time. I was reminded that a parish hall is God's house as well as is a magnificent cathedral. In a centuries old cathedral, a modern church building, or a plain parish hall God is present and we can rightfully say "...we are assembled in this Thy house."

We are accustomed to using the word "church" in various ways, not the least of which is in referring to a building in which worship services are generally held. But, in a larger sense, and in a more correct sense, the church is God's people. Further, it is only as His people gather in a building that it becomes His house. As Grundtvig has put it:

> We are God's house of living stones,
> Builded for His habitation. . .

How easy it is to forget that how easy it is to forget that the church is really not a building nor is it a remote abstraction; it is a living entity, as close to us as we are to God.

Of course it is as nice as it is practical to have a building that is beautifully appointed and set aside for the worship of God. Nevertheless, circumstances at times remind us that whenever and wherever we come face to face with God we are in His house or in His presence. You and I must never forget that, in the final analysis, we are the church. This is a fact of which we need to be especially mindful as we face the manifold tasks of the church in today's world.

Incidentally, the worship service at West Denmark fell during the annual Family Camp conducted by the congregation. I was, therefore, both interested and pleased to note that as soon as the worship service has ended, chairs were moved aside and the children's folk dancing began. Not only did this strike me as quite fitting but it caused me to reflect anew on the wholesomeness of a faith that can readily combine the sacred and the secular in this manner. Or, come to think of it — is it really healthy to separate the two?

In 1968, following in the wake of the assassinations of Martin Luther King and Robert Kennedy, the Congress passed and the president signed some rather mild gun control legislation. Now, seventeen years later, the

Senate has voted to abolish some of the provisions of that legislation thus making it easier to purchase, transport, and sell firearms. This action was taken, not in response to a lower murder rate nor to a lessened threat of assassinations, but to pressure brought to bear on the Congress by the National Rifle Association (NRA). At this point the outcome of the proposed new legislation is still to be determined but, given the present political climate, it would not be surprising if guns were made even more readily available than is the case at present.

The NRA is a group among whose belief's seems to be the idea that one's manliness is proved by the fact that he carries a gun. It reminds me of the fact that I once heard someone wonder aloud what kind of a man it was that thought he had to carry a gun. This urge to be a gun-toting American is, in part, a hangover from the days of the frontier. It is also related to the desire of some to display their machismo — though so often such individuals succeed only in making themselves look ridiculous.

The NRA and assorted "gun nuts" never tire of pointing to the Second Amendment to the Constitution which carries the phrase, "... the right to keep and bear arms shall not be infringed." They also seem to enjoy simplifying the issue with such well-known bumper stickers as "When guns are outlawed, only outlaws will have guns." To the latter one need only say, "Of course!" If guns were outlawed one would be an outlaw if he had a gun. As for the matter of the amendment, even a cursory examination makes it clear that the NRA's view is based on nothing more than wishful thinking. Those who so passionately cite the phrase in question conveniently omit the words which precede and constitute the rationale for ". . .the right to bear arms..." The Second Amendment really says, "A well regulated Militia, being necessary to the security of a free State, the right of the people to keep and bear arms, shall not be infringed." Quite apart from the fact that this is 1985 and not 1791, would all those who clamor for guns be willing to become a part of a well regulated militia?

Certainly gun control will not eliminate murder but only a willful blindness can fail to see that it could help a great deal toward that end. And, this is to say nothing of what happens somewhere every day when loaded guns fall into the hands of children.

Time and again polls have shown that most Americans favor some form of control of lethal weapons. Reason, common sense if you will, points out how unwise and even stupid it is to be without rigid controls. One would expect, therefore, that reason and common sense would bring such controls. Well, don't hold your breath waiting! The macho mentality, which I suspect is born of an insecurity, demands a gun, and how often does reason triumph over such an emotional complex as insecurity?

Volume 34 number 9, September 1985

On a recent Sunday morning I did something which I am not accustomed to doing on that day and at that hour — I turned on the television set. All at once I found myself viewing a scene which I shall not soon forget. I saw a large amphitheatre-like room filled with hundreds of people. On the platform, amid many floral decorations, a man strode back and forth, microphone in hand, ostensibly preaching. I had tuned in to one of those many programs which have come to be referred to as "electronic church."

The speaker (I can't make myself call him a preacher) spoke in angry terms. His message had to do with pornography, a subject concerning which he had all the answers. I will not dignify his talk by calling it a sermon — though he probably thought it was such. There was no love, no forgiveness, no goodness in it. Neither will I dignify it by referring it to as a lecture. It was long on wrath and short on facts logic was distorted and reason was absent. The one word that repeatedly comes to mind as I think back on the incident is "harangue," a "harangue" which Webster defines as "A speech addressed to a multitude, often a noisy, ranting speech."

The auditorium was packed and as the TV camera swept the room one could readily see that those present were transfixed by the speaker's words and manner. Time and again, as he paused to wipe the perspiration from his brow, they applauded. I could not help but thinking, incidentally, that he might have done better to perspire more in the preparation than the delivery of the speech.

When the harangue was completed (the topic was to be continued the following week) came the inevitable pitch for money. The audience, which included an untold number of TV viewers, was told that receipts had been poor lately and, therefore, they were implored to give generously.

Another somewhat similar program followed. Here the pitch for funds came at the beginning and the audience was told of the desperate need for millions of dollars, "Because God does not want us to borrow." By that time I had heard more than enough.

I found the whole experience at once amusing and disgusting. Amusing because of the antics of the speakers with their flagrant manipulation of both the language and facts. Disgusting because all of this takes place in the name of Christianity.

If I imagined for one moment that this sort of thing represented the Christian Gospel, I would quickly and decidedly renounce Christianity. How anyone, with even the slightest familiarity with the Christian faith can listen to, and much less accept, such blatant nonsense is difficult to understand. It particularly disturbs me that many people, and most often those who can least afford it, support this type of thing while the so-called evangelists live "high-on-the-hog."

What disturbs me most, however, is that the existence and the proliferation of this sort of thing is a symptom of the failure of those of us who have been preaching for years. What have we said, or failed to say, that causes so many to so completely fall victim to the wiles of the electronic medium? What have we said, or failed to say, that so many cannot differentiate between the Christian faith and the harangues of a shyster? What have we said, or failed to say, that leads, so many to so quickly substitute human hatred for Christian concern?

Fortunately, the future of the Christian faith does not depend upon you or me but upon God — God who may well be amused by the antics of the attention-getters but who may be deeply disappointed in you and me.

I take a rather dim view of opinion polls taken by office-holders. Such polls generally are not worth very much. They may well indicate "which way the wind is blowing" but they may not say much about the proper course of action. When I vote for a senator or congressman I expect him to consider all the facts and then act on his best judgment. I do not expect him to take a survey to see what people want and then act accordingly. Time and again, experience has shown the majority can be wrong. This poll taking reminds me of a remark, attributed to Winston Churchill, to the effect that he could not govern well with his ear to the ground.

Be that as it may, such polls are revealing, to say the least. A recent one, taken by an Iowa senator, indicates that the majority feels the way to reduce the federal deficit is to eliminate waste. There is no question but that there is waste in government but that there is enough so that its elimination would make any appreciable dent in the deficit is questionable. It also raises the question of what constitutes waste. What is waste to one may be essential to another.

The same survey showed that only four percent favored raising taxes. The two replies really are related. The last thing the American citizen wants is to pay more taxes — and the public sector is increasingly showing the effects of this. Sooner or later we, or our children, are going to have to pay a very high price for this neglect. Private affluence at the price of public poverty can only lead to a collective disaster.

Volume 34 number 10, October 1985

The noted historian, Barbara Tuchman, in a wide-ranging interview some months ago, told of her findings after doing some research on disarmament, beginning with the Hague Conference in 1899. She said, "...I realized - and this is what research does for you — that governments don't want it. They really don't. They go to these conferences and keep the talks going, but they don't want it." She concluded that arms control is not the answer but that "... the only way we can survive is to reach some minimum form of accommodation."

Certainly any realistic observation of the present scene would encourage the same conclusion. To every suggestion that is brought forth by one side or the other there is generally a ready response that quickly nips the latest bit of hope in the bud. For all of the time, effort, and talk that goes into maintaining the fiction, governments — our own included — do not seem to want disarmament or even arms reduction. One could take a cynical view of this, a view that may, in fact, be more realistic than cynical, and say that the reason for not wanting arms reduction have little, if anything, to do with national security.

Disarmament talks, no matter how appealing the idea may be, are simply not the answer to the tension in the world today. The real answer, the ultimate answer, to the reduction of that tension lies not in talking about the number of missiles each side may have but in discussing frankly and openly why each side feels it needs them. Only as tough words are replaced with calm discussion, only as competition is gradually replaced with cooperation, and only as fear gives way to trust will there be any real hope. No, I don't expect this to happen soon. There are too many who have too much at stake in the present arms race to expect any sudden change in the direction of sanity.

I could never be a farmer. Oh, I think I could master the necessary knowledge and skills and handle the job in that respect. What would hinder me most, however, would be the uncertainty involved. I am not sure I could stand to see all of my efforts wiped out in a few minutes by a hailstorm. I would find it hard to see my income for the year wither along with the crops for a lack of rain. The vagaries of the weather alone would make me think more than once before committing myself to an occupation that is at best a risk and at worst a gamble.

But there is more than nature to contend with. The current farm crisis has again brought to the fore the fact that the farmer is more likely to be the loser than the winner in the continuing economic struggle; a struggle that has gone on with no real abatement for several generations.

It is no exaggeration when the problem today is called the farm crisis. It is a crisis the outcome of which will decide the future of agriculture and the family farm for generations to come. Demonstrations, marches, and farm aid concerts may call attention to the problem but will do little toward solving it. Stop-gap measures and band-aid solutions will not do. Such things will only postpone the inevitable day of reckoning they will simply postpone the day when the independent farmer will become a hired hand working for some huge agricultural corporation.

If the family farm is to be saved — and let me say in no uncertain terms that I think it should be — something more than making an extra dollar has to be recognized. It is this desire on the part of all of us, farmer and consumer alike, that has brought us to the point we have reached today. We must all bear a portion of the responsibility for the situation that presently obtains. Consumers, food processors, bankers, government, and farmers themselves must share the blame. Somewhere along the line we must become aware that we are all in this together and what hurts one will, in the long run, hurt all. Sooner or later we must realize that we are one nation, one people — indeed, one world, and that we must work together to solve what is really a common problem.

Today it is the farm problem, tomorrow it may be the labor problem (which has already become serious in some industries), and always it is the arms race. The same ultimate solution, a willingness to understand and to work together toward a common goal, applies to all of these problems. To date, that solution, though obvious enough, continues to elude us. It must not be allowed to do so much longer — time is running out.

Volume 34 number 11, November 1985

Many years ago I was talking with a man concerning the improved economic conditions at that time which, in my view, had been in part brought about by political actions. The man, who obviously did not share my political views, said, "I want some credit for that."

There is no question but that what we do, the efforts we put forth and the abilities we possess do make a difference. But, when all is said and done, many, many of the bounties we enjoy have come to us through the actions of the society of which we are a part and, more especially, through the beneficence of God. It was a recognition of this latter fact that caused the Pilgrims to observe the first thanksgiving in 1621. It was this fact also that caused President Lincoln to establish a national day of thanksgiving.

Today I fear that Thanksgiving has become a largely perfunctory celebration and that the significance of the day has become lost in feasting and football. This is really not so strange. We have so much to be thankful for, while others have so little, that we easily jump to the conclusion that, in one way or another, it is ourselves who really deserve the credit. In a word, we have become proud and there is no greater barrier to thanksgiving than pride.

It is no accident that the humble, and those who sometimes have the least, are often the most grateful. It is no accident, for example, that one of the truly great hymns of thanksgiving was written by Martin Rinkhart during the Thirty Years War — a time of intense personal hardship and suffering. He was humbled by events beyond his control and was therefore grateful that there is a God to whom he could turn. Is this not really the essence of thankfulness? It is not the presence or absence of blessings but the fact the reality of God before whom there can only be humility and thus thanksgiving.

If I had a headache I would probably take some kind of pain reliever. If I still had a headache the next day I would very likely repeat the process. If, however, the headache persisted for several days I would be ill-advised to continue taking pain relievers. Headaches may be symptoms, danger signals, that something is seriously wrong.

Terrorism is also a symptom, a symptom that something is wrong with civilized society. We may respond to it, as indeed we have, by increasing CIA activity, barricading embassies, and stepping up airport security. Such activities are needed and may, momentarily relieve the pain, but — make no mistake — they deal with the symptom and not the cause. The continuing terrorist activity in the world today demands that we look for the deeper cause.

I know full-well that terrorist activity must not and cannot be condoned. If and when the guilty parties are known and can be apprehended they should be brought to justice. In spite of the fact that it involved some highly questionable practices, there is much to be said for the recent action in which four terrorists were seized. That action brought a good deal of satisfaction to the United States, and especially to those whose aim is to "save face." Yet, does anyone really believe this will bring terrorism to an end? I would hazard the guess that, if anything, it will increase it.

I hold no brief for terrorism or terrorists. That form of activity is completely anathema to civilized society. But it must be borne in mind that it is committed by those who can see no other way of expressing their demands. When on one will listen, much less discuss or negotiate with them they choose the way of violence to get attention, the attention of the powers that be. This is precisely why so much terrorist activity is aimed, directly or indirectly, at this country. We have the power, we can bring pressure to bear, in order that they may be given a fair hearing.

I do not pretend to know who is right and who is wrong in the Middle East. Neither do I know the answer to the problem in Northern Ireland, which is a periodic terrorist hot spot. But I do know that the terrorists, whoever or wherever they may be, are trying to get the attention of the world. They are trying to tell us something and unless and until we begin to listen and get down to a serious discussion of the root problem, terrorism, in one form or other, will continue. Of this we may be certain.

This is certainly not to excuse terrorism but it is to say that there is really no security against it. Only as we recognize it for what it really is, a symptom of a deep-seated and festering sore on the body of society, will there be any hope of eliminating it and thus sparing hundreds, perhaps thousands, of lives.

Volume 35 number 2, February 1986

Paul, who is generally assumed to have been the writer of the letters to Timothy, tells us that, "…the love of money is the root of all evils." Somehow, this has gotten twisted a bit so that it is often said that money is the root of all evil. There is, of course, a decided difference between money and the love of money.

But, if money, in and of itself, is not an evil, neither is it a good. Many good things can be done with money but the money itself is perfectly neutral. This fact should be obvious.

Yet one of the impressions one gets in this day and age is that given enough money all kinds of things can be corrected. If there is a problem of one kind or another in our society we seem to assume that if we simply throw enough money at it we can solve it. There are few who would seriously maintain this, of course, but our actions often give the lie to our thoughts.

Obviously, there are many problems that cannot be solved unless and until there is a transfer of money from the private to the public sector. In a word, it is futile to think that some things can be improved unless the average citizen, and that means you and me, is willing to pay more taxes. We might, for example, be able to get some of the potholes out of our streets and roads if we were willing to pay more in taxes. We could improve our fire and police protection we could raise teacher's salaries, and there is almost no end to the things we could.

Having said that, however, it must be added that some of the most serious problems — and I am not thinking of health alone — in our society cannot and will not be solved simply by the infusion of more money. Does anyone really think, for example, that we would usher in a new and lasting period of peace if we were to throw even more money at the Defense Department? (In my view, the very opposite would be the case.) Does anyone really think that the quality of education would be much improved if we were to throw more funds at it? And, we must not forget the church. The church faces some real problems today but a shortage of funds is hardly the most serious.

Make no mistake I am not suggesting that many good causes do not need more money. I know very well that education, the church, poverty programs, mass transit, and scholarship programs — to name just a few — would benefit greatly by receiving more funds. I am certainly not opposed to higher salaries for teachers, giving to the church, and to generally strengthening programs that help people.

What I am saying, however, is that we need to put forth our best efforts, our most serious thought, and our deepest understanding if we are to adequately deal with some of the profound problems that face us and our world as we near the end of the twentieth century. We need to avoid the fallacy that inheres in the simplistic thought that more money will solve all our problems. That notion is akin to what I would term the bumper sticker mentality; the notion that there is as simple solution to even the most complex problem.

We had grown so accustomed to space launchings, successful missions, and returns that it came as a shock to the nation when the last space shuttle blew up soon after launching. The deaths of seven people, the loss of an extremely costly space vehicle, and the set-back to the whole space program — to say nothing of the blow to national pride, is hardly to be minimized. Nevertheless, the fact that the whole event was seen on television, that it became a media event, tended to magnify it. It made us prone to forget that 248 servicemen died in a crash in Newfoundland in December and that upwards of 20,000 died in the volcanic eruption in Colombia in November.

Repeated successes made us forget the possibility of failure yet we knew very well that it could happen. Space flight is hardly a routine activity it is a dangerous enterprise and we should not be too surprised when something goes wrong.

The tragic events of January 28 represent a real loss to the nation and an even greater loss to the families of those who were killed. Yet, space exploration should and must go on. The spinoffs from the program alone will undoubtedly make it worthwhile. But, in a larger sense, it is that kind of research that may help make this a better world for our grandchildren. We can best honor the seven who died that day by continuing, as Lincoln said in another context, "...that cause which they have thus far so nobly advanced."

Volume 35 number 9, September 1986

Many years ago, when elections were held at the conventions of the old American Evangelical Lutheran Church it was the custom to identify lay candidates by stating their occupation. The thought was that by confining identification to this fact alone the election would not be prejudiced in favor of one of the candidates. Whether or not this was true is highly debatable. In any case, I recall very vividly a year when one of the candidates for a particular office was identified by saying simply, "He works in a Yo-Yo factory." As might be expected, this brought general laughter.

Ove Jensen did indeed work in a Yo-Yo factory at that particular time but to characterize him in this way was nothing short of ludicrous. Ove was one of those rare good people whose maturity, knowledge, and wisdom reaches far beyond the narrow confines of a work place and has an interest in and concern for all of life. In a time when the trend seems to be toward knowing more and more about less and less, Ove was almost an anachronism. His mind was not fenced in by his work, by his community, nor even by his country. He did not live in the past and neither was the future an all-consuming passion with him. He saw life in perspective and he saw it as a unity. The result was that he was as interested in and concerned about the environment as he was about status of his own lawn; he was as interested in and concerned about the black man in Africa as he was about his next door neighbor; he was as interested in and concerned about the growth of nuclear weaponry as he was about the growth of weeds in his garden.

For a number of years Ove served on the Board of Directors of the Danish Interest Conference in the position of treasurer.

The fact that Ove's formal education was not extensive by no means diminished him. What he might have lacked by way of expertise in particular areas he more than made up for by a broad general knowledge that was largely the result of self-education. He was well-read and his reading was not confined to any particular field. His home bore evidence of his reading and he belonged to a reading club in which all kinds of books were read and then seriously discussed.

His reading habits were bi-lingual as was his conversation. He was as much at home in the Danish as in his native American and, as a result, he could profit by and enjoy the best of both worlds. Piety and religiosity were as foreign to him as he was contemptuous of them. Christianity meant more to him than outward display and pious platitudes. The church and the community were inseparable and he would have been happy to see his community at West Denmark complete a new building to replace the one destroyed by fire a year ago. Ironically, the congregation was planning to break ground for the new structure on the Sunday following Ove's funeral.

My wife and 1 have had occasion to visit West Denmark many times and, especially in recent years, one of the highlights of those trips was always a visit with Ove and Solveig. We will miss Ove on such visits in the future but we will always be grateful for the life he lived among us. His was a life of integrity, a genuine life a life without cant.

A feature in the newspaper the other day was a story about movie and television personalities who casually lopped some years off their age, apparently with the thought that they could thereby retain a degree of their youth. Even the president's wife preferred to try to make herself younger in this way. There is nothing new in lying about one's age. In the time and place in which I grew up few women would tell their correct age. Women whose lives were rectitude personified in matters of morals and language would calmly lie about their ages. Men might lie about other things but, by and large, it was the women who lied about their age. This obsession with youth, which is what it really amounts to, was even carried to the extent of putting false dates on tombstones. The advent of Social Security has complicated the matter by giving a false age but it has hardly made it impossible.

This matter of lying about one's age is more humorous than it is serious. In many, if not most cases there is no real harm done except to the individual whose integrity has been compromised by a lie. Some might call it a 'white lie" — but I have always had difficulty understanding just what that is.

Any notions I might have of lying about my age were quickly dispelled the other day by a cute young thing at a cashier's counter. One quick look was all she needed before saying, "We have a discount for senior citizens."

Volume 36 number 4, April 1987

As one grows older, I suppose he is somewhat prone to look back on earlier times as "the good old days." There is a tendency to idealize the days of youth and young adulthood. I hardly need to be reminded that those "good old days" were not always so good and, in some respects not as good as the present time. Within my lifetime, for example there have been two world wars, to say nothing of minor and major skirmishes in which our country has been involved. There was a major depression, the attendant hardships of which made life anything but pleasant. Yet, it seems to me that for all of these problems there was a spirit of unity that is not as prevalent today. It is well established that when a nation is threatened by a disaster of one kind or another, its people become united to overcome the threat.

Perhaps it is because there is no real threat of this kind today that Americans have never seemed further apart on anything than it is today. We have carried this notion of democracy to a ridiculous extreme where each seeks to further his own ends without any thought of how it may affect others. The result is that we have black against white, women against men, young against old, gunslingers against non-gunslingers, smokers against non-smokers, doctors against lawyers, — one could go on and on making a long list. Yes, even the church gets into the act by seeking privileges of one kind or another. Just look at the proliferation of organizations having the aim of furthering the ends of a particular group. Some have been around for a long time, others are of a more recent vintage. That the upshot of this is the Political Action Committee should not really surprise anyone. Through such committees various groups make their voices effective when those who govern do so with an ear to the ground and a hand out for election dollars.

In my view the great threat to America today is not external. The least of my fears is that this country is or will be seriously threatened from without. I know full well that for many the arch enemy is Russia. For my money the real threat is internal. If this country is ever to go down the drain, in my opinion, it will be because democracy has run wild. The problem is to find a way to control democracy that itself is not undemocratic. There is no easy solution but the problem is very real and only a widespread recognition of that problem will bring a solution. As I have said before, sooner or later we are going to have to realize that we are all in this land, and indeed in this world, together. Our democratic system of government was not devised for my benefit or yours but for all of us together. When any one tries to make it serve his ends at the expense of others all will suffer and the system eventually will fail.

Come to think of it, there was one who had the solution a long time ago when he said, "You shall love your neighbor as yourself..."

Have you ever noticed that all of us have a tendency to complain most loudly concerning that which we know least about. We don't like to admit it to ourselves but we do observe it in others. There is a tendency, more pronounced in some to be sure, to respond emotionally rather than rationally.

What brings this to mind is the case of the Cooper children here in Iowa, a case which was recently the subject of a segment of the "Sixty Minutes" broadcast. The case involves five children who were removed, by court action, from a foster home in which they appeared to be happy and placed in two other homes pending a possible return to the mother. The case has aroused a good deal of interest and a great deal of emotion. There has been a flood of letters to the editor of the daily paper, most of them castigating the Department of Human Services and shedding tears over the adverse effects the action might have on the children. Incidentally, no one seems to be aware, or care, that the incessant publicity might have an equally serious effect on these young minds.

Almost all of the comments one reads in the daily press represent emoting. The case does arouse strong emotions, to be sure, but unless and until one knows all the facts there is not much point in simply expressing indignation and emotion. There may have been, and I suspect there was, good reason for the action by the court. Such reasons cannot be made public without jeopardizing the welfare of the children.

The point of all this is that while emotion is good and valuable in its place, it cannot be the basis for the settlement of all issues. Emotion has almost certainly been responsible for more wrongful acts than has reason.

Volume 36 number 5, May 1987

I have long found it difficult to maintain the 55 miles per hour speed limit, particularly on the interstate highway network. The combination of good weather, the open road, a desire to get where I was going, and above all, speeding traffic all have had their effect. The result was, as one might guess, that I soon joined the crowd and exceeded the speed limit. Now that the states are one by one raising the limit I will no longer need to be concerned about getting a ticket for speeding — unless I once again join the crowd and start pushing 75 miles per hour. From the standpoint of freeing the citizenry from the fear of the highway patrol, saving a few minutes, and utilizing to the full the abilities of one's vehicle as well as the road, raising the speed limit is a good thing.

Unfortunately, the matter is not quite that simple. We are prone to simplify matters, especially if it is to our advantage to do so. This propensity to simplify has hardly been retarded by the fact that our elected leaders seem to shun discussion and rational consideration in favor of simplistic solutions to very complex problems. But, that's another matter — back to the highway and the speed limit.

There can be no legitimate question but that in the years since 1973 the 55 mile limit has saved lives. I have read statements to the effect that speed does not cause accidents. One could argue that and, without a great deal of trouble, show that it is pure nonsense to try to maintain such a claim. Be that as it may, there cannot be the slightest question but that speed increases the severity of accidents. Certainly the chances of being killed in an accident at 55 miles per hour are great but at 65 they are infinitely greater. From the standpoint of common sense as well as statistics, there can be no question but that raising the speed limit will cost thousands of lives; lives sacrificed in the interests of saving a few minutes.

However, even if one ignores the safety factor, always assuming that it will be someone else's life that is lost, there is another compelling reason why the limit should not have been raised. It is a reason that vividly illustrates how short sighted the human animal can be. The 55 mile limit was enacted in 1973 in response to an oil shortage and was basically a conservation measure. That lives were conserved in the process proved to be an added bonus. In the years since the price of motor fuel has increased but we have learned to live with that. Now there is an oil glut and the price has dropped to some extent. So, once again, we can burn motor fuel with impunity. The only consequence appears to be the financial cost and that seems to be no real problem.

Yet, unappreciated as it may be, there is a serious problem. Stated simply it is that the supply of fossil fuels is finite. It is only a matter of time before the world runs out of oil. Oh yes, I know very well that by that time something else may have been developed to take the place of oil. It would, however, be completely irresponsible for me to make that an excuse for a profligate waste of fuel. In a word, we desperately need conservation measures now and not simply when the price goes up. The 55 mile limit was a conservation measure. The fact that it is now being scrapped does not alter the fact that we need to conserve.

One might legitimately ask, "How far would you carry this conservation why not make the limit 35 or ban automobiles entirely?" Admittedly, this would be even more effective but this would be neither possible nor practical. My point is simply that we are, in the interest of expediency abandoning a reasonable conservation effort, and that it will, in the long run, prove to be the height of folly.

Perhaps the best conservation measure and the most effective would be to impose a really stiff tax on gasoline. Given the political climate in this country such a tax is a very remote possibility. Meanwhile, I'll join the crowd — with others traveling at 65 miles per hour it would be dangerous to try to maintain 55. So, I'll breeze merrily along at 65, trying to forget the lives that will be lost and the fuel that is being wasted, trying to have little regard for others and even less regard for the future.

Opinion surveys in Denmark have recently shown that the confidence of the public in journalists is at a very low ebb. The majority appears rely less on the press than upon most groups in society, including politicians. What a similar survey would reveal in this country is not certain. There is no question bit the freedom of the press has brought great benefits but sometimes one could wish that the press would show a little more responsibility and demand less freedom.

Volume 36 number 6, June 1987

The constituting convention has been held, the merger approved, a bishop named, and a headquarters site chosen, all of which are necessary to the launching of the new Evangelical Lutheran Church in America at the beginning of the new year. This move has the ringing endorsement of the overwhelming majorities in the merging bodies. Only on the part of a relatively few is there weeping and gnashing of teeth.

Historians have been prone to speak of America as a great melting pot in which all of the many races and nationalities have been melted into one. In more recent times, however, this view has come into serious question and, instead, the so-called salad bowl theory has been advanced. This view holds that while the many disparate groups have been brought together to form a whole, each has, to a large degree preserved its own identity and been able to contribute a distinct flavor to the whole. It seems to me that the mergers among Lutherans are of this salad bowl variety. It would be folly to suggest that all have now become one. They may have come together in one organization but, for all the talk of unity, it is really one of form and not of substance. This diminishes neither the importance nor the value of the move. Not only is a salad nourishing in itself but it holds a great potential for real unity.

Unfortunately, there are still those who can think only in terms of a melting-pot merger but to insist on that kind of merger is to postpone the matter indefinitely. That there are and will continue to be differences in viewpoints, theological and otherwise, within the new structure is as it should be. It occurs to me that this is really the kind of organization that the Grundtvigians thought they could establish in America. They took as their pattern the Church of Denmark in which divergent Lutheran factions lived together under one roof in harmony. Unfortunately, they were far ahead of their time and even the Danes in America could not live together.

Incidentally, it is sometimes suggested that now the Danes have at last gotten together. One can imagine that if he likes, but to compare the Danes of one hundred years ago with their descendants today is to compare apples and oranges. It is certainly not as Danes we have gotten together it is as Lutherans. If the two Danish synods still existed I personally doubt they would have gotten together, even at this late date.

On the whole, the merger appears to be a good thing but there are some things about it that should give pause. First of all, one should not be misled by the emphasis of some on the theological basis for coming together. The real grounds for the merger were and continue to be sociological. Given the social climate in this country, where there seems to be a new merger of some kind every day, a Lutheran merger was almost inevitable. And, one may be sure that this is not the end of the matter. There will be continued church mergers from time to time. This is by no means to suggest that the Christian Church cannot be served by sociology or that this makes it any less Christian.

A second factor that calls for a cautious attitude is that there seem to be so many great expectations. For my part, I prefer to adopt a "wait and see" attitude. Frankly, I will be surprised if the new church grows rapidly, if indeed it grows at all. A comparison of church statistics at the time of the previous mergers with those of today is not very reassuring. I do not expect the new church to have nearly as much "clout" as some ascribe to it. Neither do I expect it to be more efficient, and therefore cheaper.

A final factor that gives me pause is the fact that this is really a merger at the top. Church bodies and synods may merger but, by and large, congregations will not. Given time and the pressures of social, and more particularly, financial forces, local mergers may take place — but don't hold your breath. Unless and until small local groups come together, which in many cases will mean "burying the hatchet" the merger will not seem very real to most.

Now, at long last, the church can shift its attention from itself to some of the problems and difficulties of this twentieth century world in which it exists. There is renewed hope that the time is not far off when the Lutheran Church as it exists in America, will be able to re-channel its efforts from being turned in upon itself to coming to grips with the purposes for which the Church exists.

The new year will usher in a new era in the Lutheran Church in this country. There will at least be a semblance of unity. And, on that foundation the passing years may see a real unity rise. Numerous church bodies have died to give birth to this and previous mergers. May their lives and their deaths not have been in vain.

Volume 36 number 11, November 1987

Thanksgiving is a time for counting one's blessings and surely we who live in the western world have many of them. Generally speaking, abundance and a high standard of living characterize western society. To be sure, we would have no difficulty in finding things that are not favorable but, on the whole, circumstances are such that thanksgiving is very much in order. Unfortunately, not everyone lives in favorable circumstances. There are so many for whom life is but toil and trouble. Have they, then, reason to give thanks?

There are few hymns which congregations sing with more zest and enthusiasm than Martin Rinkhart's "Now thank we all our God." Many a festive occasion is marked by the singing of this hymn and it has a place in many a thanksgiving service. Yet, it is somewhat ironic that few people have had less cause to give thanks than did Rinkhart.

Rinkhart lived in Germany during the Thirty Years' War and the walled city in which he lived became a place where many sought refuge and safety from the ravages of that war. The city soon became so overcrowded and dirty that starvation and disease were rampant. In 1637 a great plague took the lives of thousands of people. Rinkhart was the only pastor left in the city and he conducted burial services for as many as fifty people on some days. During that terrible year he had over four thousand burial services, including one for his wife. In addition the city was raided more than once during the year with the raiders taking all they could lay their hands on. Yet Rinkhart, who could understandably have written, "now curse we all our God," could pen the words that have become so familiar and so beloved.

It has been suggested that Rinkhart wrote the hymn to celebrate the Peace of Westphalia which ended the Thirty Years' War in 1648. That notion is refuted by the evidence but it seems to reflect the fact one must have some obvious cause for giving thanks to God. This Thanksgiving, from thousands of pulpits, there will be a recital of all the things for which we should be thankful. We preachers like to emphasize the positive aspects of our social and religious life. But, in the light of Rinkhart's experience, it seems so superficial. Of course we owe thanks to God for blessings but here was a man who could give thanks when there were no obvious blessings. Why?

Does not the answer perhaps lie in the fact that there is something much deeper here than outward circumstances. Rinkhart's god was more than a fair weather god; he was more than a safe port in stormy weather. His was a god whose love remained constant "in spite of dungeon, fire, and sword." You and I have many blessings but our greatest blessing is the constancy of God's love, and it is this, above all, of which we should be aware at

Thanksgiving time.

Few laymen have played as significant a role in the life of the church as did Erling N. Jensen, who was perhaps best known as "Dane." When "Dane" died the other day he left behind a host of grateful people; grateful for what he had given, not only in the field of education, but to the church as well.

Earning his doctor's degree as a young man, "Dane" came to Grand View College where he headed the science department — in fact, he was the science department. Many a student from those days will attest to the fact that he was an excellent teacher who did not tolerate laxity in study. He later moved on to Iowa State University at Ames. Still later he became president of Muhlenberg College at Allentown, Pennsylvania. After some years there he moved back to Iowa State. During his retirement he continued to live in Ames.

"Dane" also served as chairman of the Board of Directors for Grand View College for many years. It was under his leadership that a quiet revolution took place facilitating the movement of the College into the mainstream of American higher education.

However, "Dane" was perhaps best known to readers of *Church and Life* as the long-time chairman of the annual conventions of the Danish and later the American Evangelical Lutheran Church. His chairmanship of those meetings covers a period of some 25 years. There was never any serious opposition to his election. He steered the convention through many a stormy debate with wisdom and a firmness that was widely appreciated. Though his rulings were on occasion challenged, those challenges were rarely, if ever sustained. The correctness of his rulings and the evenhandedness of his judgments were recognized and generally accepted.

Fully conscious of the past and of his heritage, "Dane" nevertheless also had his feet firmly planted in the present and was very much aware of and committed to the future. He was one more example of the fact, that in my view, the American Evangelical Lutheran Church was singularly blessed with wise leadership. In this thanksgiving season we have many things for which to be grateful and not least the fact that we have had a "Dane" in our midst.

Volume 37 number 3, March 1988

I am currently struggling through Bob Woodward's *Veil, the Secret Wars of the CIA, 1981-1987*. It was Bob Woodward who, in collaboration with Carl Berstein, doggedly pursued the Watergate scandal that eventually brought down Richard Nixon. He has just as thoroughly pursued the actions of the Central Intelligence Agency through the Reagan years and particularly as that agency has developed under the leadership of the late William Casey.

I use the word "struggling" advisedly. For one thing it is a very thick book. For another it is, in my opinion, entirely too detailed and not too readable. Woodward's revelations, however, are enlightening and they are, to say the least, disturbing.

I have never thought of myself as being especially naive but when I learn of some of the operations in which my country is engaged I find myself being both shocked and angry. I'm shocked because I find that, in the name of freedom and democracy, all sorts of clandestine operations are being carried out by the CIA in many parts of the world. Every effort is made to prevent you and me from knowing anything about them and if we do find out, the powers that be simply find another way to obscure the truth. I am angry that my government should be engaged in encouraging assassinations; I am angry that my government should be actively seeking to overthrow other governments; I am angry that my government should be handing out millions of dollars not only to tin horn dictators but to others who are no more than hoodlums; I am angry that my government completely ignores the wishes, to say nothing of the needs, of other peoples.

Our government and the world in which it operates has become so complex that most of us cannot begin to know what goes on among nations. We have entrusted the details of governing and conducting foreign relations to those we have elected and to the duly constituted authorities they have chosen. But, it does seem to me that we do have a right to assume a respect for our own heritage and traditions; we do have a right to expect that they would not only act wisely but honorably; and we do have a right to expect that they would act with due consideration for the peoples involved. It may be that certain ideologies do not appeal to the American mind but that hardly means that any action designed to defeat those ideologies is justified. The CIA seems to operate on the premise that the end justifies the means. I believe that to be not only wrong but ultimately counterproductive and I would be not a little surprised if the majority in America would endorse such a philosophy.

Veil reveals a prime example of what can result when excessive zeal and excessive secrecy are merged.

If you want to be impressed with the actions your government is taking against communism throughout the world, read *Veil*. If, on the other hand, you want to think of your government as honorable, if you want to continue to hold an unreserved pride in America, do not read it.

A generation ago, when he headed American Motors, George Romney said something to the effect that it was absurd for a 100 pound woman to get into a 4,000 pound vehicle and drive two blocks to the drug store to buy a two ounce package of bobby pins. I've thought of that statement many times, not because the absurdity represented is unique but precisely because it is only one of the many absurdities to which all of us are prone. To be sure, we are quite good at rationalizing our absurdities but our reasoning does not always square with the facts. Consider some of the more obvious absurdities in which you and I sometimes engage.

> Item: Extolling the virtues of America but being unwilling to support it with tax dollars.
> Item: Driving downtown and ignoring the bus which is both cheaper and safer.
> Item: Driving to a gym or fitness center to take some exercise.
> Item: Judging a product by its cost.
> Item: Claiming we would have better teachers, preachers, etc., etc., if we paid higher salaries.
> Item: Supporting the church financially but not attending it.
> Item: Building a huge war machine in the name of peace.
> Item: Taking pride in democracy but finding it too much bother to consider the issues and candidates and then vote.
> Item: Enjoying private prosperity in the midst of public poverty.
> Item: Having an excellent health care system that few can afford.
> Item: Responding to the ills of society by "bad mouthing" politicians and bureaucrats.
> Item: Proclaiming the virtues of free enterprise but giving public aid to it.
> Item: Being vocal about rights but silent about responsibilities.
> Item: Demonstrating for "right to life" but favoring a death penalty.

Well, I could go on but I'll let you think about it and see how many absurdities you can come up with. It is an interesting speculation but, let me warn you, it may not lead to a very high opinion of individual or collective humanity. However, if we are to have any hope of improving ourselves, our nation, or our world we must begin by first seeing what is wrong — and that means, among other things, taking a hard look at some of the absurdities in which you and I engage. Yes, I know, this will hardly make you feel good about yourself — and that we are told is so important these days.

Volume 37 number 13, December 1988

It is because the United States has built up its military strength to an unprecedented degree that the Russians have finally been willing to come to the negotiating table. For the past several months, and particularly during the recent election campaign, we heard this view expressed many times and in many ways. It appears to be a formidable argument but it is more apparent than real. Certainly the Russians do appear willing to negotiate and progress has been made in limiting nuclear weapons but to attribute that to the growing military strength of the United States involves questionable reasoning. It is not a fact it is simply a matter of opinion. It completely omits any of the other possible explanations for the new international climate. It is a view that relies on power pure, naked military power. It is a view that reduces international politics to a kind of Russian roulette, where those who play will sooner or later suffer. The lessons of the past are clear on this point. The landscape of hum an history is strewn with the wreckage of men and of nations whose concepts of power and might led directly to their decay and downfall. Power, based on brute force, whether embodied in a punch in the nose or nuclear weapons, is neither constructive nor conclusive.

Into the midst of an obsessive preoccupation with military power comes Christmas with its reminder of another kind of power a power that is constructive and a power that is conclusive. It is difficult to imagine more lowly circumstances than those attendant upon the birth of Christ. Yet, it is doubtful that one can conceive of a power that has had greater effect upon the world for almost 2,000 years than that which has come through Jesus. Here was one who discouraged the use of brute force, to say nothing of military power. Here was one who taught that, "...all who take the sword will perish by the sword." Here was one whose concern was with that which is right and whose reliance was on the power of love.

Sometimes it seems that:

" . . . hate is strong and mocks the song of peace on earth, good will to men."

But then, as Longfellow goes on to say, Christmas comes to remind us that:

" . . . the wrong shall fail, the right prevail, with peace on earth, good will to men."

Almost 2,000 years have passed since Christ walked among men and constant repetition may have dimmed the significance of his life and words. Men and nations may even have become more enamored of brute force and military might. But, when we penetrate beneath all of the tinsel and trappings that have come to surround Christmas we again find him who taught us that the real power and the last power in this world lies in love.

In the recent election Minnesota joined the list of states to be bitten by the lottery mania. Approval by the voters makes it possible for the legislature to now set up a lottery. I must say I am a bit disappointed by that vote. I had always thought Minnesotans had more sense than that.

This whole lottery thing is getting out of hand. Not only is it here to be played but the public is actually strongly encouraged to participate. The advertising and TV commercials in Iowa, for example, must constitute an advertising agency's dream world. I can understand and would expect a tobacco company to encourage smoking even though the evidence that it is unhealthy is overwhelming. I can understand and would expect the liquor industry to encourage drinking even though statistics show it to be at the root of many traffic deaths. But I do have trouble with the idea that the state should encourage gambling — especially when serious social problems inhere in it.

Interesting isn't it! If a politician talks of raising taxes he doesn't have a chance. If, on the other hand, he seeks to install or enhance gambling, he becomes a forward looking statesman. I see a day, not far off, when there will be a national lottery. Now, if this could be a means of financing the war — oops, I mean, defense — department I might even be able to go along with it. Then those who like to play games, military or other forms of gambling, could play to their hearts content while the rest of us grappled with the real problems of this world.

Well, I suppose I should not complain about gambling. After all, the lottery mania brings in money that I should be helping to pay in taxes. So, a word to all those who are bitten by the lottery mania — thank you for paying my taxes.

Volume 38 number 6, June 1989

The late Joseph Sittler, who was noted for his good sermons, was fond of telling a story from his early ministry about a sermon of his that was not so good. After the service, as he was greeting his parishioners, one kindly old lady said to him, "You must have been busy this week, pastor." What an unforgettable way of suggesting to a pastor that perhaps he has been busy with the wrong things. This old lady had put into kind words what I am sure many parishioners feel from time to time. The sermon mattered to her and she was critical without being rude or unkind.

We can all think of ways to respond to a sermon that shows ample evidence of being a "Saturday night special" and that reflects little preparation and even less thought. Most of the time, however, we just grumble about it and go home to have what someone has called "roast preacher" for Sunday dinner. It is easy for the preacher to get the idea that no one really cares what he says. During some twenty years in the parish ministry I can only think of once or twice that anyone came to me and challenged what I had said or indicated a desire to discuss it. It would take a colossal ego for me to assume that I was always right. In spite of this experience, I continue to believe in the importance of the sermon. I know full well that not all would agree but, to me, the sermon is the most important part of the worship service.

Strangely enough, it happens many times that, when a pastor knows his sermon fell short and was anything but good, someone will say, "I enjoyed your sermon," or, "That was a good sermon." About all the confused pastor can do is smile and say "thank you." To be lulled to sleep and to relax the effort to prepare good sermons because of such remarks could be fatal to the preaching mission of the conscientious pastor. This is not to say that the pastor should not be made aware that his sermon struck a responsive note but, he should not be made smug and self-satisfied by it.

How should one respond to a sermon that has made an impression? Probably the most common comment is, "I enjoyed your sermon." But if this is the most common it is also the most inane. Aside from the fact that it is an easy and often meaningless comment is the fact that, by and large, sermons are not meant to be enjoyed. There is a sense in which it may be said that a truly good sermon is one that a person would rather not have heard. I am often reminded of the story of an old pastor and his wife who attended a service at which a popular preacher spoke. As the sermon progressed the old pastor's wife gave evidence of dismay and disgust. Finally, her husband whispered to her, "Yes, my dear, I understand how you feel, but I could not have filled this church." "No," she whispered in reply, "but you could have emptied it." Indeed, a full church does not necessarily indicate good sermons.

How should one respond to a sermon that has made a significant impression? Certainly no one response would cover all situations but a pastor recently told me of one that he appreciated more than all others. As he was greeting the members at the door someone said to him, "Thank you for giving us something to think about." Come to think of it, isn't that what preaching is all about? If a sermon can impress to the extent that people go home and think about it or discuss it, the preacher's effort will not have been in vain. There can be no greater tribute to a pastor than that his sermon moved someone to think about the Gospel.

The most common way to raise wages and salaries is on a percentage basis. Thus, the morning paper states that faculty members at the state universities are to get a ten percent increase. A percentage increase seems to be equitable and fair to all concerned. But is it, really? This seems to me to be a built-in method of perpetuating and even increasing some of the most obvious inequities in our society. The executive who earns $100,000 per year gets an increase of $10,000 while the man or woman who is struggling to hold a family together on $10,000 per year gets an increase of only $1,000. As the years go by and increases are granted in this way, the disparity between the "haves" and the "have nots" becomes ever greater. Of course, it may be argued that each gets what he deserves and the executive "deserves" more — a statement that, at the very least, is highly debatable. In my book, an across the board increase of a fixed sum would be more equitable and would do at least a little toward decreasing the gap between the rich and the poor. In another context Christ did say that to those who have more shall be given. However, it would be distortion of the teachings of Christ to use this as a justification for percentage increases.

Volume 38 number 7, July 1989

The storming of the Bastille on July 14, 1789 is generally accepted as the date marking the beginning of the French Revolution. This year, which marks the bicentennial of that event, will be marked by numerous celebrations in France. The French Revolution was, so to speak, the opening event in the long struggle to loosen the chains that bound the masses in continental Europe. A century earlier the bloodless revolution of 1688 had marked a step in the same direction in England. And, of course, our own American revolution, beginning in 1776 had freed the colonists from the yoke of oppression and tyranny.

In Europe, the French Revolution ushered in a long period of violence and revolt, not only in the French Revolution itself but in the Napoleonic wars that followed. Then came revolutions in other European nations during the 19th century, finally culminating in the two revolutions in Russia in 1917. In our day full blown revolutions appear to be a thing of the past — at least in the western world. Third world nations, for the most part, still have a long way to go.

Unfortunately, though revolutions in the western world appear to have ended, even there the violence has not ceased and oppression is not something we can speak of only in the past tense. Further, new, sophisticated, and subtle forms of tyranny abound in even the most advanced nations of the world. Witness the continuing problems in South Africa and the current upheaval in China. To make matters worse, modern technology has compounded the degree of violence that shakes and shocks the world from time to time. The recent violence in China is a case in point. While China is not strictly speaking a part of the western world it is certainly well on the road to becoming one of the more advanced nations. Some of the newscasts emanating from Bejing are set against a background of a thoroughly modern city. One may wonder how such primitive violence can exist in a modern setting.

Yet, a moment's reflection reminds us that violence is really not primitive. Violence may take many forms and range from a punch in the nose to a machine gun, but it is as modern as tomorrow. Time and again one reads of pundits and others who suggest that education is the answer. As the peoples of the world become more literate, these writers suggest, revolution, civil war, and violence will recede into the background. I wish I could agree, but I beg to differ! I yield to none in my respect for education and in my interest in advancing it, but it will not solve the problem of what has been called "man's inhumanity to man." It will not solve the problems of revolutions, wars, civil strife, and the resultant violence. Indeed, one could make a strong case for the notion that it may even intensify them.

Violence is often an emotional response to the claims of reason. Emotion is subjective and, by and large, education is concerned with the objective. The subjective may well complement the objective and we may experience the finer emotions of love and good will. But when emotions conflict or when the objective and subjective come into conflict, violence of one form or another often ensues. So what is the answer is there no hope? As someone once said, "ultimately the problem is theological." Unless and until each of us sees his neighbor, whether across the street or across the world, as also being a child of God, and unless and until emotions are held in check by a respect for life, oppression, conflict, and violence will persist.

Another tree in the forest has fallen. The name of Pastor Holger O. Nielsen has now been added to the list of those dedicated men and women who have passed through the "valley of the shadow of death." He was one of those steadfast individuals who helped to move the Danish Church into the mainstream of American church life. He served several congregations including one on the west coast and one on the east coast. He also served for a number of years as secretary and later vice president of the synod. He came out of a family whose life was centered in both church and school and through the years he significantly contributed to the life of both so that they might come to have the importance to others that they had to him. Now he has gone from among us but we have all, in one way or another, been enriched by his labors in the Kingdom.

Some years ago a church bulletin listed a talk to be given under the title, "The Life of Christ in Stained Glass Windows." In this title someone, unwittingly, has stated what all too often becomes the case. Like a stained glass window, the life of Christ becomes something to look at and that's as far as it goes.

Volume 39 number 3, March 1990

I hardly dare get into the abortion issue; an issue which continues to generate headlines of one kind or another. Yet I cannot continue to ignore the question. Almost daily, on his television screen, one sees protest marches by one side or the other. The catch phrases and slogans issued by either side would simplify what is in reality a very complex problem. It leads me to suggest that when an issue is reduced to placard and bumper sticker proportions it is radiating more heat than light.

Let me say at the outset that there is, in my view, no easy answer to the problem. Whatever the outcome may be in the states, to which the abortion issue has now been relegated, there will be many unhappy people. That, incidentally, is a price of democracy. Rarely, if ever, can a decision be made in a democratic society that will please all. Those who do not like it will simply have to learn to live with it and hope that eventually the wind will blow their way.

But, if I know of no easy answer, I do know that there are some facts which should not be lightly dismissed by either side. In truth, sometimes I am inclined to say to both the abortionists and their opponents, "a plague on both your houses." Both, in their zeal for their cause, tend to play fast and loose with the truth. Neither side comes to the struggle with clean hands. Many pro- choice enthusiasts seem to look upon the technique as a sophisticated birth control device. The pro-lifers, on the other hand, seem greatly concerned about the fetus but show little interest in human, not to say humane, life after birth.

Those who favor abortion have some good arguments. They would take abortion out of the alley and make safe abortion available to all women regardless of financial status. If abortion is banned entirely, illicit activity will flourish but only those who can afford clandestine clinics will have access to a safe procedure. They also favor granting abortions to victims of rape and incest, and when necessary, providing state or federal funds for such. These are not unreasonable claims and it is difficult to argue against them. Nevertheless, when pro-abortion enthusiasts talk about their right to do as they please with their bodies and would make abortion as widespread as the common cold, they are throwing out morality with the fetus.

Let it be very clear that the ultimate purpose of the sexual act is procreation and that the pleasure is a byproduct. And, despite claims to the contrary, what a woman does with her body is not her business alone. The father, the parents, and society, to say nothing of the unborn child, all have a stake in her action. As a matter of fact, there is almost nothing one can do in this life that does not have an effect, for good or ill, on someone else.

The pro-life people also can bring some reasonable arguments. One would be hard put to deny that an abortion destroys a life, or a potential life. Abortion must not be allowed to become a means of escaping the consequences of an action. Particularly obnoxious is the possibility, and indeed the probability, of abortion based on the gender of the fetus, an action reminiscent of those cultures in which female infants were wantonly destroyed. Ready access to abortion, they would also say, makes for loose morality. One can hardly deny that. Yet there is a question as to what extent behavior is moral simply because the law requires it.

However, in their own way the pro-life people are as heartless, and perhaps even more so, then those who favor abortion. They appear to give no consideration to the mother, no matter how she became pregnant. Their position on other social issues, in many cases, is in direct conflict with their pro-life stance. There is no question but that they are pro-fetus; whether or not they are pro-life is open to serious question.

Dedicated Christians can be found on both sides of the issue. A pronouncement by the church, no matter how carefully worked out, will be an exercise in futility. This is basically a moral issue and it is for that reason that it is such an emotional issue. We humans have a propensity for getting all steamed up about whether or not someone else is acting morally. I see no solution in this case other than that women, physicians, and all others who may be involved, act in accord with the dictates of their own conscience. Preconceived solutions, no matter how carefully thought out and no matter by whom issued, church or state, will simply not do. It is difficult, if not impossible, to legislate for moral issues. Each case must stand alone — and the final judgment must be left to God.

Volume 39 number 12, December 1990

A year ago, not only most Americans, but most Europeans were filled with optimism. It was an optimism shared by a good part of the world. The Berlin wall was crumbling and relations between East and West were beginning to resemble something other than a bellicose confrontation. In the months that followed those relations became ever more civilized and humanity began to look forward to something besides arms build-ups and the accompanying drain on the economies of both East and West. In our own country there was even talk of a "peace dividend."

Alas, now, a year later our hopes are cruelly crushed once again. This time war seems more imminent than ever. At the moment the East, western Europe, a good part of the Arab world, support the American position. Just how soon that support will begin to erode is not clear but, in any case, at this juncture the Middle East oppressor seems to stand alone. That, however, is small consolation for those who may have to give their lives to bring him to bay.

The point is that, where a year ago we could look forward in optimism and hope to a brighter and better world we must now recognize that, in some respects, the prospects for peace on earth have suffered a severe and dangerous reversal. Yet, this should really not surprise us! The notion that humanity can achieve peace on earth belongs to the world of fiction it is at complete odds with the reality of humanity and collective life. Even if humanity should at some remote point in time succeed in living together without benefit of weapons, the ensuing absence of war would not really be peace. There has been no armed strife between the citizens of this country, for instance, since the Civil War of over 125 years ago. For all of that, it would be rash to say there is peace in this land of ours. The media is replete with stories of black against white, man against woman, ethnics against ethnics, rich against poor, old against young, environmentalists against developers and despoilers, and pro-choice against pro-life, to name but a few. Despite the absence of armed strife there is certainly no peace in our country — and one can surely multiply this by as many countries as there are in the world.

Into this atmosphere of envy, bitterness, and down-right hatred, comes Christmas with its message of peace on earth. It is true that this country was in the midst of the Civil War when Henry Wadsworth Longfellow wrote those well-known lines: "And in despair I bowed my head, there is no peace on earth I said..." But, who among us, as we look at the world today, is not inclined to echo his words today.

That first Christmas, so long ago, was really not a time vastly different from our own as far as human relations are concerned. And, the very coming of the Christ, far from leading to an improvement of those relations, accentuated the differences. Nevertheless, we continue to associate the Christmas event with peace on earth, and rightly so. We do so because in our more reflective moments we know that peace, in the biblical sense, means something other than a utopian concept of human life. This thought has been expressed in many ways but, in my view, one of the best is by E. J. Tinsley, in his commentary of the Gospel according to Luke. He writes:

> Peace in the thought of the Bible means more than the absence of strife. It is entire harmony of life, something which, in its perfection, only God has. But the good news of the Gospel is that God intends human beings to have a life similar to his in its freedom and satisfaction. The meaning of the angels' song is not that men can bring about peace with God or with themselves purely by their own endeavors. God's peace is God's alone, and it is his favor to men to bring about in them a peace which has some resemblances to his own. * *

Christmas has historically been a happy time. It should be and it can be as we remind ourselves that peace is not man made but God given. In this awareness, in spite of all that would threaten and destroy peace among humans, it can indeed be as merry Christmas.

**Tinsley, E. The Gospel According to Luke, *The Cambridge Bible Commentary on the New English Bible*, .Cambridge University Press, London, 1965, p. 38.

Volume 40 number 4, April 1991

The war fought with Spain, in which Theodore Roosevelt made a name for himself in Cuba in 1898, has been called "a splendid little war." Now America has once again fought "a splendid little war." And, if one thinks only in terms of American losses, it was indeed "a splendid little war." However, I do have difficulty in trying to ignore the enormous destruction that has been wreaked on the Arab world to say nothing of the thousands of Arab lives lost in our wanton destruction of their world. Nor can I forget that American lives were also lost.

Nevertheless, this appears to be a time of great pride in America. Pride that we were able, in the words of the President, to "kick ass" so thoroughly and so quickly; pride in our volunteer fighting forces, pride in our efficient (and very costly) war machine, and pride that, again in the words of President Bush, "America is back." I must admit that I have a great deal of difficulty in feeling, much less manifesting, pride in my country today. As far as I am concerned, pride engendered by accomplishments on the battlefield is wrong. This is not to say that it may not at times be necessary to take to the battlefield, though whether this was one of those times is questionable. It is to say, however, that, to put it simply, we should hardly be proud that we were able to kill more than the enemy did. One can be happy that the death and destruction are over; one can rejoice that American men and women are coming home; and one can be grateful to them for responding to the dangerous and distasteful task which they were called upon to perform. But it is quite another matter to take pride in what they have done in our behalf.

Further, I could muster some pride if I thought that this "splendid little war" had really settled anything. Time will tell, and I hope I am wrong, but at this point a so-called "new world order" is as far off as ever. Indeed, in some respects it seems farther off because the moral of this War is that pure naked power is in the driver's seat. The rush for power, the arms race, will take on renewed meaning in many parts of the world, not least in our own country.

Webster tell us that pride is "inordinate self-esteem, conceit." I wonder if this is not the kind of thing Martin Luther had in mind when he said, if memory serves me correctly, "sin is pride." Frankly, I think this is the kind of pride that is rampant today. But Webster gives another definition of pride when he says it is "reasonable or justifiable self-respect." That kind of pride I could go along with.

I could, for instance, take great pride in America if all races and creeds were accorded equal treatment. I would rejoice if we could show as much enthusiasm for getting the homeless off the streets and getting the hungry fed as was shown for the "splendid little war." I would be greatly pleased if we could put even a fraction of the effort that went toward liberating Kuwait into liberating countless Americans from their bondage to drugs. I could take pride in an America really dedicated, rather than simply giving lip service, to assuring its children the best possible education. A meaningful energy policy, a serious resolve to reduce environmental pollution, a real effort toward mass transit, and an end to passing an enormous public debt to future generations are things in which I could find pride.

But, then, I have seldom been with the majority, I am not now, and do not expect to be in my lifetime. Meanwhile, about all I can do is hope that reason will ultimately prevail. I am buoyed by one thought, however, and that is that I am not entirely alone.

Pastor Svend Kjaer will be able to observe his one hundredth birthday on May 6th. In the April issue of *Church and Life* in 1986 (p. 11) I wrote about two grand old men who were members of the seminary class of 1919. One of the two, Ottar Jorgensen, died in 1987. The other is Svend Kjaer, the last living member of that notable class, which included such other "giants" in the Danish Church as Alfred Jensen, Holger Strandskov, and Arthur Frost. Svend Kjaer was ordained in 1919 and served five different congregations. He served in the midwest as well as on both coasts. His last period of service to the Church was rendered as superintendent of Valborgsminde, in Des Moines. Following that, he and his wife, Ethel, retired, first in Des Moines and then in Iowa City. An article about his early life, written by his nephew, will be found in the Danish section of this issue. (P. 11)

Svend Kjaer may be characterized by the Danish expression "en af de stille" (one of the quiet ones) but his service was no less real or less important. I know I speak on behalf of many when I echo the words of the Master and say, "well done, good and faithful servant," and congratulations and best wishes on your 100th birthday. (Svend Kjaer's address is: 3210 Raven Street, Iowa City, Iowa 52240.)

Volume 40 number 6, June 1991

It is "no longer acceptable, morally, ethically, or economically" for roughly 33 million citizens to live with inadequate or nonexistent health insurance. With these words the American Medical Association called for a public discussion of the issue of runaway health care costs and some kind of overhaul of the present method of delivering health care. It devoted an entire issue of its prestigious journal to the presentation of more than 70 proposals for reform.

It is heartening when an organization like the AMA, which has consistently been an obstacle to changing the status quo, now finds it "'morally unacceptable." It has long been ironic that this country, which is perhaps the most advanced in the field of medicine, lags way behind other industrialized nations in the social area. The United States and South Africa are the only industrialized countries that do not have some system of universal health care.

On the day the AMA report was made available, the *McNeal, Lehrer News Hour* (PBS) devoted its entire program to a discussion of the issue. Many viewpoints were presented and some quickly shot down. One of the sharpshooters was a representative of the health insurance industry. Naturally, he was quick to find fault with the Canadian system, which places the government in the role now occupied by the insurance companies. It does not take a genius to see that such a plan is anathema to the insurers. It was said that we cannot use the system used by another nation. We need an American system — whatever that is. To suggest that we cannot learn from others is both arrogant and stupid (things that are really closely related).

The delivery of health care is a very complex problem one that will require the best thinking of those who are intimately acquainted with the area. Certainly I do not profess to know what the answer is but there are a few things that do stand out clearly. First and foremost, I am convinced that tinkering with the present method of delivery of health care will be a waste of time, money, and lives. I am also of the opinion that the private sector simply cannot be entrusted with this task. If any further evidence of this is needed, one has but to take a look at where we are today. Oh, yes, there are those who fear government bureaucracy. Take my word for it the government is by no means the only place in which there is bureaucracy. Ah, but there would be waste in government. Sorry, but I have lived long enough and been observant enough to know that waste is by no means confined to government. There are most probably more dedicated individuals in government service than one could find in private enterprise. The difference is that government servants work in a kind of goldfish bowl where their every move is subject to public scrutiny. Fortunately for the private sector, it is largely free of such scrutiny.

It occurs to me that we already have the nucleus of a universal health care delivery system in Medicare. Medicare is not perfect by any means but we who are in the older generation know very well that without it life for us would be a great deal different — if, indeed, there was life at all. I can already hear the cry, "no more taxes." Why is it that if something can be called a tax it seems bad but if that same payment can be considered a necessary expense there is not much complaint? If this connection I suspect that if all that were now paid in health insurance premiums by individuals and employers were paid in taxes we could have a good, compulsory, universal health care delivery system — and there might even be enough left over to make a dent in the national debt. One of the problems is that it is so easily assumed that when the employer pays, health care is free to the worker. Nothing could be further from the truth.

Aside from the problem of selfish interests, is the fact that everyone seems to want a perfect system before any change is made. No system is perfect, and especially not at the beginning. But, as the "bugs" are found they can be eradicated. In any case, most anything would be an improvement over the shameful and "morally unacceptable" condition that exists today.

I ran across a revealing statistic the other day. It is one which I had often wondered about and I'd like to pass it along because you may also have wondered. "Every week," I read, "more than 500,000 trees are used to produce the two-thirds of newspapers that are never recycled." There is another related statistic that would, if available, give an even more revealing picture. This has to do with the percentage of the daily and especially the Sunday paper that is given over to advertising. I would guess it ranges between 75 and 90 percent. Just think, 500,000 trees— and for what? I don't know how much space 500,000 trees would take but I'd guess that it would take a sizable space in a forest.

Volume 41 number 3, March 1992

Have you seen the ADM (Archer-Daniels-Midland) commercial for ethanol? Ethanol is the highly touted alcohol additive for gasoline that appears to have the two fold-virtue of reducing the amount of fossil fuel used and the amount of air pollution. As the commercial puts it '"ten percent in, twenty-five percent out." In other words, by substituting ethanol for ten percent of a gallon of gasoline, the polluting effect of burning that gallon is reduced by twenty-five percent. One can't argue with that the statement is good, as far as it goes.

The problem that is not mentioned is that the use of ethanol results in a net loss of energy and a net gain in pollution. Studies have shown that more energy is used to make ethanol from corn than is saved by adding it to gasoline. Further, that energy, which comes from burning either coal or oil, results in considerably more pollution than burning a similar amount of gasoline. This is to say nothing of the additional soil and water pollution that would result from increased corn production, an increase that is being urged by advocates of ethanol. It should be noted also that ethanol use is being subsidized (at least in Iowa) by not taxing it as heavily as other fuels.

I am well aware of the benefits that a widespread use of ethanol would bring to the agricultural community (and not least ADM) but to assume and even proclaim that this alleviates a problem is a prime example of intellectual dishonesty. True, it does deal with two aspects of the problem, namely the finite oil reserves and urban pollution, but it simply transfers those ill effects and makes the over-all situation worse.

I'm afraid this way of approaching problems is all too typical. I can recall when judges and magistrates used to have troublesome individuals escorted to the county line and be told not to return. The idea was to get rid of them and let someone else worry about them. There's a word for it. It is called "passing the buck." The use of ethanol, no matter how highly recommended, is simply "passing the buck." It not only fails to be a solution to the basic problems but it postpones the search for real solutions.

Meanwhile, the one measure that would have a real effect on the future is increasingly disregarded. Conservation of energy would decrease the use of fuel and cut down on pollution but that is not very popular these days when gasoline is "dirt cheap." In my lifetime I have never seen gasoline as inexpensive as it is now when inflation is taken into account. I can recall when gasoline sold at six gallons for a dollar. But I also recall, at that same time, my pay was at the rate of thirty-seven and one half cents per hour, or fifteen dollars a week.

A good stiff tax on gasoline would do more to conserve fuel and reduce pollution then subsidies for ethanol. To be sure, conservation is not the only or final answer. Research must continue. A portion of a sharply increased gasoline tax could be used for funding such research. To use all of the tax for highways simply compounds the problem. I have little doubt that someday a satisfactory over-all solution will be found, but until it is, we must do what we can to keep matters from becoming worse.

We are stewards of the earth and all its resources. How we use the land, how we use oil, how we treat the air, soil, and water will make a difference to our posterity. To put it in very personal terms, I would not like to have my grandchildren, fifty years from now, comment on the mess they find in the environment by saying, "My grandfather helped to get us into this mess."

Some time ago I heard a rather elaborate and fanciful presentation, the purpose of which was to show that the speaker had not made an error that was in question. All of us have, I am sure, heard a number of such excuses over the years. Some of them have really been "whoppers." Nor are these rationalizations confined to children or those who do not know better. At one time or other we have all been guilty. How much simpler (and more honorable) it would be to simply say, "I made a mistake."

There seems to be an uncanny correlation between the propensity for making mistakes and the ability to fabricate excuses. Perhaps it comes of practice. In any case, the seriousness of the mistake may vary but the excuses are very often laughable.

There is something about we humans that makes it so difficult to say, "I made a mistake," or, "I was wrong." Could it be that we are reluctant to acknowledge that we are finite and that we do not want to recognize any limitations? Perhaps it boils down to this — humility is difficult.

Inevitably, our relationship not only to man but to God is affected. The reality is that while we may be able to delude ourselves and may even delude others, God expects nothing less than the truth.

Volume 41 number 6, June 1992

A period of recession seems to bring into focus things which are otherwise ignored. Of late there has been considerable publicity regarding the high salaries of some to the nation's Chief Executive Officers (CEO's) of corporations. There have even been movements for legislation that would limit such to a multiple of the average workers' salary. Free enterprise being what it is, it takes little insight to see that such a movement will not get off the ground. Moreover, such legislation would surely be evaded one way or another. Evading the law seems to be the favorite indoor sport of all too many corporation lawyers and tax consultants. What cannot be evaded is conscience, but the situation in America, and indeed the world, would seem to indicate that commodity is in short supply.

One CEO is reported to have received compensation worth $88 million for last year. When questioned about such a vast sum he replied, "I'm worth it." What he lacks in conscience the man more than compensates for in an ego which is nothing short of colossal. We pay our public servants only a tiny fraction of what some of those robber barons take home and we get all excited about that being too much. Judging by the CEO standard, the president and members of Congress receive a mere pittance. Ah, yes, you say, "but that's a public matter and what a CEO is paid is a private matter." Legally, of course it is, but morally it is another story.

Where did the corporation get the $88 million? They did not pick it from a tree somewhere. They picked it out of the pockets of everyone who ever bought a product made by the company. Where did General Motors or Chrysler get the millions they paid to their CEOs? They picked it out of the pockets of anyone who bought a General Motors or Chrysler product. In the final analysis it is the consuming public that pays these fabulous salaries just as it is the consuming public that pays corporation taxes — however much corporations may complain.

There is another aspect to this matter of high salaries that has long-range and troubling implications. The reward (translate that loot) that goes to the CEO is based on the profit made by his or her company during the past year — and sometimes even during the past quarter. What this means is that the CEO will almost invariably make every effort to have the company show a maximum profit during any given year. Never mind that the long term health and profitability of the company may be damaged by such a short-term emphasis. Never mind that the workers' wages may be cut or that pollution and safety measures may suffer. The bottom line is profit, and profit right now.

This undue emphasis on the short term carries over into our political system and, indeed, into our daily lives. Never mind that the national debt is increasing by leaps and bounds. Let our children and grandchildren worry about that. As a nation we can borrow and borrow, and spend and spend an ever-increasing sum on debt service and thus continue to have the lowest taxes of any industrialized nation. Never mind that some 20% of our taxes now go toward paying interest on that debt and that each year it gets worse. But, make no mistake, there will be a day of reckoning. (By the way, have you ever stopped to think about to whom that 20% goes. Is it too much to say that some people then have a vested interest in continuing deficits and enlarging the national debt?)

By the time these lines are read the day of Pentecost (June 7 this year) will have come and gone. If the recent past is any indication it will have been almost unnoted. In the Danish Church, both in Denmark and America, it was observed as one of the three major Christian holidays. I happen to believe that this was as it should be. Christmas and Easter, no matter how much importance we attach to them, cannot stand alone. Alone they become simply milestones on a Christian path to nowhere. Unless and until the Holy Spirit comes to life in an individual, that person's life will be, as Shakespeare put it in another connection, "bound in shallows and in miseries." Only as the Spirit is given precedence over that which we call the real world can there be any hope of solving the problems of humanity. It is not strange that the Holy Spirit, the most intangible member of the Trinity, is the most desperately needed in our time.

Volume 41 number 8, August 1992

One hardly needs to be reminded that the world has come a long way in his lifetime. Seventy-five years ago kerosene lamps and outhouses were very common. Horses still outnumbered automobiles. The airplane as a means of transportation existed only in the minds of a few dreamers. The telephone was becoming popular as a means of communicating, but radio was in its infancy and television was unheard of. Now, electricity, indoor bathrooms, and automobiles, are commonplace, and flying is perhaps the most practical way to travel. As for radio and television, rare is the home that does not have at least one of each.

I often think of a funeral service I once conducted. It was for an elderly lady who, as a child, had come to the state in which she lived, riding in an oxcart. She died as a result of injuries sustained in the crash of a jetliner. Just imagine, oxcart to jetliner in one lifetime. Developments in the years since her time have been even more phenomenal. This summer it will already be 23 years since a man landed on the moon. Progress is snowballing to such an extent that my computer, though only six years old, is already out-of-date (though, fortunately, it still serves my needs). Progress comes ever more rapidly and there appears to be no end to what technology can accomplish.

If daily we reap the benefits of technology, we do, nevertheless, live in a society which seems bent on self-destruction. Race, crime, drugs, violence, wars, unemployment, and a growing economic disparity each create problems of a formidable nature. Taken together they seem to spell disaster. As if these problems are not enough there is the environment to be considered. The signs are unmistakable that it needs attention right now and to put it off with vague references to development and jobs is to invite disaster.

The difference between our progress in the field of technology and our failures as a society are striking. Why are we not able to transfer the progress in one area to the other? One often hears the question, "If we can put a man on the moon, why can't we solve these other problems?" The answer is simple enough. Technologists do not have to deal with emotions and the human will. In a sense, their task is easy. They deal with forces that can be understood; forces that don't have a mind of their own forces that don't talk back to them. I know it is generally believed that science and math courses are the most difficult and, in so far as they require rigid discipline, they are. I have long maintained, however, that rightly understood, the social sciences are the most difficult to deal with. Scientists and mathematicians have made it possible for us to go to the moon and to have an ever increasing number of gadgets. Social scientists, on the other hand, no matter how hard they try, are not able to keep violence and wars down. They have not been able to reduce the prison population nor to abolish racial discrimination. Politicians, even with the best of intentions, are not able to come to grips with national or state deficits. Progress in these areas has been largely illusory and we are as far from answers as we ever were.

Reason, logic, common sense — these are the hallmarks of science and technology. They make it possible for researchers to be completely objective. Yet, if humans were completely objective in all things some of the finest and best values in life would be lost. Both fortunately as well as unfortunately, we are creatures of emotion. The emotions enable us to love, rejoice and be grateful they enable us to show anger, hatred and engage in violence. Unless reason is tempered by emotion we become like "My neighbor, old Pat" who could see none but objective values. But, unless emotion is tempered by reason, the ills of society will persist. This is the human dilemma this is the reason we could send a man to the moon but cannot deal with individual and social problems.

It strikes me as being somewhat ludicrous:

- To complain about the high cost of college tuition and regularly cut class.
- To extoll the virtues of democracy but not be willing to accept the will of the majority.
- To suggest that the basic problem today is one of communication.
- To call a war machine with more than enough weapons to destroy all humanity a defense department.
- To raise the fare and cut the schedule in an effort to save a mass transit system.
- To vehemently assert one's liberalism.
- To discuss the evils of pollution in a smoke filled room.

Volume 42 number 8, August 1993

Water, water, everywhere
Not any drop to drink.
Samuel Taylor Coleridge, 1798

These lines from Coleridge's "The Ancient Mariner" describe in a few words the situation in which a quarter of a million people in the Des Moines area found themselves in mid-July. The massive flooding that took place in the Midwest created untold damage and, among other things, inundated the Des Moines Water Works, contaminating the water supply and forcing the water works to cease operation on July 11. At this writing (July 20) the city is still without water, though service is expected to be restored by the end of this week. However, we are told that the water, while it can be used for many other things such as bathing, toilet flushing, laundering, etc., will not be fit for drinking for another three weeks. An extensive clean-up and purifying operation must first be completed. Meanwhile drinking water has come from other communities and is available at numerous distribution points throughout the city.

The worst seems to be over, but the destruction remains. The minor inconvenience most of us have experienced pales by comparison with the damages and loss others have suffered. Indeed, some of us were even able to escape the inconvenience for a time by visiting friends and relatives elsewhere.

So much for a brief review of a crisis which has been national headline news for days. What may be in order now are some random reflections and observations engendered by what without question may be called a major catastrophe.

Perhaps most important of all is the remarkable spirit of cooperation that has been called forth. Hundreds, yes, thousands of men, women, and children volunteered their efforts in filling and placing sandbags on the levees, around homes, other buildings and at the water treatment plant. That in some cases their efforts were in vain does not minimize the valiant work of the volunteers. Nor were the volunteers only those who were directly affected by the rising waters. Many busloads of volunteers came from as far away as Minneapolis and St. Paul. Those of us whose physical activities are limited can only marvel at and be grateful for the work of the volunteers. Crises are not unlike Christmas in that they tend to bring forth the best in humanity.

The losses in Des Moines alone are tremendous, but they become almost insignificant when one adds to them the cost in property damage and crop losses in the entire Midwest. Federal and state deficits notwithstanding, governments will have to step in. The restoration of roads, bridges, and other public facilities, as well as giving aid to those who have lost all, is more important at the moment than missiles super colliders and space stations.

Fortunately, there was very little looting, a condition which often accompanies disasters. There were, however, those whose greed got the best of them and who decided that rules were for others than they. As water entered the mains in some sections, and officials sought to get the entire water system operating, strict prohibitions against turning on taps were issued. Some chose to ignore these prohibitions and thus set the whole process back by a day. Why must some act so irresponsibly in a crisis?

As the crisis passed its peak, the finger pointing began. Inevitably, there are always those who, blessed with hindsight, are ready to point fingers and cast blame. Cooperation, born of an emergency, is seldom able to withstand the ordinary. It seems that it is always so much easier to be united against something, in this case a destructive flood, than to be united for something. One sees this time and again in political actions. What a different world it would be if humanity could center its attention on positive undertakings rather than always simply reacting to the negative.

Finally, the flooding has made me mindful of the difficulties faced by our grandparents. They were not accustomed to get light at the flip of a switch they could not get water with the turning of a faucet. A daily shower was out of the question and even the Saturday night bath presented difficulties in many cases. Life was not easy, but they took it in stride. Now, a couple of generations later, we have conveniences of all kinds and therein lies a problem. As long as these things function as they should all is well, but let one of them fail and we feel put upon; let two or more fail at the same time and we may feel utterly lost. The pioneers would be amazed and perhaps not be able to function in the world of the 90s, but they could tell us a thing or two about how to function in a more natural environment.

In the name of jobs, more and more corporations are resorting to what is in effect governmental bribery, saying that unless a state or city comes across with aid in some form or other they will move. In a recent case a corporation executive called councilmen who questioned the corporation's need, "'not very bright." It seems to me that a CEO who cannot run his firm without governmental assistance is in a poor position to call others "not very bright."

Volume 42 number 9, September 1993

"Oh well, said Mr. Hennessy, "we are as th' Lord, made us."
"No," said Mr. Dooley, "lave us be fair. Lave us take some iv th'
blame oursilves."
Finley Peter Dunne, 1867-1936

The blame game, is hardly confined to Washington even though the two
political parties lose no opportunity to blame each other for everything from
taxing and borrowing to graft and corruption. The casting of blame seems to
have become a way of life. The daily press is generally filled with examples
of how responsibility for misfortune or tragedy of one kind or another is
cavalierly attributed to this or that person or institution. In all too many
cases such attribution is aided and abetted by a legal profession more
interested in reward than right.

God comes in for a good share of the blame. It seems that humans, when
they can find no one else to blame, attribute the tragedy to God. There are
those who have no trouble attributing the recent floods in the Midwest to the
wrath of God. Again, how often have we not heard a death characterized as
an act of God. "The Lord called him home," or "the Lord had need of her,"
are phrases one can hear at most any funeral.

Increasingly, — or at least so it seems — blame is being placed on others
than God. Malpractice suits are a growing concern to the medical
profession. Certainly, there are incompetent doctors and inexcusable
mistakes are sometimes made. Nevertheless, the overall impression that one
gets is that no one dies naturally any longer. Death is always someone's
fault. Someone must be blamed!

Then, too, there are accidents. These may be as serious as one involving
motor vehicles and death or as minor as a fall involving bruises. In either
case, the placement of blame seems to be a top priority.

In some cases the desire to shift the blame is questionable, to say the
least. Thus, the lawsuits frequently brought against tobacco companies for a
death seem to me to be nothing less than an evasion of personal
responsibility. I hold no brief for the tobacco industry! One would have to
search far and wide to find a more irresponsible trade group. In the face of
overwhelming facts, this industry continues to deny those facts and is now
turning its attention to markets in which the hazards of smoking are not as
well publicized. Be that as it may, when labels have appeared on cigarette
packages for a couple of decades warning of the threat to health that is
involved in smoking, it seems to me that suing a company is simply an
evasion of personal responsibility. Oh yes, I know that the label does not

warn that smoking is addictive, but suggest this is to grasp at straws. One would have to be completely out of touch with reality to not know that smoking is both addictive and dangerous. The desire to pass the buck and place blame on the tobacco companies is, as far as I am concerned, understandable but hardly valid.

Examples of blaming others could be multiplied almost endlessly. In some cases it is more than justified in others it is simply a way of excusing one's self or denying that much does happen by chance. No matter how much we might like to, we cannot evade the fact that we, too, have some responsibility and that some things do happen by chance, which Webster defines as: "'something that happens unpredictably without discernible human intention or observable cause." Blame should be placed where there is good cause, but, in the words of Mr. Dooley, "Lave us be fair. Lave us take some iv th' blame oursilves."

Some TV commercials annoy me some amuse me and most of them raise questions. It seems clear that each one is growing shorter, but that there are more and more of them. This is one reason that at our house we increasingly watch PBS. It is true that there are many reruns on PBS, but generally those programs are worth a rerun. But, back to the commercials.

The loud, raucous commercial, such as those advocating "Pepsi" I switch off as quickly as possible. Of course they are not made to appeal to senior citizens anyway so a reaction of annoyance is to be expected. I also become annoyed at performers who shout and in a very loud voice proclaim the alleged merits of a product. Some are local, but I am sure examples of such are to be found in every community.

There are also those that amuse me those that purport to show "proof" of a product's ability to, for example, get out stains, or the ability of a pickup truck to climb over huge boulders thus showing how rugged it is.

Then there are those commercials that raise questions. Why, for instance, would any well-known personality allow herself to become an advocate, with the implication of use, of Polident or Preparation H or Attends? Those who wear dentures or have hemorrhoids or are incontinent generally do not spread the news far and wide. The confusing thing is that those who do this have already made their mark. Is the lure of dollars so great that they are willing to pretend most anything?

However, I am forced to admit, that TV advertising, ludicrous and loud as it is, does work. The makers of products would not spend millions of dollars on it if it did not bring results. The real question then is, "What does it say about the viewers?"

Volume 43 number 1, January 1994

Our time seems to be preoccupied with the casual. "Come as you are," appears to be the dress code for every occasion. Professors go to class looking as if they just crawled out from under a car; entire wedding parties combine tuxedos with tennis shoes; clerical robes don't quite cover golf socks and loafers, and neckties are becoming an endangered species.

Nor is it just in dress that this obsession with the casual is seen. People one has never heard of and probably will never meet again, are on an instant first name basis, and especially if they are doing telemarketing. Casualness in the use of the language is rapidly corrupting both speech and writing. Advertisers play fast and loose with spelling. Light become lite, night become nite and so on, *ad nauseum*. Grammar is something left to English teachers and pedants instead of being used to shape the written and spoken word. One writer has compiled two volumes of what he calls *Anguished English* containing hundreds of examples of tortured language gleaned from advertisements, students' papers, the media, and literature. Certainly we all can and do make mistakes, but in many cases it goes beyond a mistake. The underlying thought seems to be, 'it's not important."

The bedroom was once a private sanctuary; today it has become an amphitheater to which television producers and novelists invite an insatiable public. Sex is portrayed as a casual act and displayed as a spectator sport.

This emphasis on the casual has come to permeate a good deal of life. It is a corollary to a society that is hell bent for something and knows not what. Some even make a case for the casual by claiming it is more natural. It is said it is more natural to dress casually; it is more natural to say whatever comes to mind; it is more natural to turn to sex, abuse, and violence. One can indeed make a case for the casual by appealing to the natural.

This raises two questions in my mind. The first concerns how far we want to carry this obsession with the casual. If, as the proponents of the casual seem to believe, one should dress only for comfort, just how many articles of clothing should one remove — weather permitting? If casual speech, spelling and writing are to be the hallmarks of this bright new age, how will we ultimately understand one another? And, if the cult of the casual succeeds in removing all the barriers to sex and violence, will society gradually make its way back to the jungle?

Then there is the related and more important question as to just what is meant by "being more natural." It can hardly be denied that it is more natural to think of the self. The punch line of a popular TV commercial put the rationale of this concern for the self well when it says, "I'm worth it." Though we may not put it in those terms, we have come to believe that we can indulge ourselves in luxuries, comfort, ease, uninhibited behavior, and whatever else comes most naturally. If I am not mistaken, however, the whole thrust of civilization, and indeed of Christianity, is to exercise some control and to move beyond the natural. Both civilization and Christianity would loudly proclaim that we are more than animals. To the extent that each of us thinks first of his own ease and comfort, to the extent that we indulge in what is most natural, to that extent these stabilizing forces are diminished.

No, I am not arguing for a stuffy conformity, nor do I desire a return to Victorian morality (which was not as moral as it is purported to be). There are times when the casual is very much in order. But I do think there should be a decent respect for the conventions of a civilized society. I may very well be wrong, and I hope I am, but I fear that a society that is in constant pursuit of the casual is entering upon a slippery slope and poses a threat to civilization itself.

Volume 43 number 7, July 1994

In a democratic society one never knows what to expect. However, I have always felt that there were limits beyond which the lust for power would not extend. How naive! Now, a convicted felon has been nominated by his party for the United States Senate and he has a good chance of being elected. This is a new low in American politics. It is true that Oliver North did not serve a prison term because his conviction was overturned on a technicality. There is no question but that he is guilty. He is an admitted liar who shows no remorse and, indeed, he is proud of what he has done.

If North alone was involved the matter would be laughable. But he has the support of many who should know better. Leaders in his party, who would leave no stone unturned, regardless of what might lie under it, support him to strengthen their own position and power. So one is treated to the spectacle of the Senate minority leader endorsing the candidacy of North. Any lingering respect I had for Senator Dole has now vanished. And then there is the Senator from Iowa, Charles Grassely, who also supports North. He is quoted in *Newsweek* as saying, "The bottom line is there have been a lot of nuts elected to the United States Senate." Well, he should know! Be that as it may, there is a very real difference between a "nut" and a criminal.

The most disturbing aspect of the whole comic-tragedy is that North was chosen as the nominee of his party with the strong support of some who call themselves Christian. It is now evident that these people will stoop to any level in order to ram their agenda through the Congress. They may have latched on to the name Christian, but it is not too much to say that they have not the slightest idea of what that name implies. If I thought for a moment that their position represented Christianity I would lose no time in renouncing that faith.

I can recall a time when this country was unified. Oh, to be sure, we had our differences. Our hopes and our goals may have differed, but we had a degree of respect for each other. We might not have agreed with the party in power, whether in the city, the state, or the nation, but partisanship had its limits. I, for instance, have voted for losers more often than for winners, but I was usually able to have respect for those who won. Now, if North should win a Senate seat I could have nothing but contempt for him and his ilk.

His message may have some appeal to the politically naive. He's not the first demagogue to exploit popular disenchantment, but to think that he and his followers would be the savior of this country is not only the height of stupidity, but means making a pact with the devil — who can't deliver in any case.

The health care debate becomes more complicated by the day. There is a very real question as to whether there will be any legislation this year. One group objects to this, another to that, and a third to everything. Some even maintain there is no crisis, saying, "if it ain't broke, don't fix it." With medical costs skyrocketing, those who can't afford astronomical health insurance premiums would hardly agree.

This is the only western nation that has consistently refused to provide health care for its people. Other nations have simplified, and government operated programs which provide health care for rich and poor alike. Theirs is a single payer system that eliminates duplication, a good deal of paperwork, and the profit motive. The latter, in my view, has no place where health care is concerned. Opponents of a single payer system like to refer to all sorts of horror stories from other lands; stories that in most cases are myths and even outright lies. Propagandists have long since discovered that if a lie is repeated often enough people will begin to believe it.

Yes, of course there would have to be new taxes! What is forgotten is that these taxes would be more than offset by the fact that no one, employer or employee, would have to pay the present high insurance premiums. Yes, there would be a vast new bureaucracy, but hundreds of bureaucracies now extant in a multitude of insurance companies would be eliminated. Bureaucracy, which incidentally, is not synonymous with evil, but actually makes the wheels go round, is by no means confined to government the private sector is full of bureaucracies.

No, I have no expectation of seeing a single payer health care system in the near future. But, who knows, someday truth may replace myth and need may become more important than greed. Meanwhile, one should not hope for too much to come out of the present debate.

Volume 43 number 8, August 1994

It is becoming increasingly popular in political life to advocate the death penalty. This is quite understandable in an era of high murder rates and when society gropes for a solution to the problem posed by crime. Such advocacy is given impetus by politicians seeking election or re-election and who seek to impress upon the electorate their "tough" approach to crime and offer a quick and easy solution to the problem. It is in order, therefore, to take a look at the death penalty, or capital punishment as it is sometimes called.

One of the arguments often advanced in favor of the death penalty is that it is biblical. It is certainly true that reference to an eye for an eye, and a tooth for a tooth may be found in the Bible, but it is important to realize these are Old Testament beliefs. Jesus rejected them, saying, "You have heard it was said, 'An eye for an eye and a tooth for a tooth.' But I say to you..." The point is that while support for the death penalty may be found in the Bible, there is no Christian support for it. Indeed, the very opposite is true. Thus, to advocate the death penalty in the name of Christianity is the height of distortion and certainly unbecoming to any who espouse that faith.

It is often maintained that the death penalty acts as a deterrent to crime in that it makes the potential criminal think twice before taking the life of another. This is a popular misconception. Study after study has shown that this simply is not true. The fear of death may be intense, but, as one writer puts it, "...one cannot argue from the terror of the murderer on the morning of execution to the deterrent effect of fear of problematic execution at the moment of crime." Indeed, there is evidence that the homicide rate is higher in states having capital punishment. A bit of reflection will make it clear that one who has murdered once has little to lose by striking again. This is one reason for the higher rate.

There are a number of reasons why capital punishment does not act as a deterrent. Prominent among these are the belief of the killer that he will not be caught; the uncertainty of conviction; and the fact that many crimes are crimes of passion in which attention to possible consequences plays no part.

Unfortunately, the racial factor is evident in the application of the death penalty. An undue proportion of those convicted and later put to death are blacks. Just what the reason is for this is not at all clear, but, whatever the reason, race and poverty play a significant role and the application of justice is clearly not color blind.

One often hears the thought expressed that putting a criminal to death is less costly than a long period of incarceration and that states could, therefore, save money by use of the death penalty. Crass as this is, it may be an appealing idea to some, but it is patently not true. Rarely is there a capital case in which there is not one appeal after another in the attempt to stave off execution. Such appeals are very costly to the state which must bear not only the cost of prosecution, but, since many defendants are indigent, the defense costs as well. Appeal costs totaling millions of dollars are not uncommon and, while costs of incarceration are high, they hardly approach cost of the numerous appeals.

One thing proponents of the death penalty say is more true. A murderer put to death is one who will not murder again. From this point of view, capital punishment is punishment, pure and simple. There is no room for atonement; there is no thought of rehabilitation. Probably the majority of cases would not result in rehabilitation in any case, but the death penalty rules it out. It also rules out the possibility correcting a mistaken judgment. Because a jury finds one guilty does not necessarily mean that such a person was guilty. There have been all too many cases of mistakes being made and when a life has been taken by the state it is a bit late for an apology.

The desire to deal with the crime problem by imposing the death penalty offers a simple solution to a vexing problem. Like simple solutions generally, it will not bear examination. More importantly, it attacks the problem from the wrong end. It deals with the crime after it has been committed. Society must turn its thoughts from how to respond to crime to how to prevent it. Admittedly, this is an area where there are no easy answers. Some crimes, like crimes of passion, we will always have with us, but there are others concerning which society may eventually be able to do something. Education would help some. So, too, would the Grundtvigian idea of few having too much and fewer too little.

Before we come with answers we need to be sure we are dealing with the right questions. The death penalty is at best a reaction to crime. It is an answer that takes an easy, but wrong approach to the pernicious problem of crime. The courts have ruled that capital punishment does not violate the Eighth Amendment, but that is beside the point. What it does violate is man's humanity and his common sense.

Volume 43 number 10, October 1994

I have never attended a Folk School. I did attend Grand View College when the spirit that undergirds the Folk School was very much alive there, but otherwise, neither in America or Denmark have I been involved in a genuine Folk School experience. I have attended a series of seminars, arranged by the Danish Cultural Institute and held at Folk Schools at Krogerup and Askov. While I believe these had some of the same flavor as a Folk School, the experience was not the same as being enrolled for full-time study.

This failure to attend a Folk School does not grow out of any antipathy toward such schools. Indeed, I have long had the highest respect for them. Years ago, when I served in the parish ministry, I had occasion to come into contact with men and women who had spent some time at Folk Schools, either in Denmark or this country. There was something different about them that is difficult to put one's finger on. They were not learned or better educated than their peers, but they did have a broader outlook on life. By and large, they did not pretend to have all the answers. But they tended to be less provincial and saw themselves as part of a larger world.

This year the Folk School can celebrate 150 years of serving youth of all ages in Denmark. The concept of the Folk School came from the fertile brain of N.F.S. Grundtvig. Ironically, Grundtvig himself never founded a Folk School and, as far as I know, he never taught at such a school. Yet it was he who first saw the need for such a school and it was he who first articulated the ideas which were to undergird it. Among these ideas are a respect for the student as an individual, with a natural and evenly balanced relationship between the teacher and the student. The aim is to awaken the student through enlightenment and inspiration to an awareness of and an involvement in the fullness of life. It is no wonder that Folk Schools are often referred to as schools for life.

The Folk School has had its greatest success in Scandinavia, and in Denmark in particular. Here and there, in other parts of the world, attempts have been made to establish or imitate the Folk School. Such attempts have met with varied success. What was perhaps the most serious attempt was made in the United States from 1878 until about 1935. While there are one or two schools in the United States today, patterned on the Folk School, the attempt to transplant such schools in America has largely failed.

The most common reason given for this failure is economic. This, I believe, is only part, and a small part at that, of the reason why they failed. While it is true that Folk Schools in Denmark receive some aid from the state and that students can get state help, there is much more involved. The Folk

Schools in America flourished as long as they could emphasize Danish language and Danish culture in contrast to all that was perceived as being American. When the immigrant flood dried up and there was no longer a strong interest in Danish culture the Folk School was robbed of its mission. The school was unable to translate its mission into emphasizing the English language and American culture. This was partly because that language was not challenged and because it is difficult, if not impossible, to define a common American culture.

Another reason for the failure of such schools in America is, in my view, the competitive spirit that is so common in this country. Though it is often deplored, there is in reality a competition for grades and credits; credits which constitute tangible evidence of attendance and learning. Such tangible evidence is widely sought by employers and the community at large. It lends status to the individual and standing to the job seeker. In a word, one may say that education in America is a means to an end rather than being a broadening experience for the individual which is, in essence, the aim of the Folk School.

Adult education is seen by some as embodying the Folk School principles. To some extent it does, but it lacks certain components that are vital to the Folk School concept. It lacks, for example, the residential characteristic that is so important to the Folk School, with its common living and sharing. The approach that is perhaps most like the Folk School is the Elderhostel. This is a relatively new movement which has had an ever-growing and worldwide popularity in recent years. This combines common living with enlightenment and inspiration and serves to awaken an appreciation of variety of themes. However, the courses generally last only a few days and the participants are limited to the older generation, a generation that is no longer competing for position and status.

In any case, the Folk School has made significant contributions to life in Denmark for 150 years and it continues to do so. And, we must not forget that for a time it made a significant contribution to life among the Danish immigrants in America. It has been and is indeed, a school for life.

Volume 43 number 11, November 1994

I recall once hearing of a science teacher who told his pupils, "If you see it in someone else's basement it's a cockroach. If you see it in your own it's a water bug." This came to mind recently, when in the debate over the crime bill there was so much talk of "pork" and "pork barrel" legislation. We take precisely the same attitude toward what has come to be known as "pork" as we do toward basement bugs. If particular legislation benefits another state or district it will almost certainly be classed by some as "pork." It is of benefit to one's own state or district it becomes quite another matter.

The "pork barrel" is of course the national treasury and "pork" is the favors that a representative is able to get for his or her district. They are able to get this through a process of mutual aid known as "logrolling" by the members of the Congress.

Senators and members of Congress tend to build their careers on how much of the federal largess they can get for their state or district. They become known for their ability to get a slice of the federal pie. A common campaign tactic has them boasting of how well they have served their state or their district. I recently saw a billboard urging a vote for a member of Congress, -which simply bore his name and the words, "fighting for Iowa." The problem is that his opponent is no better. Rarely do they speak of what they have done for the country as a whole. This is not entirely their fault of course. We tend to expect our elected representatives to deliver for their state or their district and we are prone to judge them by how well they have done in that respect.

This way of judging leaders is not exactly new. In Marc Anthony's funeral oration, speaking of Julius Caesar, he says, "He has brought many captives home to Rome whose ransoms did the general coffers fill." In effect he was saying, "Look what Caesar has done for you." It is a statement akin to that which the modern politician makes as he seeks to promote his own record. Be that as it may, of one thing we can be sure, the "pork barrel" is with us to stay and, in the final analysis, we all help to fill it.

The larger question is whether or not something is really "pork." It may appear so, especially if it benefits someone else. If that is the only criterion the answer is easy enough. There are times, however, when something lightly labeled as "pork" is of real value not just to a state or district, but to the country as a whole. Such, I believe, was the case with much that was referred to as "pork" in the crime bill. By and large, the "pork" was aimed at preventing crime. One item that was much ridiculed was midnight basketball. Admittedly, it does have a boondoggling ring to it, but one must look beyond that to the real purpose. Experience has shown that if young people, who otherwise would be on the streets and subject to the temptations of crime, could be offered an alternative, to that extent crime would be reduced. In this case the alternative was basketball. The idea was to get young men shooting baskets rather than shooting each other.

It was no great problem to get money assigned to providing more police or building more prisons. There was no problem expanding the sentencing provisions. But those things, as obvious as the need for them may be, will not solve or even reduce the crime problem. They present a "knee jerk" reaction. They do not deal with the root causes of crime and one does not have to be a genius to see what some of these are. Unemployment, poverty, the breakdown of the family, the exaltation of materialism, drugs, the proliferation of firearms, to name just a few, are causes we can do something about if we put our collective minds to it. The trouble is it is so much easier to wring our hands and then build more prisons — which is not cheap, by the way. If a fraction of that money were used to prevent rather than react to crime we might get somewhere.

The point is that pork barrel politics are here to stay and you and I are ultimately part of the reason. More importantly, we may well be calling the wrong things pork. The real pork is funds that will go to your state and mine to build bigger and better prisons. That pork is the funds that will be spent reacting to crime instead of trying to prevent it. The old adage, "An ounce of prevention is worth a pound of cure," still applies. But, somehow, ounces are harder to grasp than pounds.

Volume 43 number 12, December 1994

Some years ago *Time* magazine presented an article about the many problems engendered by the Christmas celebration. These were summarized in a quotation from a psychoanalyst who said, "Christmas put the damndest demands on everybody." As one contemplates the things that have become almost vital to our celebration, one is inclined to agree. What one must note carefully, however, is that it is the celebration and not the event that makes so many demands. But to get beyond the celebration to the event is to appreciate ever more its significance and our proper response to it.

Luke's narrative of the event tells of a census, a long journey, and a weary young woman. That picture speaks loudly to us of the fact that, time and again, we must take life as it is. It speaks to us of the fact that circumstances are not always such as we would have them. But it also speaks to us of patience, determination, and of obedience all sustained by an underlying trust.

Again, Luke's story of the Christmas miracle brings to mind an obscure town in a land remote in time and place. We see the town of Bethlehem which can lay no claim to fame other than the event which we now celebrate. It is a picture that reminds us that the mighty acts of God have nothing to do with time or place. It reminds us that such acts have nothing to do with greatness, glamour, or prominence. Bethlehem is any town in every time, in any land and every land. It is the meeting place of humanity's greatest fears and highest hopes.

Looking again at the story we see an especially unpleasant scene intrude. We see a crowded town, a busy people and an inn in which all rooms are taken. It is a scene that speaks of business as usual, first come first served. It shows us in graphic terms how unconcerned we can be to the plight of others.

Then we come upon a stable, a manger, and a new mother who has found a quiet comer in a noisy world. A child has been born in the midst of the squalor of humanity. It speaks to us of a God who came to humanity not to command or threaten or even to miraculously save, but to share the worst even as He might raise us to the best.

From the stable our thoughts move to a dark and lonely hillside, where men are at their posts, far removed from home and family, out of touch with the town below in the darkest hours of the night. For all of us there may be similar lonely hours there may be sleepless nights in which we are plagued by all sorts of fears and imaginings. Like the shepherds however, little may we be aware that at such times God may be very near. When it is dark enough you can see the stars, runs the old adage. The shepherds saw them and we, too, may see them.

Then there are the angels with their message of glory to God and peace on earth. That scene speaks to us of awe and wonder, something that is easily lost in this sophisticated age. No, one does not have to believe in angels or midnight songs to have a sense of awe and wonder. We simply need to be aware that there is still action in this universe that is beyond the mind of man or woman.

One could cite other things in the Christmas story that also speak to us. The Bethlehem star, for instance, still lights the way to Christ for wise men everywhere. Or, the scene of the shepherds and the wise men paying homage to God reminds us that contrasts in conditions are created by humans but unity is found in Christ.

Finally, there is the focal point of the whole story — the babe himself. One must always be aware that the babe grew to manhood and revealed God to humanity. The deep significance of the event lies in the fact that through it God manifested himself. As one of the translations of a line in John's Gospel puts it, "the idea became alive." In a word, Christmas tells us that God is not an idle dream.

Soren Kierkegaard tells us that commitment is at the heart of the marriage ceremony. There is a similarity between the joyous event of a wedding ceremony and the happy event of Christmas. However much one may fall in love with and become emotional about the babe in the manger, what really counts is one's commitment to the man he became. In the final analysis, what really matters is that we follow wherever he leads.

Volume 44 number 4, April 1995

This was the tenth year for the meeting at Solvang. The fall meeting at Danebod has been a reality since 1946. The Menucha Conference has been drawing those of Danish background for a number of years. The Danish Interest Conference has been around since 1962. So too, has *Church and Life*, which began as *Kirke og Folk*, in 1952. It came into being when *Dannevirke* could no longer carry on and therefore, the *Kirkelig Samler* page which it carried also expired. To all of this one must add the museum at Elk Horn, the language camps at Menucha and Minnesota, and the Family Camps at Tyler and West Denmark. In all of these one may see a common thread, namely, the desire to experience and preserve our Danish heritage.

It should be noted that, by and large, the meetings are carried out without benefit of clergy. There is clergy involvement in some of these efforts but, for the most part it is the lay people who plan, direct, and attend the meetings and conferences. One reason for this is that there are few remaining pastors of the old Danish Church. Unfortunately, few of the newer pastors have any knowledge of or interest in the Danish heritage and give more than lip service to it. The tie that bound those of Danish background was originally the church. In the nature of the case, this is no longer possible. That which binds in fellowship today is the heritage itself. As Kristian Ostergaard wrote so many years ago, and as Johannes Knudsen has translated those lines, "Where heritage and spirit unite us, we are one."

While we have not been very successful in disseminating our common heritage and traditions, there are few indeed who have turned their backs upon them. This is evident in the large number of people, from all walks of life, who attend the meetings and camps today. Many of the same names and faces appear at more than one event each year. At present attendance appears to be growing and a new generation is making its appearance in many cases. Whether this trend will continue or whether the newcomers will be the last generation that knew and loved the Danish Church and its heritage is hard to say at this point. But, for the moment at least, the Danish heritage is alive and well.

What more could have been done to disseminate our heritage is problematic. Two of our leaders were instrumental in having the constitution of the Lutheran Church in America reflect our Danish and Grundtvigian background. However, most people are not conversant with, nor interested in, the finer points of theology. A few theologians, notably Joseph Sittler, Phillip Hefner, and Walter Capps have been impressed by Grundtvigianism, but even their influence has not been enough to spread our heritage far and wide. *A World of Song* was not as widely appreciated as one might have expected. I recall that one of the LCA camps was presented with a large number of copies, but these came to be looked upon as "the Danish hymnal" and stood on a shelf unused.

I suspect that one reason for this has been our lack of zeal in this matter. Perhaps we were not aggressive enough. But this, in itself, is part of our heritage. We are, by nature, a low key people and to attempt to be otherwise would be contrary to the heritage we hold dear. More importantly, those whom we seek to impress with the Danish heritage generally have a heritage and traditions of their own. So, in effect, we would have to convince them that ours is better. It has been my experience that no indigenous and certainly no ethnic group is willing to say that their particular heritage is not the best. Witness, for example, the frenzy of feeling that surrounds "Americanism." or the "American Dream." To suggest that these should be replaced or even modified by the heritage common to Danes is, at best, to invite ridicule, or, at worst, to be branded as unpatriotic.

Meanwhile, let the meetings, the camps, the singing and the many other traditions we hold dear continue among us. It is all too true that they may eventually wither and die, but they are serving a purpose in the here and now. I have never subscribed to the idea that only that which reaches large numbers is worthwhile. Neither do I believe that only those things which are passed on to future generations have any validity and serve any purpose. The time and treasure expended in planning and attending the various gatherings, building and promoting a museum, and publishing and subscribing to journals and papers gives ample evidence that our Danish heritage is not yet dead and that a large number of people still appreciate it.

Returning from the meeting at Solvang aboard Amtrak we were stopped for, a long time near Granby, in the mountains in Colorado. There was a problem with two young and very unruly men on the train. The train personnel decided to put them off. Accordingly, they radioed ahead to the sheriff in that county and we waited for the deputies to appear. After what seemed a long time to be stopped in the middle of nowhere, they finally did come. Then, a group of male passengers were huddled about a window, looking out to see what was taking place. Suddenly came a female voice from a nearby coach seat saying, "And they say women are nosey." Touché!

Volume 44 number 6, June 1995

Some weeks ago, in the pursuit of additional genealogical information, I contacted the Public Library in the city in which I grew up. I knew that the information which I sought could be found in the old directories for that city. I further knew that it would be a simple matter for a library staff member to find that information, make a photocopy of the relevant pages, and send them to me. I expected to pay a reasonable fee for that service.

The reply which I received did really not surprise me, but it did force me to seek another avenue of approach. I was told in the reply that recent cutbacks in the budget made it impossible to serve clients outside of the normal service area of the library except upon the payment of a rather large fee. The fee mentioned was such as to make me happy that I was informed before the work was done.

This experience points up the fact that budget cuts, on whatever governmental level, have their consequences. The moral of that story is that whatever pittance one may save in taxes will be more than compensated for in private expenditures. Like many another city, Des Moines is in trouble. It, too, has cut back on library hours and services. Potholes abound and are given only cursory treatment. The local bus service, which depends in part on contributions from local and Federal governments, is poor and threatens to get worse. The state legislature, prompted by the governor, voted a tax reduction, but meanwhile the infrastructure crumbles. On the Federal level, the question is not whether to cut expenditures, but where to cut them. The inescapable conclusion is that the coming election in 1996 looms larger in the minds of the politicians than the national welfare.

Certainty state and federal budgets need to be balanced. We cannot continue to borrow our way into the future. To say the least, it is unfair to our children and grandchildren to make them pay for our extravagance. But there are, after all, two ways to balance a budget. One, and the most popular in some quarters, is to cut expenditures, so long as those expenditures benefit someone else. The other is to increase income. In the current debate concerning the Federal budget, I have yet to hear any politician of either party suggest this latter course. Oh, a few brave souls have suggested that cutting taxes at this time is a bad idea, but none has dared to suggest raising them.

Like most people, I am not enamored of the idea of paying taxes. But, as Oliver Wendell Holmes has said, "Taxes are what we pay for civilized society." Further I reject the myth that in America we are overtaxed. Even a cursory look at what citizens of other developed countries pay in taxes would quickly dispel that notion. Not only so, but the lavish expenditures which are evidenced in our homes and on our highways give the lie to our pleas of poverty. In so many areas, from automobiles to furnishings, luxury appears to have become the standard rather than the dream. Encouraged by the state, many are putting supposedly scarce dollars in the lottery. Casinos are proliferating at an amazing pace and during the past month the local county owned gambling casino (yes. I'm ashamed to say we have such) boasted of earning a profit of over ten million dollars. That is hardly a sign of poverty, and hardly a sign of inability to pay for a civilized society-though it may be a sign of stupidity.

Be that as it may, anyone who thinks that a cut in Federal expenses is going to save him money is living in a dream world. The current debate on cutting Medicare is a case in point. Such cuts will mean higher out-of-pocket expenses for the elderly and others who depend on it. Some of us can live with that, but all too many cannot. Again, in other areas, cuts on the Federal level, will mean more expenses for the states. Cuts on the state level will simply mean that the counties and cities will have to raise more money. Cuts on the county and city level will mean that you and I will either have to do without some services or dig deeper in our pockets for some things.

One example will suffice. Potholes are hard on a car. They are one of the prime causes for faulty wheel alignment. Getting the wheels realigned is a rather expensive proposition. Yet, strangely enough, many would rather pay $50 to have their wheels realigned than pay $10 more in taxes to eliminate the potholes. The point is, that while the budget debate rages in Congress, it is well to not begin to count any savings to you as the various proposals are advanced. You will be affected; there is no doubt about that. But the effect will almost certainly be adverse.

Volume 44 number 7, July 1995

In the section on Denmark in *Nordisk Konfact,* a headline says, in translation, "The pension bomb ticks steadily on." The article goes on to say that attempts to deal with the problem have been largely unsuccessful and that early in the next century the pension fund will be in real trouble. Sound familiar? In this country both friends and foes of our Social Security system warn that the long range future is not bright. Actuaries and others tell us that unless changes are made, the "baby boomers" will find the cupboard bare when it comes their turn to retire.

I know that politicians of both parties have said that Social Security is "off the table" in the current drive to slash the budget. The current focus seems to be on Medicare, but, sooner or later Social Security will become a candidate for cuts and the tinkering will begin. And, judging by the treatment Medicare is receiving, such tinkering could be disastrous.

There are those extremists who would abolish both Medicare and Social Security and thus eliminate the burdensome tax on workers and employers. This might solve one problem, but it would compound another – the problem of what to do with the aged. Social Security was conceived during the depression. There were other old age pension plans advanced at that time. Remember the Townsend Plan—facetiously called the ham and eggs plan? It would have given what was then a fabulous sum of $200 a month to all who were over 60 on the condition they retire and spend the money each month. Social Security, when it was finally enacted into law, was a more modest proposal. However, the conditions set forth in the Townsend Plan were basic to any such idea. The high level of unemployment meant it was necessary to get older people out of the work force to make room for younger people. And, there can be no question but that Social Security provided and continues to provide a healthy stimulus to the economy.

These two things are easily overlooked today. While at the moment we have a high employment rate, there are still countless younger workers who could move up the ladder if older workers would bow out. As for older people who still wish to be active, there is no end of work that cries out for volunteers. That the economy is enriched by Social Security spending can hardly be gainsaid. Millions of older people are able to meet their needs and even some of their wants because, though they are no longer employed, they are assured of an income every month.

Abolishing Social Security completely would bring several problems in its wake. For one thing, in millions of cases, it would cast the burden of supporting their parents directly on their children, and in most cases, on children least able to bear that burden. There are those who maintain that they could do better by personal savings and investment. This is questionable and it leaves out of consideration the fact that Social Security provides for the younger worker who is suddenly disabled. Few people could provide that kind of protection for themselves or their families. Voluntary saving for old age represents dreaming more than reality.

The real problem comes when plans are advanced as to how the system can best be saved. This is a task for experts and not for two-bit editors or politicians. I take it as a given, however, that the system in some form must be preserved. Changes will have to be made; changes that may be distasteful in many case, but that are needed. Among the changes suggested are a reduction in benefits, a tax on benefits, a more severe limit on earnings permitted, a means test, etc. From where I sit, it would appear that a uniform benefit to all, regardless of earnings and contributions, would be a possible solution. Of course, I know some would cry to high heaven about such a plan.

Whatever the solution offered, it should be borne in mind that the purpose of Social Security is to solve a vital problem. The aim should be to find the most equitable solution and the most workable one. In a civilized and Christian nation, there is no excuse for having some live on the verge of starvation and others in the lap of luxury all in the name of equity.

Last evening as Johanne and I were leaving a restaurant, the clerk at the desk said, "You guys have a nice evening." That is hardly the first time that has happened. I am not so concerned with the fact that a couple of senior citizens are addressed as "you guys" as I am with the casualness and the poverty of language which it represents. English is a language rich in words, expressions and aphorisms. Why must so much of our language be reduced to slang, colloquialisms, and the lowest common denominator? The clerk could have said, "you people," or "you folks," or simply, "have a nice evening." Instead, she reverted to the teen age expression with which she was apparently most familiar and we, who were old enough to be her grandparents, became "guys," just like her schoolmates.

Volume 44 number 9, September 1995

How much easier and more pleasant life would be if all things were either black or white. One could come to a decision knowing in advance that the action would either be good or bad. There would be no middle ground; there would be no agonizing questions as to whether one had done the right thing.

Of course some things are black or white. They are either demonstrably true or it has been decided by fiat that this should be the case. It can be demonstrated that $2 + 2 = 4$. It can be demonstrated that the world is round. It has long since been decided that a gross is 12 dozen or that one horsepower is the equivalent of 550 foot pounds per second. Generally speaking, in the area of mathematics and established scientific principles, things are either black or white, right or wrong.

In the area of social thought, however, life is not that direct and far from being that simple. There are those who are dead certain that enforced bussing or affirmative action are proper answers to the racial problems in America. There are those who have no question but that more sex education in schools is the answer to the rising illegitimacy rate in the country. And a large segment of the populace, with many political leaders among them, have no question but that the death penalty and ever more and bigger prisons will reduce our crime rate. In all of these cases there are others who take an opposite point of view. They say flatly that bussing is wrong and that affirmative action is in reality reverse discrimination. They say sex education has caused the problem; that the death penalty is morally wrong and that building prisons is a reaction to the problem rather than dealing with the causes of crime. In all of these things, and many more, there is a large gray area in which certainty is no more than a matter of opinion.

Strangely enough, in the area of religion this is generally recognized. We say we believe something; we recognize that religion is a matter of faith. Most of us know very well we can't prove there is a God. We can't prove any number of things that we commonly associate with faith. Unfortunately this wisdom does not always carry over into social and political issues.

One of the most recent disputes by partisans of one view or the other has been occasioned by the fiftieth anniversary of the dropping of the atomic bomb on Hiroshima. Actually, the flap began some months ago when the Smithsonian Institution planned an exhibit centered on the Enola Gay, the plane which dropped the bomb. Protests by veteran's groups and others resulted in a watered down exhibit. But the controversy continues, not only in the press and on television, but among Americans in all walks of life. Just the other day I heard two veterans proclaim with a high degree of certainty that their lives had been saved by the dropping of the bomb. One could hardly blame them. When President Truman gave the order to bomb Hiroshima the reason given was that it would save American lives which might otherwise be lost in an invasion of Japan. Estimates of the number of American lives saved range from 25,000 to the popular myth of one million. In any case, the ostensible reason was to minimize the loss of American lives in an expected invasion of the Japanese homeland.

Now, fifty years later, scholars generally dismiss this position. According to one source, "The consensus among scholars is that the bomb was not needed to avoid an invasion of Japan and to end the war within a relatively short time." This may be discounted as "Monday morning quarterbacking" or second guessing. What is not so easily dismissed is the fact that, at the time, a number of high-ranking military officials felt that it was a completely unnecessary step. Most prominent among them was General Eisenhower, who has written of how he expressed his "grave misgivings" to the American Secretary of State and who felt America would shock world opinion "…by the use of a weapon whose employment was… no longer mandatory to save American lives." Beyond this is the larger question as to why a second bomb was dropped. Political and diplomatic considerations, it is argued, played a large role in the president's decision.

What one's position is today may be quite another matter from what it was fifty years ago. Then it was seen by most of us as the key to victory. Many still see it as such. Others of us are no longer so sure. For many of us the bombing of Hiroshima and Nagasaki falls in the great gray area where there is no definitive answer. Life would be more simple and more comfortable if all could be reduced to black and white, but we have to learn to live with the gray.

Volume 45 number 2, February 1996

Ostensibly, the struggle in Washington, which may still be going on when these lines are read, is about the deficit and a concern with not saddling our grandchildren with a huge debt. More realistically, it is about the next election.

But, leaving aside the matter of the next election, certainly we could all agree that it is not fair to make future generations pay for what are considered to be the excesses of this generation. However, the struggle is not quite that simple. One cannot really be concerned about the economic welfare of future generations while providing a huge tax cut for the more affluent members of this society. By and large, I suspect that most everyone could get along without such a cut. Many of us would not even object to higher taxes if they were applied progressively. There are so many indications in our society that an untold number of Americans are far from being in a financial bind. It would appear that the only ones who do not see this have been blinded by their focus on the next election. Be that as it may, the line we hear over and over again is that the deficit and the resultant debt will have an adverse effect upon future generations. This is a statement with which few would disagree. Who is there among us who would say that, except for a war or natural disaster, we have a right to expect our grandchildren to pay our bills. Moreover, neither can one be concerned with the economy with which the children of the future will live and not be concerned with the world in which they must live.

Being concerned for the financial health of the nation in which our descendants will live is only one way, and really the easiest way, of bequeathing them a better world. A better world involves many things, the importance of which cannot be measured in dollars and cents. In a number of instances they are things which the people of the present can act to correct if there is a collective will to do so. Let me be more specific.

In all the talk about deficit and debt, one rarely hears a word about the environment, about the finite resource of fossil fuel, about global warming or about checking the population growth. These are all crucial factors in the world our children, grandchildren and great-grandchildren will inherit.

Our more affluent and supposedly well educated leaders and their followers express no compunctions about wasting the finite supply of precious fossil fuels future generations may desperately need. Both the Congress and the President caved in to the pressure to raise speed limits. Now the states are hastening to place their own upper limits higher — and one may be sure, incidentally, that speeders will travel the highways well above the legal limits. They seem to have lost sight of the fact that originally this was intended as a fuel saving measure. Now, aside from the fact that the cost may be measured in terms of lives lost, raising the speed limit is a further license to waste more fuel. Our progeny will hardly thank us for that.

Or, what about global warming? To be sure, the jury is still out on the greenhouse effect, but there is an increasing body of evidence that global warming, far from being a figment of human imagination is a product of man's unconcern. There is every indication that global warming, with its threat of inundated coastal cities, increased skin cancer, and agricultural chaos, is one of the least attractive legacies we can leave behind. The future will not thank us for ignoring global warming.

Then there are such things as water pollution, air pollution, the rape of our natural resources and much more, all in the name of profits. Or, take the root of them all, the exponential growth of the world's population; a growth that is by no means confined to the third world. The refusal to do anything to arrest this trend is shameful and the fact that a large segment of the church continues to block such efforts is unconscionable. Nevertheless, that too, is a vital part of our legacy and one for which we will be given no thanks.

This is not to suggest that the deficit and the debt are not important. What is suggested is that this is only a part, and perhaps the least important part, of the picture. It is nothing less than reckless and irresponsible to abdicate our responsibility to conserve fuel, to provide clean air and water, to fail to husband our resources, and to ignore the burgeoning of the world's population.

It is indeed a laudable goal to pass along a debt-free society to those who come after us. But, to paraphrase the Master himself, "What will it profit them to have a debt-free nation if the world in which they must live has already been laid waste?" The really sad part of all this is that we have the means as well as the knowledge to both eliminate the deficit and to deal with these other things so that those who follow us may live in a habitable world. The only thing lacking is the will.

Volume 45 number 4, April 1996

"The Holy Spirit is bringing us together. We are letting the love of Christ unite us," said a Des Moines priest recently. He was referring to the growing ties between conservative Roman Catholics and the so-called evangelical Protestants, two religious groups which have historically been widely separated. Of all the Protestant groups, the evangelicals, the "born again" group, are the ones that would have been considered least likely to find common ground with the Romans. This does not embrace the entire Roman Church, of course, but only the most conservative element in that Church. What's going on here? How can two groups, whose differences have been deep and bitter cooperate on any level?

It is certainly not because each has re-examined its theological position. Theologically they are still as far apart as the poles. The one element of the equation still pays homage to a pope while the other pays homage to the Bible. Bible belt Christians are not about to become Roman Catholics and embrace the papacy nor are the Romans about to swell the ranks of the inhabitants of the Bible belt. It is not the Holy Spirit that has brought them together and it is not the love of Christ that unites them. They are united by something much more mundane; they are united by a social and political struggle in which they share similar views. A social stance, and a political position expressive of that stance, makes strange bedfellows.

The common aim of this strange alliance is to impose a conservative social and political agenda on American society. They are united in their opposition to abortion, and homosexuality. They stand firmly for family values — as defined by them. The tacit implication is that those who do not stand with them in unconditional support of their position are in favor of sins of the flesh and have no interest in family values. The fact of the matter is that it is not quite as simple as that. It reminds one of that classic question, "Have you stopped beating your wife yet?" Just as it is impossible to give a simple answer to that question, so, too, one cannot give simple assent to the conservative position without doing an injustice to the many related questions that arise.

Abortion, however much one might like to think so, is not a "yes" or "no" matter. It is a very complex issue, something which both sides of the question would do well to realize. It is an issue to which there is no solution that will satisfy all. Least of all is it an issue which can be resolved by legislation. The matter of homosexuality is a similar issue. There is increasing evidence that it may be genetically based and as such beyond the control of the individual. Be that as it may, one can be sure that homosexuality cannot be legislated out of existence.

It is interesting and informative to note that, in this case, the separation caused by differing theological viewpoints, has given way to a unity in a certain political and social stance. While attention to the social problems of the day may bring about a political realignment, it would be a mistake to assume that such attention will bring to the fore any reassessment of theological positions. Ironically enough, religion, which should be the great unifying force in our world, is still that which divides people within both the church and the state.

When the late Enok Mortensen wrote his book about the folk schools in America he called it. *Schools for Life*. This is essentially what the folk schools were. They were not schools to teach agriculture. They were not schools designed to make one proficient in teaching, blacksmithing, shoe repair, or any other of the myriad of "how to" subjects. The lecture was the preferred method of instruction and the students were given a nodding acquaintance with great literature, biography, history, and religion. They were schools designed to give the student a richer and deeper view of life. The need today is not for folk schools, as such, but for the spirit and purpose of the folk school to permeate education.

One could wish that today's schools, especially Colleges, were schools for life. This is certainly not evident in any look at today's world. It is especially not true if one reads college advertisements or turns to the catalogs of such institutions. Far from being schools for life they are institutions which stress training for making a living. Certainly training to function in the world of today is important, but there is much more to life than earning a living.

Schools for life and schools for earning a living need not be mutually exclusive, but unfortunately, the competition fostered by the social order, as well as the explosion of information today, tends to make them so. We are in danger of rapidly becoming a nation of experts; experts who know more and more about less and less. This has its advantages, to be sure, but in a democratic society such as ours it is essential, as Grundtvig became aware long ago, to have an enlightened and responsible public as opposed to one that is simply trained to pursue a livelihood.

Volume 45 number 5, May 1996

Newsweek, in a recent article, referred to them as educrats, by which the writer meant the teachers and administrators who are charged with running our public schools. The burden of the piece was a report on an Education Summit held in the East and attended by the President, many of the nation's governors, and powerful executives of some of our largest corporations. Except for a very few, the educrats, or educators, were left out of the conference.

The concern of the meeting was that high school graduates do not have the minimum, skills needed to compete in today's world and to hold a job. It was pointed out, as it has been time and again, that European and Japanese students do much better than graduates of American schools. Youth are given diplomas who are better fitted for life on the street than they are for the workplace. Some states, notably Iowa, boast of their educational system, claiming that it is one of the finest in the nation. If that is true, one can only say, alas.

The recommendations of the summit were threefold: (1) set state-by-state standards, (2) test, (3) and make teachers and schools accountable. Thus, the student would be required to meet certain goals and failure to meet them, as indicated by a test, would result in flunking. Finally, if schools and teachers failed too often, they, too, would suffer the consequences.

This is all very well, but the case is not quite that simple. Certainly there is no question but that changes need to be made. The suggestions emanating from the educational summit may have some merit, but the fact that one has been able to get elected to an office, in the case of the governors, or bring the bottom line into balance, in the case of the business leaders, really does not qualify them to prescribe all the answers in the case of schools. While the things which they have suggested may help, the things they have ignored will eventually sabotage the effort.

While I certainly do not pretend to know the answers to this complex problem, but I do know that there are certain questions that cannot be ignored. One is the question of the tax base for the public school. Another is the role of that school in today's society. A third, which I would cite, is the role of the parents.

Schools cannot continue to be adequately supported by a local tax base. I know of rural school districts in which residents rarely attended a meeting unless there was a suggestion that the tax rate be increased. The same is largely true of school board elections. Just today the newspaper reported more budget cutting by the local school board. One cannot blame teachers for turning to multiple guess, machine graded tests, for example, when the class size is excessive. Public schools are too important to be funded in this way. The tab must be picked up entirely by the state and/or the nation. In a highly mobile society such as ours we can no longer permit students in a city school to receive a more complete education than their rural counterparts. And, to take it a step farther, we cannot countenance students in Mississippi being short-changed on education as compared to those in Minnesota simply because of a disparity in the tax base.

As for the role of the schools — that is an area that needs closer scrutiny. We have come to expect the Public School to assume responsibility for all sorts of things from baby sitting to sex education. Whatever parents feel they are too busy for or would prefer not to do, is dumped on the school. Some of these things may be justified, but many are not. The school must not become a surrogate parent. Perhaps most important, the school must be seen as something other than an entertainment center for the parents. School sports have their place, though only relatively few can participate. All are involved in the academic pursuits which deserve priority.

Then there is the role of the parent, or parents, as the case may be. One cannot underestimate this factor. For a variety of reasons, the parent may not be able to be actively involved in the child's education. However, at the very least, unless and until that parent recognizes the importance of the school, enforces attendance, and makes homework a priority for the student, the efforts of the teacher will be in vain.

It is all very well, and popular, to blame shortcomings and failures on the school and on the teacher. Some of this blame may be justified, but closer to the heart of the problem are the taxpayer and the parent. Unless taxpayers are willing to assume their responsibility for the schools and parents are willing to assume their responsibility for their children, there will be no quick-fix. There is no panacea for what is fast becoming a serious problem.

A final word of caution. Important, necessary, and good as they may be, computers and all the technological paraphernalia that have come to be associated with the modem school, in and of themselves, will not solve the problem. Indeed, they may, in fact, compound it.

Volume 45 number 6, June 1996

Many years ago I read a novel called, *The Last Angry Man*, by Gerald Green. I don't remember much about the novel, which was revolved around a dedicated doctor in a poorer area of a big city. I do recall, however, that he went to visit a classmate in a more affluent part of the city and how he was urged to move and tailor his practice to the wealthy. The wealthy physician was showing him around his office when he said, "See the little red light on the machine over there? It doesn't mean a damn thing, but it impresses people."

It doesn't mean a thing, but it impresses people. How often are we not confronted with things intended to impress us, but which, in the final analysis, are rather meaningless. Unfortunately, the institutional church, with its emphasis on processions, eternal flames, paschal candles and similar items, is a major offender in this area. However, that is another matter. My concern here is with the political world; a world in which each side pulls out all the stops in an effort to try to impress the other with the notion that theirs is the most reasonable and logical solution to any problem. Thus, the so-called think tank has blossomed in recent years. A good many of these are located in Washington, where they can deal directly with Senators and Representatives. Some are located elsewhere, notably the Hoover Institute in Palo Alto, California. Some are backed by liberals most are backed by conservatives.

A think tank sounds like a good idea. The notion is that those most qualified should get together, share ideas and come up with the best possible solution to a problem. Legislation growing out of this kind of thoughtful consideration would have more merit than is evident in a good deal of what emanates from Washington and other power centers. Serious thinking about a problem is much to be preferred to a rush to judgment.

Regrettably, this is not the kind of think tank which is so prevalent today. Today's think tanks, impressive as they may sound, cater to the political parties. What passes for thought in them is not directed at finding a solution to a particular problem. They begin with the solution and seek to rationalize it. Put in terms of a syllogism, the desired conclusion is accepted first and the thinking involves trying to find the premises necessary to justify that conclusion.

The point of all this is that one should be not a little wary of accepting the findings of a think tank, impressive as the concept of a think tank may be.

English is a language rich in meaning. Thoughts and ideas can be expressed in many different ways. Some words have different meanings in differing contexts. In some cases, however, one meaning has so pre-empted the field that a person hardly dares use the word at all.

For example, "affair" means a matter or action. The word has taken on sexual overtones implicit in it to the extent that one is reluctant to use it in any other context. When I was writing about a particular incident my first thought was to call it "the Karl Nielsen affair." I had second thoughts and called it "the Karl Nielsen matter."

"Cleavage" is a word used among other things as a biological term. A biology teacher tells me he was reluctant to use the word because when he did so a titter would go round the classroom

"Ejaculated" may mean said, ejected or uttered vehemently. When I was a boy I was addicted to Tom Swift books, a series about an inventor hero. The author often used that word instead of "said." I'm not sure he would do that today.

"Erected" generally means constructed. I used the word often in writing of new buildings at Grand View until a friend advised against it because it has other meanings also.

"Fairy tales", as stories of mythical beings, would only cautiously be called such at present. While the basis for this escapes me, the word has taken on a homosexual connotation.

"Gay" is a perfectly good word, as in "Don we now our gay apparel." However, except to speak of a homosexual, any other use of the word is unwise.

Then there are words that one is reluctant to use because they may reveal a gender bias. Some of these are generic terms which have nothing to do with gender, but sound like it. Such expressions as "chairman", "mankind", and even "men", come to mind. The elimination of these can make writing cumbersome and stilted. The substitution of the word person every time the expression "men" is used is not really a satisfactory solution. The efforts made to eliminate what are conceived to be masculine terms in hymns sometimes borders on the ludicrous. Incidentally, I have not yet heard "a person" being used in place of "amen."

Volume 45 number 8, August 1996

Terrorism is a pervasive threat in the modern world. It is as much a threat in the skies over America and on the streets of our cities as it is in Northern Ireland or the Middle East. No nation or group of people is immune to acts of terrorism in one form or another. Terror in the sky over Scotland, bombing in Oklahoma City, car bombs in Israel, and now a bomb at the Olympics, bear ample witness to this. The threat exists whenever and wherever a group, operating in secrecy, nurses a grudge against society. Nevertheless, terrorists have a success rate of zero because, much as they may think so, the changes they desire will not be brought about by their nefarious activities. Terrorists don't seem to understand that threatened peoples simply grit their teeth, dig in their heels and continue to pursue the course they have chosen. The battle of Britain in 1940 was the ultimate in terror, but the British did not capitulate as Hitler had expected.

Meanwhile, society seeks security against acts of terrorism. Steps of all kinds are taken or contemplated. Security measures are taken at airports, accessibility to public buildings is limited, and identification becomes a way of life. While the terrorists do not succeed in their goals, they do succeed in the destruction of trust and in making the social order behave like an armed camp. But in reality there is no security and we would be deluding ourselves if we thought this was possible.

Terrorism is not new. Regardless of what it might have been called, whenever the few have taken destructive action against the many, terrorism has existed from ancient times. What is increasingly new, however, is the means to threaten and perpetrate such action. Invention and technology have advanced to such a degree that those who seek to pursue their own agenda through terror too often are able to make good on their threats.

With the exception of the Japanese terrorist subway attack of some months ago, in which a poison gas was used, terrorism has been largely confined to explosive devices and guns of one kind or another. This may not continue to be the case according to no less a person than the Secretary of Defense. Not only poison gas, but germ warfare is not beyond the reach of the terrorist. Uninhibited by scruples, and taking full advantage of technology, there is no end to the death and destruction that the modern terrorist can impose. Meanwhile, the social and the economic implications of terrorism are staggering.

It is difficult to keep all the implements of threat to society out of the hands of those who would use them for their own ends. Some, however can be more rigidly controlled without the sacrifice of civil liberties. Machine guns, assault rifles, tanks and other weapons of war, should be kept out of the hands of civilians. If grown men want to play children's war games, let them use broomsticks and water pistols. Handguns, which we have in abundance in this country, also should be more strictly controlled. The second amendment, which is so often mistakenly appealed to as giving the right to bear arms, does not give blanket permission to acquire weapons for either assault or defense.

Nevertheless, terrorism is and will continue to be a serious problem in our time. The major reason for this is that the terrorists see no alternative to taking matters into their own hands and apparently have no concern for human life, no matter how innocent of wrong their victims may be. In some cases they may feel that their position has been dismissed out of hand. Society must not surrender to their demands, but there is often a very fine line between surrendering and giving them a full and fair hearing. The problems, whatever they may be, are not insolvable. In fact, sometimes most of us don't even know what the problems are.

Reacting to terrorism will inevitably bring all kinds of restrictions and rob us of a good deal of our vaunted freedom, but in the long run little in the way of security. Acting to prevent terrorism with a critical examination of the issues is the only path to a safe and secure world. Violence and terror are born of intransigence by either or both parties.

Were I to be in any doubt that I belonged to a much earlier generation, the act of looking around in a public restaurant on a Sunday noon would quickly bring me back to reality. The kind of attire one sees today is beyond my comprehension. Tank tops, tee shirts with advertising or obscene writing, and, of course, the ubiquitous jeans, to say nothing of men eating with their hats on, seem to be the order of the day. There one can see men wearing things that I would not wear to crawl under my car to change the oil. This is all done in the name of being casual. I'd have another name for it, but perhaps it is best to just put me down as an old fogy and not one of "youse guys."

Volume 45 number 9, September 1996

"The reader feels like a resident in the White House." This line was not written about the Clinton White House, but about that of Eleanor and Franklin Roosevelt during the Second World War. It was written in praise of a book by Doris Kearns Goodwin, called *No Ordinary Time*. This hefty volume, which deals with the Roosevelts and the home front during World War II, is certainly no ordinary book. Each of its 638 pages of closely written text and more than 100 pages of notes, bibliography and index attests to the author's scholarship. Further, the fact that it is difficult to leave it alone, attests to the fact that the book is at once readable, informative and enjoyable. The author has written other similar volumes and she is a frequent guest on, among other things, the *Jim Lehrer News Hour* on the Public Broadcasting System.

It is not my intention, however, to present a review of this work. Rather, I would like to say something about some of the contrasts with our own time that occurred to me. It must be recognized, of course, that the events described in this book took place over 50 years ago. Circumstances were quite different, technology has advanced in ways undreamed of and politics is much different. With these cautions in mind, one may contrast that time with today.

It should be noted that the book deals with a period of war. There were disagreements, to be sure, but, by and large the nation was united against a common, external enemy. This is hardly the case today. We have no common enemy now — at least not one that we are willing to recognize. I cannot recall any time that this nation has been so divided as it is today. We are divided by races (or races) by gender, by age, by political leanings, by religion or lack of it, by social status, and by economic factors, to name some of the major divisions. For all of the hoopla that is engendered by our political conventions, there is precious little unity in America today. Do we need a war to unify us and to bring out our best? Must there be an external enemy to cause us to unite against the common enemy within, selfishness, greed, position and power?

The personal lives of both Eleanor and Franklin were far from ideal, a fact to which the book bears ample testimony. In a word, they were hardly saints. Yes, there was some talk and there were complaints from time to time, but the scandalmongers were not out in full force. For the most part the country saw the President as doing his job, and their personal lives were their business. There was a war to win and people were not inclined to make private matters public matters.

Then there is the matter of the President's wife. Eleanor Roosevelt was constantly on the move. She was the eyes and ears of her husband. She was where he could not be she brought him reports and made suggestions almost constantly. Many of these things were seriously considered and redounded to the benefit of all. Oh, of course there was criticism of her and suggestions that she should stay at home, but, by and large, they were not given much attention. It was certainly not anything like the sustained attack that continues to be made on Hillary Rodham Clinton.

There were opinion polls back in those days, but they were neither as ubiquitous and immediate as they are today. Today one gets the impression that anyone, of either party, in a position of power or leadership consults his polling experts before he dares open his mouth. They seek to lead and govern with an ear to the ground. "Nothing is more dangerous in wartime," said Winston Churchill in 1941, "than to live in the temperamental atmosphere of a Gallup Poll, always feeling one's pulse and taking one's temperature." Polls may be less dangerous in peacetime, but they may be no less destructive. Constant poll taking may help win elections, but, in my view, it is destructive of good government.

The period of the Second World War was certainly no ordinary time. Then, we as a people, had something more to think about than our own interests. We knew that we were all in this effort together. We seem to have lost sight of that fact in recent years. Nevertheless, the war years can be turned to for the valuable lessons they can teach us. Like history in general, we ignore it at our peril.

Not another one! Iowa, a state with less than three million in population, and comprising only 1.3 percent of the total United States population, already has 15 gambling casinos of various kinds. Another is waiting in the wings and now comes the news that still another will be waiting to be approved. Added to this is the fact that the state already has a state run lottery. This may not set a record among the states, but it does show how far some will go in pursuit of development, jobs and dollars. Oh, well, as P. T. Barnum once said, "There is a sucker born every minute." I guess we have to accommodate them somehow. Come to think of it though, if the suckers want to help pay my taxes, I guess I should let them.

Volume 45 number 12, December 1996

The world of bumper stickers is generally a pretty simple one. In that world the most complex of problems is often reduced to a simple phrase or slogan. In the year of a presidential election these rear bumper messages proliferate far in excess of any imagined value that they may have. Other causes also have their devotees who want all and sundry to know about that subject and they have taken a stand to the extent of plastering the rear of their car with a message. Then, too, there are those messages which are intended only to be humorous. They more often succeed in generating laughter than the others succeed in generating action. By and large, however, these rear end messages benefit no one except the printers who make them. Once in a great while one does happen behind a car with a real message; a message that brings second thoughts — and even an editorial. Such a one was seen recently, even though it was not yet the Christmas season. Simple, and to the point, the message said plainly, "Wise men still follow Him." It was, of course, an allusion to the story of the Wise Men as told in the second chapter of Matthew's Gospel.

"Wise men still follow Him!" In my view there is no more important message that emerges from the Gospel. Yes, one may be impressed by what was accomplished on the cross. One may be very much aware of the forgiveness of sin. Or, one may become sentimental about the babe in the manger. But, when all is said and done, belief that does not lead to action is an easy and empty faith. The true test of wisdom lies in following Him.

What does it mean to follow Him? Some aspects of following Him, good and wise as they may be, are not really very difficult and may not be very rewarding. Regular attendance at church, adequate support of the church, and attention to the customs and traditions of religion, are things easily associated with following Him. But, if that's all, if that is as far as the following goes, a vital point of His teaching has been missed.

"Jesus was more than a great teacher," has become a cliché among preachers and theologians. Such an emphasis has been put upon this, however, that the fact that he was a great teacher is often overlooked. There have been other great teachers. Socrates, Plato, Aristotle, Mohammed, Buddha, and Christian theologians down through the centuries. Preeminent among them stands Jesus and it is Him that wise men still follow.

There are many ways of observing the birth of Christ. Some of them are good and even profound. Others are shallow and silly (e.g. a birthday party for the Christ child). As far as I am concerned, however, there is none that can compare to a commitment to being a disciple of the one who was born in the stable at Bethlehem.

The story of the Wise men is almost peripheral to the Christmas Gospel. In some respects it reads like an afterthought. Following the Master, however, is no afterthought and it is by no means peripheral to the Gospel. Indeed, wise men still follow Him.

Volume 46 number 1, January 1997

In the process of downsizing for eventual apartment living (for which there is no immediate prospect), I have been trying to sort through and dispose of some books that have accumulated over the years. I find it to be a difficult job. It is difficult, not because of the work involved, but because I find it extremely difficult to part with books. It is not because they have the monetary value they once did, though my investment in books over the last fifty years has been more substantial than I realized. Small town and rural pastors do not have access to large libraries as do others. Now, for the most part, my books are old and practically worthless. Nevertheless, I am reluctant to part with them and the real reason for my reluctance is that they are like old friends. They are reminders of another day and another time but most importantly, they have been sources of information.

Books open the world to us. In 1838 William Ellery Channing wrote, "It is chiefly through books that we enjoy intercourse with superior minds." That statement is even more true today. Even in this day of the personal computer and its spinoff, the internet, the wisdom of the ages is embodied in books. Libraries, from the smallest private collection, to large community and college collections, are repositories of information. Through such one may be enlightened, entertained and amused as nowhere else. From the ridiculous to the sublime, it is all there.

Some years ago the Grand View College Library made available some bookmarks which urged the recipients to "Be all you can be — read." There is much truth in that. Sometimes I feel that reading is becoming a lost art though the proliferation of bookstores and their customers seems to negate that view. The audio-visual appears to be the preferred medium of the many. Witness the phenomenal growth of video outlets in the past few years.

I recall an advertisement of a half-century ago that stressed the fact that it was fun to be fooled but that it was more fun to know and then proceeded to make the reader aware of some little known fact. Books may call attention to little known and obscure facts, but they may also make one aware of profound truths. Many an "old wives tale," for example, may be refuted by an acquaintance with scientific facts gleaned from books. Superstition may die hard, but the knowledge to be found in books is eternal. Yet it is not just in the interests of knowledge that one may consult books. Through books one may become acquainted with other lands, their culture, their virtues and their vices. A rich goldmine of information and inspiration may be found in biographies and autobiographies. Again, one may climb Mt. Everest in the high Himalayas, or journey to the wildest Africa in the safety of a comfortable arm chair. Whatever one's needs or desires, the world lies at one's fingertips where books abound.

Of course some are excluded from the world of books by visual impairment. But, even in such unfortunate circumstances there is help. Modern technology has made available a plethora of books on tape which often can be had just for the asking.

Meanwhile, however, the downsizing must continue. The limitations of space will eventually demand that I part with books which have served me well. Fortunately, there is an organization here in town that accepts used books and has a gigantic sale every year. Perhaps the friends that I have had may thus fall into new hands that will cherish them as I did. The great thing about a book is that it may be passed on and can be just as valuable to the new owner as to the one who parted with it.

In connection with the disposal of books, I have in my study a box in which originally motor oil was shipped. I note that the box touts the oil as giving "World Class Protection." So now even a particular brand of motor oil is called world class. Have you noted how this expression is being widely used these days? Seemingly, everything from motor oil to education is being advertised as world class. I'm not at all sure just what the expression is meant to convey I suspect that it has become a kind of shorthand or synonym for the best in this land and all lands. Thus, to call something world class is to give it the ultimate praise.

However, if some of the things that are being stressed as world class are really such, one can only say "alas." If some of the newspapers and magazines which claim this accolade are indeed world class, I shudder to think what the rest must be like. If some schools that claim to be such are really world class then mediocrity is certainly the order of the day. We already have world class medicine — and here the expression may refer both to the procedure and the cost. What's next? Will it be world class religion? Just what would that involve?

When all is said and done, in my view, the expression "world class" is one of those phrases that are meant to impress. They may indeed do so, but they hardly enlighten in the process and don't mean much, if anything.

Volume 46 number 2, February 1997

I have long had an interest in songs, and particularly in hymns. It may seem somewhat of an anomaly that one whose musical abilities are almost nil should have a shelf of books, in both Danish and English, consisting of songbooks, hymnals and reference works pertaining to the same. This by no means makes me an authority on the subject, but it does mean I do have some opinions regarding songs and hymns. For what they may be worth, I present some of my views concerning hymns here. They may at least serve to set some minds in motion.

I have experienced the transition from the *Hymnal of Church and Home*, and its antecedent, *"Den Danske Salmebog,"* through the *Service Book and Hymnal*, to the *Lutheran Book of Worship*. Though that transition has not always been easy, it is one with which I and many others have learned to live. I am sure it has not always been easy for those in other constituent synods of the Evangelical Lutheran Church in America to lay the old aside and take up the new. I do believe, however, that we who were a part of the former Danish Church suffered a disproportionate loss. One could wish there had been a somewhat greater inclusion of translations of Danish, and especially Grundtvigian hymns. But, that is so much water over the dam and now my concern is with what exists today. My comments concern the *Lutheran Book of Worship* and its use. I am sure not all will agree, but so be it.

To arrive at the point we are at today there has been not only selection, but alteration of a considerable number of hymns. Long hallowed phrases are gone and in their place have come new, and often stilted, wordings. The most obvious and the most numerous changes have come in an attempt to strip the hymns of what is considered to be sexist language. I most heartily endorse a religion that is not gender based. Christianity is not and was never intended to be for males only. What gives me pause however, is the refusal to recognize that such words as "men," and "mankind" are generic terms as well as terms referring to males. But, as far as I am concerned, the changes that have been made in that respect are more amusing than serious. As *Newsweek* once put it, "What the revisers seem to have forgotten is that good hymns are works of art, not ideology." Oh well, at least "Amen" has not yet become "A-person."

More serious are alterations, for reasons that escape me, that change the meaning of a hymn. John Fawcett's "Blest be the tie that binds," is a case in point. Anyone familiar with the story of that hymn will know at once why he wrote "the fellowship of kindred minds, is like to that above," because he was on the verge of leaving old friends and discovered he could not do so. Why a committee of self-styled experts wrote "the unity of heart and mind are like to that above," I'll never know.

Another example, which is more serious in that it changes the focus, is that great Welsh hymn, "Guide me, O Thou great Jehovah." William Williams framed his hymn around the journey of the Israelites in the wilderness. This theme carries through the entire hymn, even in the revision which appears in the *Lutheran Book of Worship*. However, the first line has been altered to read, "Guide me ever, great Redeemer," thus effectively substituting Christ for God. Perhaps that is what the author meant, but I doubt it.

I have some reservations about how hymns are sometimes used — or misused. One of the most common practices is the elimination of one or more stanzas. Generally, the author wrote the hymn as a unity and the elimination of stanzas often destroys that. An example from a Ladies Aid Christmas party comes to mind. The leader suggested we sing the first three stanzas of "I heard the bells on Christmas day." Those familiar with that hymn will know that only as it gets to the fourth stanza does the hymn get beyond gloom and doom. I also find objectionable what I would characterize playing games with hymns such as having men sing one stanza and the women another.

A part of the reason for many difficulties with hymns is that we tend to sing melodies or tunes. When a person says he likes a particular hymn the chances are that he means he likes the tune. There is nothing wrong with liking a tune, but it must never be forgotten that what we sing are words. Hymns, as someone has said, are the congregation's conversation with God. We need to be reminded that the words of our conversation are important, otherwise we could just as well sing some gibberish.

There is still plenty of room for improvement in the *Lutheran Book of Worship*. Warlike hymns could be eliminated, though many would call them old favorites. Words like "wretched" could be dropped. Indeed, hymns that in the final analysis reflect on God the creator could be eliminated. I tend to agree with a pastor in Greenland who was once interviewed about hymns. At that time Frederik Nielsen said, "I would like to see hymns of penance eliminated from the hymnal because they downgrade human life instead of thanking God for it." But then, as I have said before, I'm an unrepentant liberal.

Volume 46 number 4, April 1997

A new television rating system has been developed by the industry. The stated purpose is to provide parents with some guidance as to which programs children may safely watch. The foul language, the violence, the horror, and the sex life shown in many television programs are felt to be harmful to children and, indeed, are having an effect on society. Foul language is replacing civility in American life and sexual scenes and references are being increasingly acted out in the lives of teenagers. The so-called V-chip, which is scheduled to be added to television sets in the near future, will provide that young children will not be free to view such programs.

Such a rating system and a V-chip are certainly called for in this day when in countless homes the television set has become the chief baby-sitter and millions of children, from toddlers to teenagers, are fed a steady diet of inappropriate language, blood and gore, and sexual activity. But don't expect too much! An industry rating system, developed under pressure, can hardly be expected to do more than filter out the most offensive programs. Beyond that, a rating system is only worth as much as the enforcement it produces. Parents will still have the obligation to keep these shows from their children. As any who have been parents will know, this is much easier said than done. Then, too, parents may not always be in a position to exercise control. The existence of millions of "latch key children" has created a new kind of children's hour during which period parental influence is reduced to a vague hope. Further, it is well known that the surest way to attract readers is to ban a book. There is no reason to assume that a television rating system will not have the same effect. For these reasons and more, television ratings and the V-chip are but a step, and a very small step, in the direction of dealing with a serious problem.

A more simple and effective solution would be to discontinue the production of such programs. If they did not crowd all others off the television screen there would be no problem. Such a solution, however, is not to be expected. There are two basic reasons why such shows are increasingly entering American living rooms. The reasons are related and this makes them even more difficult to deal with. The first is the desire for ever greater profit by the television moguls. Intimately related is fascination with that type of program by a large segment of viewers.

In his, *A Reporters Life*, Walter Cronkite, refers to his experiences on the Board of the Columbia Broadcasting System. The Board, he says, was made up of top-notch business leaders and they discussed only financial matters. "We never," he writes, "discussed violence or children's programming or

permissible language or the frequency or the suitability of commercials."
Again, he writes, "...it is whistling in the graveyard to assume that very
much product is going to come over the airwaves that isn't aimed at
improving the bottom line." In a word, under the free market system, profit
is the dominant aim.

The television industry has long since discovered the interest in and
fascination with the kind of program that many parents decry. In effect they
say, "We want it, but keep it from our children." Witness the popularity of
many of the idiotic, so-called comedy shows. Witness the acceptance of sex
as a spectator sport. Witness the growth of murder, the car chase and its
variations, and violence of all kinds. Make no mistake, producers and
advertisers know what the viewer wants and, in the interest of profit they
are determined to give it to him.

The further question is why the viewing public finds pleasure in this sort
of thing. Here one gets into the fields of psychology and psychiatry, but one
can speculate. May it not be that such programming provides a vicarious
experience for those who otherwise lead humdrum lives? Henry David
Thoreau, in his perceptive book, *Walden* written in 1854, said, "The mass of
men lead lives of quiet desperation." If Thoreau was right, and there is much
to indicate that he was, this could explain many things, including the low
level of television in America.

Television has a great potential. No generation has had the unlimited
opportunity that we have today. Television can provide access to great
music and drama. It can provide a ringside seat to events from across the
world. It can unite us as a nation and a people and increase our
understanding of other nations and peoples. And, it occasionally does these
things. But most of the time it is simply a reflection of society itself.

Fortunately, there is Public Television — though there is an element in
the Congress that would like to dispense with it. Public Television does
provide an alternative to a steady diet of sex and violence. It has an excellent
news program, the comedies it shows are really funny, the nature programs
are outstanding, and dramas are good. Were it not for PBS, in my view,
television would be a lost cause.

At times we do watch something other than PBS. Is it my imagination or
have scenes in which smoking takes place on television increased of late?
Can it be that the tobacco companies have found a new way to "hook" the
young?

Volume 46 number 5, May 1997

Anyone who lived through the great depression of the 1930's should not need to be reminded of how difficult it was to come by a dime — to say nothing of a dollar. Those of us who were growing up at that time may not have been so aware of it as were our parents. In his second inaugural address, the late President Franklin Roosevelt was moved to say, "I see one-third of a nation ill-housed, ill-clad, ill-nourished." Millions of Americans throughout the land knew from personal experience that this was no exaggeration. Then, while the depression was still sapping our energies, came the war in Europe and ultimately our involvement. If there ever was a time when America could not afford the outlay that was necessary it was in 1941. Yet, to our lasting credit, finally aware of the alternative, we gritted our teeth and did what was needed.

The war in Korea, the Vietnam War, and the Cold War were other such times. To be sure, the economy was in much better shape then, but the outlays of money alone to maintain and bolster the defense department were staggering. But there was no real objection, no whining about "hard times" or taxes. This was something that had to be faced and the American people generally took it in stride.

Now all that is over — at least for the present. Not only so, but we are in a time of low unemployment, progress on many fronts and unprecedented prosperity. Unfortunately, we have also been turned in upon ourselves. There is much complaining about the deficit, the national debt and the cost of defense. From both ends of Pennsylvania Avenue come finger pointing and other signs of disagreement and discontent. The Congress spends its time on endless investigations that thus far have served only to eat up millions of dollars. In the face of this, the powers that be say we need a tax cut. That cut, of course, would be on a percentage basis, a system by which those who benefit most need it least, whereas those who are in real need benefit little or not at all. Wage increases on a percentage basis work the same way. Nevertheless, as political leaders are fond of saying, the people are better custodians of money than the government. That sounds great until one sees how money is often spent on whims and fancies, on casinos gambling and gambling on Wall Street. Government could hardly be more wasteful.

Meanwhile, we have, in the minds of many, become poor. We can no longer afford to help those in poverty. We have to cut back on things like headstart, school lunches, veterans hospitals, aid to immigrants, and other projects that promote the general welfare. There is little money for education. Efforts to curb pollution are targets for a cutback. The arts and the humanities have fallen victim to the budget axe. Amtrak, as many would have it, would be best eliminated, but meanwhile can be cut severely though we subsidize much else in the area of transportation. The Public Broadcasting System must learn to get along on less, though some, believing it to be too liberal, would shut it down entirely. Research, which is so vital to the future, must go begging. Never mind such things as public health, nuclear fusion and other pure science research that may one day pay great dividends.

On the state level it is the same. In Iowa, there happens to be a surplus at the moment and the governor and the legislature are falling all over themselves in granting a tax cut. Again, it is a cut which will benefit those who are better off while the have-nots can look on. Meanwhile, Medicaid has been passed to the states and no one knows how much it might cost. The state's infrastructure is in poor condition, with buildings and roads crying for repair. School buildings, are in need of a huge infusion of funds. Financial aid for students suffers while the cost of tuition at state institutions, and elsewhere, is constantly on the rise. It would appear that more prisons is all we have money for.

The point of all this is simple enough. If we can't afford some of these things on the state and national level at this time when will we ever be able to? The ugly fact is that too many of our political leaders do not want to do these things now or at any other time. It is much easier for a politician to go to the voters and say he voted to save money than to say he voted to help people. It is much simpler for him to explain his concern for the present than for the future. Above all, it is much more pleasant to be able to count our dollars than to invest them for the common good.

We are still the richest nation in the world. Can we, in all decency, afford to neglect the poor among us, the struggling institutions, the structures that are falling apart and the many other things that clamor for attention, in the name of tax cuts and the mite this will bring to each of us? Dare we neglect the future for a pittance in the present? Sooner or later we will pay, and perhaps dearly, for what is done or not done today.

Volume 46 number 6, June 1997

The postal service has now announced that there is a probability that the present thirty-two cent stamp will cost thirty-four cents next year. Remember when you could contact friends across the state or anywhere in the nation for three cents? Then, too, there was the penny post card. I recall that some of us used to carry on an extensive correspondence via the penny post card. It is surprising how much can be crammed on a post card. Those were the days when every penny counted and to telephone was unthinkable. Now those days are gone forever and, in many respects, it is just as well.

One can complain about the cost of postage, but there is really not much to do about it. Everything else has increased. Wages and salaries are up, social security payments regularly increase and the cost of living has increased far above what it was 40 or 50 years ago. So, from my point of view, the steady increase is called for by the postal department are not unreasonable. It would be nice if the rate could be greatly increased on "junk mail" which comes in an ever broadening stream. But, we are told that this kind of mail helps the postal service to pay the bills. It would be nice if there were some other source of revenue, but perhaps then the economy would suffer.

If I do not find the cost unreasonable, I do, however, find the service increasingly poor. It is almost as if there is an inverse relationship between cost and service. As the cost goes up the service goes down.

I often think back to the way it was when I was growing up. Then, as now, we lived in a city. We had two mail deliveries each day. The letter carrier was on foot, though he did ride the city bus to the point where his route began. Not only so, but the route of this particular carrier included a steep, quarter mile long hill, which he had to climb twice a day. The mail was always on time. It was a time when the inscription over the Main Post Office in New York City, which was adapted from the Greek historian Herodotus, meant something. It read: Neither snow, nor rain, nor heat, nor the gloom of night stays these couriers from the swift completion of their appointed rounds.

In this day and age, when speed seems to be the dominant factor in so many things, the postal service seems to be the exception. We never know when to expect our mail, which arrives once each day. Once in a great while it does arrive before noon. Usually it is late afternoon, and on occasion it has been almost six o'clock in the evening before we hear the mail dropping into the box. This, like other cities, is one in which every letter carrier has his own vehicle, which he then parks at a corner while he delivers the mail on that street. I am told by the post office that there are 342 such vehicles in Des

Moines, a city of less than 200,000.

In Denmark the letter carriers use bicycles as they make their rounds. This seemed to me to be a good idea until one day, while in Denmark, I saw a letter carrier's bicycle, loaded with mail, parked outside an apartment house while he delivered inside. Our system, in which vehicles are carefully locked each time the carrier leaves, does provide a better insurance against theft.

The pre-vehicle American system provided frequent locked storage boxes on many street comers. In these the mail for a particular area was deposited and from them the carrier could retrieve the quantity for each segment of his route. Thus, he was not burdened with the whole amount for his route any one time. These storage boxes have disappeared. So, too, have the drop boxes. There was a time when there was a drop-box on many a street corner. Now, if one misses the carrier, mailing a letter in this town entails considerable walking. Our closest dropbox is a half mile away. In good weather this is no problem and the walk is good for me. If the weather is bad, I often drive to the branch post office a mile away. This does have the added bonus that the mail is picked up more frequently.

There is a booming parcel service in this country the managers of which would like to take over the first class mail service. Then the postal service would be left with the dregs — and mailing a letter would become even more costly.

Of course I am not privy to all of the problems that may be involved. I have no reason to think that the current postal powers are any less dedicated to their work than their predecessors were. The present condition does point up the fact, however, that there is more than money involved in efficient service from the postal department. It may, indeed, be necessary to go to a thirty-four cent stamp, but don't look for an improvement in the service any time soon.

Volume 46 number 7, July 1997

The travel season is upon us. Schools have closed for the summer vacation, workers get a respite from their labors for a shorter or longer period, and other scenes and experiences beckon for a brief time. To me, summer vacation time has always been a glorious time. I can recall how 60 years ago the one week long summer vacation was something which one could enjoy in anticipation and relive in retrospect.

With the coming of spring and summer, the call of the open road takes on new meaning. To be sure, the interstate highway system makes it more possible than formerly to travel regardless of the season, but even those highways are more certain during the spring and summer. The interstate highways, a legacy of the Eisenhower Administration, have made travel much easier, faster and safer. Today it is difficult to recall that the system was first conceived as a defense measure. Congress, it seems, can be persuaded to do anything in the name of defense. (Perhaps health care and education proposals should be advanced as defense measures — which, indeed, they really are.) Nevertheless, whatever the reason, the construction of the interstate highway system is one of the greatest assets of which our country can boast today. Of course it does have some drawbacks. When one sees the never ending parade of huge trucks, with their threat to safety, their waste of fuel, their needless pollution, and their squandering of manpower, one may have some second thoughts about it. Yet, in spite of this, we can be justly proud of our interstate highway system.

Whatever their shortcomings, I, along with millions of Americans, do prefer those highways when traveling. In spite of their ever-increasing commercial use, statistics leave no question but that they are safer. There are many who object that they are boring and that one does not get into small towns where there is life and action. This is true enough, but I would contend that from an interstate one can get a broad view, a kind of panoramic view, which is often not possible on ordinary two-lane highways. Not only so, but small towns, with, their speed limits and traffic lights are not only time consuming and dangerous, but wasteful of fuel and profligate with pollution.

Be that as it may, travel by motor vehicle is only one way to get about the country and the world. Unfortunately, the rise of the automobile has led to the decline of public transportation in general and the railroad in particular. Amtrak, the quasi-governmental corporation, was formed in the early 1970's to take over the declining passenger railroad system. Today it is all that is left of the elaborate passenger service this country once knew. Hundreds of empty railroad stations around the country give mute testimony to this.

Amtrak itself is now in decline and if some members of Congress can have their way, it will decline still further to the point of extinction. This is in decided contrast to Europe, where the trains are thoroughly modem and almost always on time.

Travel by bus is not an option that one would normally choose for a vacation. It is hardly the most leisurely way to get about and, as is the case with the train, the number of cities and towns served has declined greatly. A growing number of cities and towns are already isolated and the end is not yet. Indeed, without an automobile, one's travel can be quite circumscribed — even in the city

The fastest way to travel is by plane. This is fine for those who cannot travel in any other way or who prefer flying. In some circumstances it is practically the only remaining way to travel. The plane has virtually eclipsed the steamship for overseas travel. Despite the headlines which a major airline crash calls forth, flying is a safe way to travel. Statistically, it is far safer than the public highway. Though normally rates are high, one can often purchase advance fares somewhat reasonably. It does have one major limitation as far as leisure travel is concerned. Generally one sees a crowded airline terminal at each end of the journey and nothing in between. Sometimes the clouds may part enough to grant a look below, but most often all one can see is clouds.

Not everyone enjoys traveling of course. Many take great pleasure in relaxing at home or taking on projects that have long been put off. There is value in this and, not least, there may be a sense of accomplishment. As for me, I've gotten beyond the major physical project stage and I do like to travel. There is so much that I have read about that I would like to see in this vast world. I shall never forget the thrill of seeing the parliament buildings in London and hearing Big Ben sound the hour, sights and sounds which previously had been only pictures in books and sounds on the radio.

Meanwhile, the height of the summer season is here. Whatever your preferences may be, staying at home or responding to the siren call of other places, enjoy your summer.

Volume 46 number 8, August 1997

Not long ago my wife and I met a lady who had once been a member of Luther Memorial Church in Des Moines. She had moved, leaving that church, and joining another. The church to which she now belonged, was the Church of the Open Bible. That's quite a change!

Changing of churches and even denominations is certainly not a new development. I am acquainted with a number of persons who, for one reason or another, have over the years gone from being Lutherans to becoming affiliated with a Methodist, Presbyterian, or a Roman Catholic congregation. I am sure also that some have come into the Lutheran fold from other bodies. This movement, while not new, does appear to be gaining steam and, to me, it signifies that denominations do not have the importance they once did.

I can recall that even as a child this matter had great importance to me. I often rode the city bus to go downtown and in the course of its travels the bus would pass three Roman Catholic Churches. As it passed each church the Catholic men on the bus would all tip their hats.

(This, incidentally, was a nice gesture of respect for the church.) However, Protestants on the bus would be very careful to not make any move that could be interpreted as tipping one's hat. Protestants were not about to be branded as Catholics and vice versa. Years later, when I began my ministry, the rivalry was still there and one would go out of the way to avoid being identified as anything but a Lutheran. Reformation Sunday was, in many a Lutheran stronghold, an open season on the Roman Church.

Happily, denominational members no longer look down their noses at each other. While there still is some rivalry and a good deal of 'sheep stealing,' i.e. getting members of another church to join one's own, the days of bitterness have largely passed. Such rivalry as there is today is a product of demographics and economics more than theology. People often tend to gravitate to a nearby church. This is particularly true if there are children who attend Sunday School. Congregations, whether they recognize it or not, often seek members to help pay the bills more than to insure that they have the 'correct' theology.

Today, even the denominational bodies meet together and engage in discussions aimed at a mutual understanding the acceptance of one another. The ELCA has long been engaged in discussions with the Episcopal, the Presbyterian, the United Church of Christ, and the Reformed Church in America regarding full communion. The church-wide assembly of the ELCA will vote on the matter this August. Meanwhile the issue has been hotly debated.

I rather suspect that, in spite of confirmation instruction and other religious training, aside from pastor, theologians and a few others, the average Lutheran cannot draw any serious theological distinction between his church and the Reformed or even the Roman Catholic. This is not to say that all should subscribe to the same views and be a part of one great church body. While this would have some advantages, it would not allow for any individuality and would almost certainly result in new divisions somewhere down the line.

It has been my experience that many lay people tend to judge churches by the order of service used. Thus, some have attended a Roman Catholic service and concluded that there is little significant difference between the Roman and the Lutheran Church. The theological distinctions, so important to the priest and pastor are lost on them and of no consequence. This is not to say that such distinctions are unimportant. They serve to define the pattern of beliefs of the church body and theoretically, it is up to the individual to hold to these. From a practical point of view it does not work out that way. The national body becomes, in a sense, an umbrella church, sheltering a variety of the religious beliefs. It is not strange then that time and again some should transfer their membership to other churches for reasons less than theological.

The old Danish Lutheran Church was, more or less, an umbrella church. It was Lutheran, but within its membership there were many varieties and interpretations of Lutheran beliefs. This was as true of pastors as of lay people. Today, the ELCA is really an umbrella church within Lutheranism.

In past centuries wars have been fought and slaughters permitted because of the differences between the churches, all of whom sought to serve the same Lord. All kinds of crimes have been committed in the name of religion. Fortunately, that day has passed, and in this more sophisticated era people tend to move freely from one church to another.

Theological distinctions have their significance, but to the extent that these are binding, they are divisive and destructive of the unity that is to be found in Christ.

Volume 46 number 9, September 1997

For a special occasion in 1820, N. F. S. Grundtvig wrote a song, which to my knowledge has not been translated. The song is called, "Langt Højere Bjerge," (Far higher mountains). The essence of its six stanzas is that there are higher mountains, prettier meadows, greater achievements, wiser people, and finer languages, than are to be found in Denmark, but that none of these can offset the values which exist in that little lovely land. In the English language we have a saying that gives expression to a somewhat similar thought. We say good things often come in small packages.

I think of these things in connection with the 125th anniversary of the founding of what became the Danish Lutheran Church in America, and ultimately the American Evangelical Lutheran Church. For those on the outside looking at it, there was no question but that it was small. It was one of the smallest, not only of Lutheran groups, but of Protestant groups in general. Those within that church recognized these limitations and often they labored to be bigger, but nevertheless they treasured the values that were theirs.

That there were such values was more than evident to those within. Oh, to be sure, there were some who chafed at the bit and who longed to be a part of what they considered the real world. For the most part, however, its adherents could say that while there were larger, finer, richer churches, the Danes were not envious of such.

At the beginning the Danes found in their Church a language and a freedom with which they were familiar. For at least two generations the church served the immigrants and the children of immigrants on these shores. This is something that is often overlooked. Sometimes one gets the impression that the exclusive concern of the church must be with the future. It certainly is true that the church dare not ignore the future or it will die. However, the church that ignores the present is already dead. The church must serve in the present with an eye to the future. In any case, the immigrants and their progeny were well served for many years by a church that had been transplanted in a new world.

Even in later years, though the Church remained small, it had many advantages. Because it was small its pastors at least had to be well informed regarding the world about them, and particularly about other Lutheran bodies. I, for example, was often surprised at how little pastors of other Lutheran churches knew about Lutheran bodies in general.

The Danish Church and its successor, the AELC, was a national body. Its congregations, though they might be few, stretched from shore to shore. We were not holed up, as are now, in some little corner of the nation. We had contacts and friends in many places, contacts and friendships that persist to this day.

In some respects the Danish Church and its successor body, the AELC, became a source of leadership for both the Lutheran Church in America and the Evangelical Lutheran Church in America. A disproportionate number of influential people came out of the Danish Church. Two seminary professors moved directly from the Danish Church to positions of influence within the merged church. So, too, did four of the men who eventually became bishops in the merged churches. An assistant to the presiding Bishop of the ELCA, the Director of the Department of Ecumenical Affairs, grew to manhood in the Danish Church. A son of the Danish Church became a regional executive while his brother, also a Danish Church pastor, headed the "Strength for Mission" drive in the LCA. Two other sons of the Danish Church moved into positions among the leaders of Lutheran World Relief where they played a major role in dealing with the problems of world hunger and of refugees. Through all of these people, and many others who served on merger committees, the little Danish Church had a decided influence.

Far higher mountains? Yes, of course! Far larger churches? Of this there can be no question. Nevertheless, the values of the little Danish Church were as real as any and its influence was widespread. It is little wonder that so many recall it with affection and gratitude.

Volume 46 number 10, October 1997

Our local newspaper never loses an opportunity to promote Iowa. If an individual has the slightest connection with Iowa through living there, having been born there, or having lived there, this is always pointed out, and often in bold headlines. When the person's deed would have a negative impact, the Iowa connection is played down or eliminated. This provincialism in newspapers is especially to be noted in smaller cities and states. Such provincialism is hardly confined to newspapers. One may see this manifested in immigrant groups, for instance, and the smaller the group the more prominent is the concern with its own image.

Americans of Danish ancestry are a case in point. We are quick to claim as one of our own the explorer, Jens Munk, who, seeking a northwest passage, came to what is now Hudson Bay in 1619. Another, Hans Christian Febinger (or Fibinger) was one of General George Washington's trusted officers. Here in Iowa we can claim Carl Rohl Smith as the Danish sculptor who was responsible for the brass figures on the monument to the Soldiers and Sailors of the Civil War. In California the name of Peter Lassen is well known. For that Dane a county, a park and a peak in a mountain range have all been named. The noted Lutheran minister who worked among the Norwegians in America during the last century, Claus L. Clausen, was a Dane by birth. Danish also were the Socialist pair, Louis Pio and Paul Geleff who attempted to begin a colony in Kansas in the summer of 1876. Among the more modern names are those of Lauritz Melchoir, Jean Hersholt, Victor Borge, and the lesser known Buddy Ebsen.

All of which brings me to Jonas Bronck. While most Danish immigrants or their children would not be enamored of New York City, they would be quick to point out that one borough of that city, the Bronx, was named for a Dane who settled there in 1639. Of all of the great and near greats associated with the Danes in America, the name to Jonas Bronck is probably cited most often. To have the origins of the Bronx, with its teeming millions today, connected with the life of a Dane in the seventeenth century is a real head-sweller. To have something in common with such a man is quite notable.

There is only one trouble with that. Recent research has shown the notion that Bronck was a Dane cannot be substantiated. In 1984 the Canadian researcher and president of the Federation of Danish Associations in Canada, Rolf Buschardt Christensen, wrote to the Bronx County Historical Society for information regarding Jonas Bronck and other Danes who settled there. Mr. Christensen received a lengthy reply saying that "...two hitherto unpublished documents there (the Notarial Archives in Amsterdam, Holland) disclosed conclusively that Jonas Bronck was born in Sweden and,

187

therefore, was not a Dane."

One of the documents describes him as coming from "Smolach in Sweden" and that his birthplace was "Coonstay." An archivist at Upsalla, in Sweden, has indicated that these misspellings almost certainly refer to the Swedish province of Smaland and the village of Komstad in that province. There was indeed a Brunk (or Brunck) family in that area and the records indicate a son named Jon Jonssen (which in Dutch would be Jonas Jonass) to which was added his mother's family name Brunk, which may also be written as Bronk or Bronck.

A theory was advanced in 1914 that suggested Bronck was the son of a Faroese minister, Mortan Bronck. However, there is evidence that the alleged father, Mortan Bronck, died in 1583. The marriage banns for Jonas Jonass Brunck are dated June 18, 1638 and state that he was 38 years old at the time. This would indicate he was born about 1600, long after Mortan died — and before sperm banks were invented. The marriage banns also give his birthplace as "Coonstay."

It is believed that Bronck had been taught to read and write by the local clergy. The books in his library suggest that Bronck taught himself navigation and the documents indicate that he was called "Captain." He left Sweden and settled in Holland. From there he plied the trade routes in the Baltic Sea and accumulated some wealth in the process. In 1639, with a few indentured servants, he left for the port of New Amsterdam, as New York City was then called. He died in 1643 during an Indian revolt, but there is no reason to think that he was slain by the Indians. Indeed, his farm was unharmed and his family and servants continued to live there. His widow remarried later that year.

Rolf Buchardt Christensen was kind enough to send me a copy of the letter detailing this research some years ago. This material is now filed in the Danish Immigrant Archives at Grand View College. It has recently come to my attention again and accordingly, it occurred to me that I should share this information, disconcerting as it may be.

Though as Americans of Danish descent we may experience a degree of disappointment that we can no longer claim Jonas Bronck was one of us and that the Bronx had a Swedish beginning, the important thing is not where the man was born, but where he lived and what he accomplished. Provincialism is not an attribute that should be cultivated by immigrants or their descendants.

Volume 46 number 11, November 1997

Harvest Festival was a tradition of long standing in the Danish Lutheran Church. Unless I am mistaken, it is a tradition that was part of the baggage which the immigrants brought with them from Denmark. Rural churches, especially, often went all-out to observe the festival. The church would be suitably decorated with corn stalks, pumpkins and colored leaves, the sermon would be geared to the festival; there would be a fellowship dinner, and an afternoon meeting with a featured speaker. It was one of the high points of the year in the life of the congregation. It was eagerly looked forward to, thoroughly prepared for, and enjoyed by all.

Though the superficial aspects of the event seemed to predominate, there was nevertheless a deeper significance to the custom. It was a recognition not only of the harvest, but of the fact that the harvest was beyond the control of man alone and ultimately resided in the hand of God.

Harvest festival is not observed to the extent that it once was. In many congregations Thanksgiving Day has become the only occasion for giving thanks to God for not only the harvest, but for His continued goodness and mercy. Thanksgiving Day perhaps has a broader significance than Harvest Festival in that it may be concerned with all aspects of human life.

Thanksgiving or Harvest Festival, it is fitting and proper that we do pause to render thanks. Thanksgiving Day is a peculiarly American custom and it is a custom that deserves to be observed.

It is generally agreed by educators, political leaders, and the general public that today's educational system is in trouble. The degree of difficulty varies with states. In the more affluent states the problem may not be quite as great as in poorer states, but a problem is in some degree everywhere present. Various solutions have been proposed and these range from supplying more computers, providing smaller classes, and administering statewide, or even nationwide tests. Each of these has some merit, each would be costly, and each has its partisans. Probably the most debated is the standardized test.

Certainly I do not claim any expertise in the matter of standardized testing. However, having grown up under such a system, and placing a high value on my pre-college education, I do have an opinion.

Beginning in the seventh grade, when we had completed a subject, be it geography, algebra, history, etc., we took a so-called Regent's Examination in that subject. No one in the school, from the teacher to the administration, saw the test in advance. We could see tests from previous years and thus know what to expect, but otherwise secrecy was rigidly enforced. If a student failed by a few points, the teacher, on the basis of the student's record, could make a recommendation to the state agency. By the end of the high school course, if one had passed all the Regent's Examinations, he or she earned a regent's in addition to the regular diploma, the latter being sufficient for graduation.

Fortunately, I took and passed all of the Regent's Examinations. I fail to see that it has hurt me one bit. In fact, I am convinced that I received a better education because of it. Further, as far as I know, my teachers were never bothered by it

Today, opponents of such a plan argue that with such testing in place, the teacher will "teach to the test." Of course — what else. If a test is comprehensive, and if the teaching is also comprehensive, a student who passes that test will have a good understanding of the subject. The essence of the subject is embodied in the test. By teaching the subject the teacher has, in effect, been teaching to the test. That is as it should be. This assuredly would not prevent the teacher from using whatever methods he or she found most effective.

It would prevent teachers from going off on a tangent. It would prevent them from "riding on their own hobby horse." I have known college teachers who more than once have said, "I wonder what I should talk about today." It would mean that they should know and teach their subject. I have known teachers who have said, "Give me the textbook and I will teach any subject." Most teachers do know their subject and they would not need to change one iota under a standardized testing procedure. To be sure, this assumes general agreement on the content of a subject and it assumes that those who design the tests are as dedicated as are the teachers. If this is too much to assume then we are indeed in real trouble.

Would this solve all of the problems in education? Of course not! There would still need to be smaller classes, fewer machine graded tests, more "essay" questions, and above all, more tax dollars. The latter is the real stumbling block, but, when all is said and done, there is no more important investment we can make than insuring the future for our children and grandchildren.

Meanwhile, one should not put education at risk on the basis of what is really a bumper sticker phrase, "teaching to the test".

Volume 47 number 3, March 1998

The local paper this week has made much of the fact that the Bishop of the Southeast Iowa Synod of the Evangelical Lutheran Church in America, held a trial and removed a homosexual pastor from the clergy rolls of the ELCA. Newspapers, incidentally, never lose an opportunity to take advantage of disagreements within the church. It is as if it is widely believed that the church is made up of perfect people who never have disagreements or differences of opinion. It was natural, therefore, that the press should have a field day with this event.

In this case I fail to see that the Bishop had any choice. In fact, I don't even see why a trial was necessary. The whole matter could have been disposed of rather quietly if the pastor and his congregation had agreed. However, they did not agree and, at this point, there is some question as to whether the congregation will defy the ELCA and retain the pastor. The pastor admittedly was homosexual and he had a live-in-friend. He was, in short, a practicing homosexual. ELCA rules permit the ordination of homosexuals, but do not permit practicing homosexuals to be pastors. This was obviously an open and shut case if the rule was to be followed. There was no question about the facts.

Be that as it may, it does seem to me that the ELCA would do well to rethink the rule at its next general assembly. If homosexuality is not an acquired, but an innate trait — and there is much to indicate that it is — then the requirement of celibacy would seem to me to be wrong. It would seem to deny to homosexuals the same privileges and pleasures that accrue to heterosexuals. Historically this has been the case, but in the light of more recent developments and studies it has become increasingly difficult to maintain an historical position.

Homosexuality and lesbianism are traits that have historically raised a red flag in the heterosexual world. They have been seen as evils from biblical times to the present but, this may simply reflect the temper of those times. In recent years this is more and more being called into question. The jury is still out on the final disposition of the matter and meanwhile it behooves the church, and that includes you and me, to observe a variation of the well-known dictum, innocent until proven guilty.

It has often been said that if archeologists some 2,000 years from now were to come upon our landfills (one no longer calls them for what they really are - dumps) they would be amazed at the number and kinds of things we had disposed of. Everything from watches, to furniture and even the remnants of destroyed buildings may be found in our landfills. We have indeed become a throwaway society. When something no longer pleases us or fails to function as we think it should, we consign it to the scrap heaps of civilization. Strangely enough, the higher the degree of civilization, the bigger its scrap heap.

Some of this is justified, at least from the standpoint of economics. After all, if it is cheaper to buy a new watch than to have the old one repaired; it does make good economic sense to get rid of the old one. If it is cheaper to tear down an old building than to remodel it, then it will pay to construct a new one in its place and let the old one go the way of the wrecking ball.

However, much of it is simply fascination with the new. The media loses no opportunity to let us know that something is "all new" or "new and improved." Somehow, the new is generally viewed as being better than the old. In many cases it is. New technological advances have had their impact on everything from automobiles to computers. In the latter case, changes come so fast that a computer is almost out-of-date the moment it is taken out of the box.

Changes in the order of worship in the church are something we have all experienced. Some changes are long overdue; others are born of arrogance. Changes are one thing, but an attitude that says, "now we will start doing it the right way" is quite another.

There are some exceptions to "new is better," particularly in the area of foods. When the aim is to impress us with the quality of an item it is often touted as being "old fashioned" or "country style." A corollary to this emphasis on quality is that often the TV promoter of a particular American made automobile speaks with a foreign accent. Strangely, foreign is equated with quality, which may or may not be so.

For the most part, however, the new is seen as much better than the old. Meanwhile, the landfills are filling, one after another, pockets are empty, credit is exhausted — but the one bright spot is that the economy is booming.

One final happy note! Thousands of we alumni are happy to note the "old main" at Grand View College is being remodeled and has not gone to swell some landfill.

Volume 47 number 4, April 1998

There are at least three major creeds in Christendom, the Apostle's, the Nicene and the Athanasian. "Creed" comes from the Latin, credo and means simply, "I believe." It is intended to be a statement of faith as it has been understood by the church. The church member, by confessing this faith, signifies his acceptance of it and his unity with the church.

The Apostle's Creed claimed the attention of N. F. S. Grundtvig and his followers. For a time he believed that this formula of faith was given to the disciples by the Lord himself and was accordingly dedicated to it. Though he later rejected this view of its origins, he continued to place emphasis upon the Apostle's Creed. He saw it as preceding the Bible and thus as the foundation of the church. The Apostle's Creed was seen by Grundtvig and others as an ecumenical document. In any case, for Grundtvigians in Denmark and America, the Apostle's Creed became the standard of faith. Several generations were accustomed to confessing their faith in the words of that creed.

It is not strange, therefore, that the substitution of the Nicene Creed for the Apostle's Creed on many occasions should be met with some raised eyebrows. Indeed, *The Lutheran Book of Worship* and its predecessor, *The Service Book and Hymnal*, say that the Nicene Creed shall be used when communion is celebrated and on other festive occasions. Just why this is so is far from clear. Perhaps the liturgical experts sought some variety or decided that the Apostle's Creed was not suitable for use at every event.

If this were a simple matter of preferences, further discussion would hardly be merited. We all have our preferences and, in many cases, including services of worship, the preference of the majority should be the deciding factor. Just how that majority arrived at a particular preference is another matter and need not concern us here. What is of concern is the nature of that preference.

The fact is that the Nicene Creed is, to say the least, a very questionable document. It was promulgated by the Council of Nicea in 325 a.d. That council was called because the Emperor Constantine faced religious division in his Empire. At that time Constantine was not a confessing Christian though he did become such later. The Council he called is considered by many to have been the most important council in the history of Christendom. Essentially, the dispute had to do with the nature of Christ. Was Christ to be considered identical with God or was he simply an intermediary between God and man? The Creed, which was eventually adopted, said of Christ that he was "begotten, not made," and of "one essence with the Father." It made the Son the equal of the Father. The Holy Spirit was dismissed with one line, "we believe in the Holy Ghost." The status of the third person of the Trinity was, therefore, not defined. Of the Creed's adoption the church historian, Williston Walker, writes:

To Constantine's influence the adoption of the Nicene definition was due. That he ever understood its shades of meaning is doubtful but he wanted an expression of the faith of the church on the question in dispute, and believed that he had found it.

Unfortunately, instead of improving matters it made them worse. The debate regarding the Nicene Creed was sometimes violent in the period between 325 and 381 and resulted in several changes. Finally, under the leadership of Basil, the bishop of Caesarea, it took a form which gave equal emphasis to the Father, the Son, and the Holy Spirit. This is basically the form which it has today. Unfortunately, disagreements engendered by it led to the formation of a number of provincial churches, among them the Coptic, the Armenian, the Ethiopian, and eventually the Greek Church. The Nicene Creed is, therefore, first and foremost a political document. It came into being in an attempt on the part of the ruler to deal with a political situation.

While the Apostle's Creed, does not specifically call Jesus the "only begotten son," in the Catechism, Luther's explanation does say that he was "begotten of the Father." The Danish version, which was used in translation in the Danish Lutheran Church in America, speaks of Jesus as the only begotten son (Gud's enbaame søn). The point is that, whether we confess the faith using the archaic, complex and meandering language of the Nicene Creed, or the more straightforward language of the Apostle's Creed, we are saying essentially the same thing.

It should be noted also that the Apostle's Creed is an ecumenical document. It is widely used in both Protestant and Roman Catholic churches. It has not been infused with theology as has the Nicene Creed. As one writer has put it, "the more theology invaded the Creed, the more Christians were required to believe, the sharper became their differences." Therefore, in this day of ecumenicity, it is completely out of place drag out the Nicene Creed as the expression of the faith. It is political in origin, archaic in language and divisive in theology. In my view it has no place in the twentieth century church.

Volume 47 number 5, May 1998

These days the movie *Titanic* is drawing huge crowds around the country. It has also won a number of awards for its portrayal of the 1912 tragedy. More than fifteen hundred people lost their lives in the sinking of that great ocean liner. That catastrophe occurred before many of us were born, but, down through the years, we have all heard of it time and again. Several movies in the past have dealt with the subject. A large number of books have been written that tell, in great detail and in pictures, what happened on that April night when the Titanic went to the bottom on its maiden voyage.

The name "Titanic" comes from Greek mythology. Titan was one of a family of giants and the ship's name designates something gigantic in size and power. The ship, which was built at the shipyard Liverpool, was a giant in size and power. It was so constructed, with a number of watertight compartments, that it was assumed to be unsinkable. As the liner set out from Southampton on April 12, its owners could boast that it had been outfitted with the latest, the biggest and the best that modern technology had to offer. It provided the height of comfort, the ultimate in safety and the maximum in speed. Indeed, it is widely believed that as the ship sped through the Atlantic night the captain was attempting to break the speed record for the crossing from England to America.

Interestingly enough, in Greek mythology, the giant Titan was overthrown by the Olympian gods, thus indicating to the ancient Greeks that even a giant was vulnerable. The iceberg in the cold waters of the Atlantic proved more than a match to human ingenuity. When the Titanic sank a stunned world belatedly recognized that mechanical and technological progress were no guarantee of security.

We welcome the many advances that have been made and that continue to be made. Even if we could, we would not wish to stop the march of progress. Too many good things have come from it and we look forward to more. The steady advance of science in so many areas, ranging from space exploration to the frontiers of medicine, brings new challenges and new hope to humanity. We enthusiastically embraces such advances and rightly so. However, lest our enthusiasm run away with us, we do well to temper it with some reservation. We do well to remember and learn a lesson from the Titanic disaster for it represents more than the sinking of a ship. It is a reminder that, important as it is, progress does not constitute the preservation nor the salvation of the human race.

April is the month for income tax filing. I'm told that in Denmark a similar date is referred to as "the devil's birthday." Whether in Denmark or

America, the day is one that is not looked forward to. Perhaps this is the reason for so much procrastination being associated with it. For one reason or another, especially those who anticipate having a balance due on their returns, put off filing such returns until the last minute.

Procrastination is one thing, but fostering it is quite another. Each year on April 15th, the post office not only remains open, but has employees stationed at the drive-by mail boxes to assist last minute filers mail their income taxes. This is a common practice in Des Moines as I suspect it is in most cities. To my mind, this fosters procrastination. It is, in effect saying, "If you want to let it go until the last minute, no problem, we will help you." The three and a half months during which it could have been done are somehow forgotten. Yes, there can be some legitimate reasons for delay, but that is quite a long time. Such delays often have another consequence. Something that is delayed until the last minute may be hastily and poorly done.

Procrastination is encouraged in other ways. Some colleges and universities have so-called "dead days," days in which there are no classes scheduled. The thought behind this is that students and faculty will have such clays to catch up on their work. It is a nice idea, but not very realistic. Does anyone seriously think that a procrastinator is going to make use of the day as was intended? Further, it is teaching the wrong lesson. When the student leaves, he or she is going to find that there are no "dead days" offered in the work-a-day world. The worker, be he or she a farmer, laborer or professional, is going to find that he is not, given extra time to do what should already have been done.

Procrastination is no respecter of persons. We can all stand the old adage on its head and put off until tomorrow what we know we could and should do today. We do not need to be encouraged in such action, either by the postal department or an academic institution. We can do badly enough without such help.

Volume 47 number 8, August 1998

Have you read any modern novels in the past few years? I'm almost tempted to say that if you haven't you shouldn't bother. Oh, as stories they are good enough and the plots are generally well constructed. Some of the authors have even achieved Pulitzer Prize status. The problem is that all of this tends to get lost in the language. Why novelists think they have to use gutter language to tell a story — or sell a book — is far beyond my understanding.

There are hardly any exceptions to this. American detective thrillers are notoriously bad in this respect. British authors are not as bad — yet. However, it isn't only detective stories that sin in this respect. One may select a highly recommended best-selling novel only to find, after having read a few pages, that it contains language that is less than civil and fit only for the gutter.

I cannot plead guilty to being a prude. As I have written elsewhere, I worked for six years alongside of World War One veterans and if there is any obscenity which I have not heard I have not yet read it in a book. My point here is that modern writers are not adding to my store of knowledge by making the f... word and similar four letter obscenities a staple of their vocabularies.

In my experience it is not customary to talk or write that way. Certainly the circles in which I move are generally somewhat limited, but, on the other hand, I can hardly be charged with leading a completely sheltered life. From time to time I do hear occasional expletives, but these are generally for emphasis rather than out of any evil intent. Incidentally, I have long felt that even the most serious expletives grow out of a desire to emphasize or a burst of passion and not out of a desire to take the name of God in vain. Expletives and obscene, four letter words, are not used in ordinary conversation as is the case in many modern novels. By and large, it would appear to me that obscenities are not as common in everyday experience as novelists would have us believe.

The rationalization is often expressed that it is more natural to use this kind of language. I would beg to differ. In fact, the very opposite is true. What is it that brings a laugh on TV? Invariably it is some obscenity or other four letter word. If such words were natural they would be accepted without laughter. In books they serve as attention getters and let us know that the writer is modern and "with it."

The intent of the writer may be to descend to the reader's level. To write to the lowest common denominator, as it were, is precisely what I think is wrong. In my view a writer, whether famous or not, has an obligation to the reading public. That obligation is not to simply entertain by appealing to the lowest common denominator in popular language. He or she has an obligation, indeed a responsibility, to try to raise the level of language. A writer need not be a snob or take a superior attitude to do this. English is a language that is rich in expression. There are many ways of saying things there are other ways of getting attention, than descending to the gutter. The English language hardly needs to be reduced to four letter words.

It is ironic that the very people and institutions that rail against deficit spending on the part of governments, go out of their was to encourage private debt. Advertising is notorious for this. All kinds of things, from automobiles to clothing are available for no money down. Banks, whose very existence depends upon promoting consumer debt, lose no opportunity to encourage borrowing. The most brazen in this respect are the credit card companies. The most significant fact about credit cards is that they unabashedly promote consumer deficit spending.

Credit cards do present a great convenience. There is not much question but that it makes shopping easier when the bills can be paid with one stroke of the pen at the end of the month. If the bills can't be paid, and the credit card companies are hopeful that this will be the case, a debt ensues. This is what it is all about. Now there is not only a debt to pay, but interest on it as well and that interest is generally figured in double digits.

At the very time when governments appear to be getting a handle on deficit spending, consumers, encouraged by advertisers, lenders and credit cards, are spending as never before. At the moment that American economy is booming, but it is driven by consumer debt. The economy appears to me to be like a train, speeding down a mountainside, gaining speed every foot of the way. One can only hope that somehow brakes can be applied before, with a crash, it is over and we all suffer the consequences.

Volume 47 number 11, November 1998

We are stewards, and what we are worth,
We shall prove as we plough the good earth,
And are sowing.
Where for others the grain will be growing.

One may be inclined to view this song of Kristian Ostergaard, which is often sung at Thanksgiving services, as having to do with the farmer as a good steward of his soil. Again, one may think of it in terms of the stewardship of our resources, particularly monetary resources. This latter is the kind of stewardship that seems to appeal most to the church, especially at budgeting time. These certainly are valid enough ways to look at stewardship. Perhaps the least common approach is to think in terms of our own abilities and the use of our time.

I have just finished a lengthy study of the life and work of Pastor Rasmus Andersen, using materials available to me in this country. Much, much more is available at the archives in Denmark. The resulting article is entirely too long for use in *Church and Life*. Therefore, probably a year from now, it will appear in *The Bridge*, the semi-annual journal of the Danish American Heritage Society.

Whether he consciously thought of such or not, Rasmus Andersen is an example of a man who gave his all in service. Andersen was one of the four founders of the Danish Lutheran Church in America. He first served as pastor in Waupaca and Neenah, Wisconsin but moved from there in 1878 and spent the rest of his long lifetime in the East. He organized and founded Our Savior's Lutheran in Brooklyn. For some years he was the only pastor serving a number of congregations and preaching places in the East. He met and gave guidance to hundreds of Danish immigrants at Castle Garden and its successor, Ellis Island. He gave spiritual aid and comfort to Danish seamen for some 50 years. In addition, he wrote or published 13 books, ranging from a guidebook for immigrants to full-fledged histories and even two novels — and never earned a penny on them. In the days before the advent of the copying machine, he made long-hand copies of many, if not most of the letters he wrote. He kept diaries, he wrote numerous articles and had a voluminous correspondence. It is little wonder that the Andersen collection in the Danes World Wide Archives at Aalborg is the largest they have.

One does not have to agree with Andersen to appreciate his efforts. He was by no means a Grundtvigian, though he was not anti-Grundtvig. He was pietist as is revealed in his writings and his behavior. By today's standards he was not very well educated, but he made up for it by the certainty of his positions. He was absolutely opposed to such things as divorce and cremation. He was high-church and he was enamored of bishops. He was one of those few who felt the Danish Church in America should have a bishop. He was fond of Episcopalianism and often attended Episcopal services. There were some who believed that Andersen was a member of the Episcopal Church, but his writings give no evidence of this, though he did nourish the hope that the Danish Church would draw closer to the Episcopal. With the Episcopal exception, he was quite intolerant of such non-Lutherans as the Mormons.

Whatever one may think of Andersen or his methods, one would have to recognize that he had an overwhelming concern for the welfare of people. Service to man is a response to God for what he has done. This, I believe, is what motivated Andersen. He was tireless in the service of humanity because he saw this as service to God. Service was his way of saying thanks to God and in that action he was in effect serving God. It is perhaps not the easiest way, but one would be hard put to find a more important and better way. We who live in America have been blessed in so many ways. It is fitting that we should have a day of Thanksgiving, a day that calls up pictures of the gratitude of the Pilgrims. More significantly, our thanksgiving should not be confined to a particular day, to the definite place or even to a special prayer. Rasmus Andersen's life reminds us that most of us have a long way to go in serving our fellow humans. Service and indeed life itself is the most fitting response for the blessings that have come to us. Each of us, no matter what our limitations, is a steward, not just of the soil, not just of abilities and opportunities, but of life itself.

Volume 47 number 12, December 1998

More than 200 years ago the French philosopher Rousseau, began his book *The Social Contract* with a sentence which has long since become a classic: "Man is born free but everywhere he is in chains." Living at the turn of the Nineteenth century, the German thinker, Goethe, could say: "No one is more a slave than he who thinks himself free without being so." They were both echoing the thoughts of the Roman, Seneca, who some 2000 years ago wrote: "Show me anyone who is not a slave."

In the ancient world there was a good deal of physical slavery. It was by no means just the blacks who were enslaved. Many slaves were brought to Greece and Rome because the side on which they had fought had lost a war. Slaves were taken for the work they could do or for the ransom they could bring. Mark Anthony, in his funeral oration, could say of Caesar, "He has brought many slaves home to Rome, whose ransoms did the general coffers fill."

But it was not just physical slavery that was so prevalent in the pre-Christian world. Fear of the unknown enslaved humanity to superstition; fear of nature enslaved humans to primitive rites and rituals, fears of all kinds made slavery of the mind a way of life. The fact is that freedom is not found in the absence of restraints any more than it is found in self-assertion. In the final analysis, freedom depends upon the human inner spirit more than it does upon external pressures and restraints.

It is as simple and as profound as that Freedom comes through truth, or, to turn it around, there is no freedom apart from truth. To grasp the truth is to see things in their proper perspective. It is, after all, fear of one kind or another that lies at the root of all slavery. It may be fear of another, fear of being different, fear of disapproval, or even the fear of missing something that might be important. The world of the twentieth century has not become so perfect that humans will not continue to enslave one another. There may still be outward bondage, but for a large segment of our world the bondage of the mind has been vanquished.

Why is this so? What has made the difference? The difference may be traced to that seminal event which occurred in Bethlehem on a bleak night so long ago. An unmistakable message, the essence of which was, "Be not afraid; for behold, I bring you good news of a great joy which shall be to all the people, for to you is born this day in the city of David a Savior, who is Christ the Lord."

That Christ has saved humanity from sin is a fact which is emphasized in the churches of the world every Sunday. This fact must never be discounted. Men and women are sinful animals and the promise of Christ to free us from sin is a major factor in the history and the continued existence of the Christian Church. However, we must never overlook the related fact that the coming of the Christ child was accompanied by the dawning of a new era, an era in which humanity would be forever free. Through him who came on a Bethlehem night some 2000 years ago, "… [we] will know the truth, and the truth will make [us] free." Free - free from the bondage which comes with physical slavery, free from the bondage to slavery of the mind and free from fears of all kinds. This, along with the assurance that sins are forgiven, is an essential message of the Christmas miracle.

Volume 48 number 1, January 1999

Let me make one thing clear at the very outset. I hold no brief for President Clinton. He has brought shame upon himself, disgrace to his family and cast the country into a prolonged tug-of-war between two bitter factions, whose continuing dispute has short-circuited the American Congress. These lines are not being written to excuse or absolve Bill Clinton. Forgive, yes, forget, no. Whatever his fate may be, we can say as did Rollo in the old comic strip, *The Katzenjammer Kids*, "(He) brought it on himself."

Having said that, let me also make clear that the partisans in the House of Representatives can hardly be excused from their guilt in this sordid and prolonged drama. They have spent six years and millions of taxpayer dollars in trying to "get" Clinton. Now, for a far different reason than they once thought, they are able to say "gotcha" and they are not about to let go. It would be a somewhat different story if some of the principals in the dispute could approach it with clean hands.

One of the principal exponents of impeachment, and one who was in a position to influence the result, is Henry Hyde, the chairman of the House Judiciary Committee. Hyde reluctantly admitted to what he called a "youthful indiscretion" (at the age of about 40) and a great fuss was made that the White House dug up this information (as if that altered the fact) when it was really revealed by a magazine. Hyde did not have the decency to step down, but continued to chair the committee. This was his hour in the sun and he was determined to make the most of it. His behavior brings to mind Robert Louis Stevenson's "The strange Case of Dr. Jekyll and Mr. Hyde." Nor is Hyde the only of the principals in the case who has been guilty of adultery. The Speaker-designate of the House did have the honesty to resign. Who knows how many others there might be, on both sides of the aisle, who are guilty of similar indiscretions.

One thing that was emphasized time and again in the hearings is the legal concept of perjure lying under oath. This brought many references to "the rule of law" and "no man being above the law." There is some merit to such claims, but one thing that emerged, as far as I am concerned, is that if one is to lie, it should not be done under oath. What ever happened to the concept that a lie, no matter where told or under what circumstances is wrong? Are we to tell our children "be careful where you tell an untruth?" Incidentally, I do not subscribe to the notion that swearing an oath is a gateway to the truth.

A fact which was often emphasized by the partisans of Clinton is that he was twice chosen by the electorate and the polls show he still has overwhelming support of the people. The Clinton detractors chose to ignore this fact. I think they were right. Congress should not be influenced by polls! Ours is a representative democracy in which members of the House and Senate are chosen by the people to exercise their own best judgment. The fact that the electorate does not approve should not influence that judgment. Americans elect representatives, not delegates. The proper recourse can be taken at the next election. Meanwhile the elected official must exercise his own judgment.

At the impeachment hearing before the full House there was much emphasis on conscience. One Representative after another rose to say that in good conscience he could not do other than vote for impeachment. Who am I to be the judge of their conscience? If their vote was not in accord with their conscience they will have to live with it. I do wish, however, that conscience would come into play more often. Does the opposition to campaign financing have its roots in a good conscience? What of health care reform, social security, environmental legislation, welfare reform, and a host of other critical issues. If positions on all or even some of these grow out of good conscience, Lord help us.

Now the impeachment, which is a kind of indictment, goes to the Senate for trial. Just how it can when the Congress is not a continuing body is not clear, but there may be ways around that. That will at least spare the country a rerun of the whole depraved mess. What will happen in the Senate is uncertain, but, at this juncture, it appears likely that the Senate will not convict and may even dismiss the matter. The Senate is generally more mature and less rabid than the House. Fortunately, we do not have a unicameral Congress.

Regardless of what happens, December 19, 1998 will long live in many minds, exceeded only by Pearl Harbor, as a day of infamy. Others will look upon it as a day of victory for the law. Meanwhile, that day will live on in the history books as a day in which no one, friend or foe of the President, could really take pride. It has forever made clear one of the major weaknesses of our democratic system, namely that the impeachment of Andrew Johnson in 1868 and that of Bill Clinton 130 years later illustrate partisan politics at its worst.

Volume 48 number 3, March 1999

In a recent issue of *The Lutheran* I read an interesting article which was excerpted from an autobiography of the former United States Senator from Illinois, Paul Simon. He indicates that he was born and raised as a Missouri Synod Lutheran, that his father was a Missouri Synod pastor and his brother is such also. Paul Simon continues in the Missouri Church while his wife and daughter are Roman Catholics. He, himself, deviates considerably from Missouri Synod Doctrine.

At the same time I received a letter from a man in Norway. He had read my selection in the 1998 issue of *Grundtvig Studier*. He writes that though he now lives in Norway he has had a longtime interest in Danish immigrant actions, particularly with respect to the Church. A relative is a member of the Missouri Synod, but my correspondent writes that he finds it, "too intense for (his) taste." He, himself, is a member of the Norwegian Baptist Society, which he says is related to the Southern Baptist Convention. Further, he stresses an interest in Grundtvig and is a member of the Grundtvig Society in Denmark.

These two items, one a autobiographical sketch of a man who is a member of the Missouri Synod and the other from a Baptist who has an interest in Grundtvig, reinforce my own thinking as concerns doctrinal positions. Yet these are far from being the only two for whom doctrine is not dominant. Indeed, Baptists have long stressed the separation of church and state, but they are in the forefront of the struggle for school prayer.

I have long felt that, aside from theologians and some pastors, the average church member is not much interested in or concerned about doctrinal positions. By and large, church members belong to the church they grew up in, or in some cases were led into by a spouse. In spite of confirmation instruction and doctrinal sermons, I would wager that the majority of church members could not give a satisfactory explanation of the doctrinal position of their church. Lutherans may know something of the importance of faith, but the majority would be uninterested in the Augsburg Confession and similar documents. Reformed groups may know something of the importance of good works, but it is doubtful there would be much interest in Calvin's Institutes of the Christian Religion. Roman Catholics may know of the authority of the papacy, but choose to ignore it when it doesn't fit their lifestyle.

The current plethora of "feel good" churches, under the guise of Christianity is a part of this picture. The most glamorous of such shows originates in California, but most cities of any size has one or more. Des Moines has several. Just what constitutes their doctrine, if any, is unclear, but one can be sure that most of the thousands who attend are either unaware of it or chose to ignore it. They attend because they find it comfortable, it makes them feel good, it is not 'boring.'

It may be argued that this is a modem trend, linked to the current tendency to ignore authority and put one's own interpretation on things. To some extent this may be true, but I do believe that the laity, as a whole, has never really bought into doctrine. Even within seminaries of a common background, there are various notions about the status of the Bible, for instance.

This is not to say that doctrine is unnecessary. It is necessary in so far as it defines a particular church body. "The Latin word doctrina means 'teaching' and religious beliefs are often first specifically formulated in the process of instructing initiates." It tells its members and the world what it believes as a church. Though all churches which call themselves Christian, believe in Christ as Lord and savior, there are vast differences among them. The doctrines of a church body serve to set it apart from others and to spell out very specifically what that body believes about God, Christ, the Bible and human life. This is the positive side of doctrine, and as important as it is, there is another side, a negative side to doctrine.

Doctrine, particularly when it becomes dogma, may become divisive. When one aspect of a doctrine is emphasized to the exclusion of other possibilities, it becomes a dogma. Some church bodies have become extremely dogmatic. The Missouri Lutherans, for instance, on communion, the Baptist aversion to infant baptism, the Roman Catholic insistence upon papal infallibility. Members of such churches are expected to subscribe to those positions— but they do not always do so.

What it all seems to mean is that, for a large percentage of the laity, in spite of what may be seen as divisive barriers that have been erected, there is one Christian Church. Certainly they may lay claim to being Lutheran, Methodist, Roman Catholic or what have you, but above all they are Christians. Time was when there was indeed one Christian Church, but a breech was made at the top and the result has become many denominations. Now the impulse for removing barriers and for unity is coming from the bottom. While the top fumbles for unity, such unity is already a reality for a large segment of the Christian world. Christian churches are a long way from being one, but, in matters of religion, Christian people are not far apart.

Volume 49 number 3, March 2000

In connection with planning our trip to the Solvang for the Farstrup-Mortensen Lectures we consulted a travel agent recently, a procedure we generally follow. After considering the possibilities, of which there are few, we decided once again to fly to Santa Barbara and rent a car there.

We would rather have taken Amtrak, but this is no longer feasible. It is not that Amtrak is less costly. Indeed, it can be argued that, when one considers the necessary meals and two restless nights, that it is more costly. However, in addition to traveling through the majestic Rocky Mountains in daylight, Amtrak does provide for stopovers. We generally took advantage of this to stop at Salt Lake City to pursue further genealogical research. This is no longer possible unless one goes by way of San Francisco where there is a necessary overnight wait. The problem stems from the fact that Amtrak has discontinued the run from Salt Lake City to Los Angeles. There one had a good connection to Santa Barbara, from which one could then take an Amtrak bus to Solvang.

This whole episode brought to mind once again the sorry state of public transportation in this country. Unless one cares to drive everywhere, there are many places in this country to which one cannot travel. As examples of this, one can cite those places which are familiar to readers of these pages. Without a car it is difficult, if not impossible, to get to the Danebod Folk Meeting at Tyler, Minnesota. There is no passenger rail service and, to the best of my knowledge there is not even bus service. The same is true of the meeting at Menucha. One can get to Portland, Oregon, but then it is a matter of renting a car or depending upon the good will of friends. So it is in a myriad of places in this country. Without a car one cannot get to Luck, Wisconsin, let alone to West Denmark. Even Des Moines, a metropolitan area of well over 200,000 people, does not have passenger rail service. One needs to travel some 50 miles to find a passenger train. How? By car, of course! Yes, there is bus service but the destinations are limited to the larger communities.

Within many larger towns and cities the matter of movement is just as difficult. Some cities do have public transportation that is worthy of the name. This city does not! When one thinks of the area involved, the only conclusion is that the bus routes are few. There are timetables for the various routes, but their greatest value is that one can figure out how late the bus is. I have on occasion in the past followed the timetable and still waited as much as a half-hour for the bus to come.

It was not always so. I recall growing up in the urban community of Troy, New York. Troy itself was a city of only some 70,000, but it was a part of a large metropolitan area which included the state Capital at Albany. There was bus and street car service to all sections of that area. During the depression, as a WPA project, the street car tracks were removed, but busses continued to serve the area. As far as I know they still do.

General Motors, in its desire to promote the sale of cars, is to some extent responsible for the demise of public transportation. In some places it purchased and then discontinued street-car service. Certainly there are other factors involved, such as the American love of the independence and convenience which a motor car gives. Whatever the reason, the result is that public transportation in this country is nothing less than a disgrace. This is without question one area in which Europe has left us far behind. We have, for example, never rented a car in Denmark because we have discovered that public transportation is excellent and widespread. True, it is not quite as convenient as a car, but it does have some decided advantages, such as visiting with fellow travelers.

The television and the newspaper have been full of the election for months. I have heard the candidates for both parties and they wax eloquent on such matters as abortion, school prayer, tax relief, foreign affairs, and many other things. However, not one of them, from either party, has uttered one word about public transportation. They are all fond of saying that they will provide leadership. This is all very well, but where leadership is really needed there is none.

There is a reason why the candidates do not mention the subject. They know very well that this is not a concern that captures the imagination like abortion or tax cuts do. Meanwhile we oldsters can grumble, but our grumbling will not be heard. And those who cannot drive or who do not have a car have to make the best of a sad situation.

It is one thing to have freedom of movement, of which we are so proud in this country — and rightly so. But, to have the means of movement is quite another matter. For all too many, there is no choice but to stay home.

Volume 49 number 10, October 2000

Free public education has a checkered history in America. It has not always been seen as good. It has not been viewed as an obligation of the state and has certainly not been understood as something that should be free. In Colonial days parents were required to teach their children or send them to community schools maintained for that purpose. Under the Confederation, in 1787, the historic Northwest Ordinance was passed. One of its provisions stated that, "Religion, morality, and knowledge being necessary to good government and the happiness of mankind, schools and the means of education shall be forever encouraged." Later, under the United States, though schools were encouraged, the means to support them were generally lacking. Only in New England was the public primary school system free and open to all. In other states, both in the North and the South, the schools charged fees, but parents who were willing to plead poverty could be exempted from paying. Thus there came to be a stigma attached to the Public School and the children of parents who were too poor to pay fees or too proud the accept charity were largely uneducated.

Opposition to the Public School came largely from those who owned property and who did not wish to be taxed so that others might send their children to a community school. Indeed, I can recall a time, at least in one state, when only those who owned property could vote in school board elections, it being assumed that those who were only renters were not involved in paying for the schools. The idea that the tax was a part of the rent seems not to have mattered. But this was not the only objection to the Public School. In Pennsylvania, for example, the opposition came not only from those who were well-off, but from the Germans who feared the loss of their language and culture.

This was certainly also the case among the Danes a couple of generations later. Many parents and pastors were vehemently opposed to public education because the curriculum did not include the Danish language and elements of the Danish culture. There were Danish schools in such places as Racine, Tyler, Clinton, West Denmark, Perth Amboy and other places. In fact, there are those still living among us who attended such schools. The education given to the children there was good, but it was definitely parochial. In other places Saturday Schools and Vacation Schools were held to accomplish some of the same ends. Many Danish immigrants and their descendants tended to look askance at the Public School for many years.

In the 20th century race became a critical issue in the public education. The U.S. Supreme Court, in the 1896 case of Plessy v. Ferguson, which was not about schools but railway accommodations, ruled that though such things were separate they must be equal. This thinking was applied to the Public School. The 1954 case of Brown v. Board of Education, overturned Plessy when the Court ruled that "separate is inherently unequal." This led to bussing, and a controversy which continues to this day.

Today the Public School is besieged by a variety of problems the essence of which is that the school is not doing its job, a job that could be done better by other means. This charge ignores the fact that the school has gradually been called upon to perform a multitude of tasks for which it was neither designed nor equipped. In all too many cases the school today must function as a surrogate parent. What are really the shortcomings of many parents are being attributed to the school with the result that the Public School is much maligned.

Accordingly, the idea is being bandied about that a non-public enterprise can do a better job than a public one. Some would, therefore award funds to the parents, in the form of vouchers, that might be applied to fees for a private school, religious or otherwise. Not only is the constitutionality of using Federal funds to, in effect, promote segregation questionable, but ultimately, this would destroy the Public School. It would result in a skimming off, as it were, of the brightest and the most affluent of the students, leaving behind those who desperately need an education in a school bereft of funds. This is really the ultimate in class warfare.

Quite apart from the educational issues involved, the Public School has for at least 150 years been the great unifier. Rich and poor, black and white, native or immigrant, the Public School has welcomed them all. In 1954, Brown v. School Board asserted that separate is not equal. Now, in the name of improvement, there are those who would thumb their noses at equality.

One does not have to be a genius to know that public education has its shortcomings. But the answer is not to be found in substituting something else - which in many cases is simply an unknown quantity. The preferable solution lies in a re-examination of its curriculum and an adequate funding of the Public School.

For a couple of generations the emphasis has been upon integrating the school. Now comes the voucher system with a renewed emphasis on segregation. Two thousand years ago, the Roman, Seneca wrote, "What fools these mortals be!"

Volume 50 number 6, June 2001

I can recall that as a boy, when a carnival or other event came to town, I would often seize upon the opportunity to make a few pennies — and pennies were scarce. I would buy (I can't recall where the money came from) a case or two of soda pop, some ice, load it in my express wagon, and take off for the event. Setting up shop on the fringes of the crowd, I would be in business selling pop of various flavors. If I had a good day I could sell a case of pop and that netted me a profit of $2.40. A day when I could sell two cases was almost unheard of and the profit from such would be big money — $4.80. Suffice it to say that my entrepreneurship was never very successful.

What brings this to mind some seventy years later is that today one is almost surrounded by pop. Coca Cola and Pepsi are engaged in the never ending battle of the bulging stomach, but others are active as well. Wherever one goes, on the street, in the mall, in corridors of hospitals and classrooms of colleges, one can see people walking about with a pop can in hand. The only place in which I have not seen someone drinking pop is at a worship service. Machines that dispense the pop are almost as numerous as the people who drink it. There can be "big bucks" involved here. Just the other day I read in the newspaper of a contract worth millions that Coca Cola negotiated for an exclusive right to place its machines at a certain institution for a few years. And, even in a state like this one which has a deposit return law, picking up empty pop cans can be more lucrative than my early pop sales.

I have long since concluded that there are some things I will never get accustomed to and one of them is seeing a young person or an adult walking around with a pop can or a water bottle in hand. I suppose it is all a part of the casual, and often, rude and crude society we live in.

Another thing I can't get used to is the cell phone. On the streets, in cars, in the aisle of a grocery store, in restaurants and even in church basements, one finds the ubiquitous cell phone. I would certainly agree that cell phones have their value, but that value is very limited. If for instance, one is stranded in a car it is a way to summon aid. It could also be a way to summon aid in other cases. Even that must be qualified, however. Recent news reported a young lady who lost both legs as a result of being trapped in a wrecked car for five days and unable to reach her phone. By and large, the cell phone strikes me as being a prestige item. Are those who make constant use of then really that busy? Appearing busy and being busy are not the same thing. The cell phone reminds me of the thought that when something is invented, advertising is then used to convince people they need it. Well, they have surely succeeded in convincing a lot of people. And, judging by the newspaper and magazine ads, the makers of cell phones are by no means giving up.

Yet another thing to which I have trouble adjusting is the variation in church services from Sunday to Sunday, as has become the custom in many places. I can recall the time, not so long ago, when we were told the Lutheran service would now be the same, from Maine to California and from Minnesota to Texas. My principal objection was not to the change, but to the unspoken attitude that said, "Now we are going to do the liturgy the right way" — whatever that is. Well, the "right way" has long since fallen by the wayside as has the concept of a uniform service. Now there are not only differences among congregations, but also within congregations from week to week. Time was when the service was uniform and one knew what to expect and could follow along. Now one never knows what will happen. One Sunday it might be the misnamed contemporary service; another it might be something someone dreamed up in Chicago; and again it might be the women singing one verse and the men singing another. No wonder the weekly bulletin is mistaken for a program and longtime members become strangers in their congregation. The hymn writer would have new grounds now for writing, "Change and decay in all around I see." Of course it is all designed to keep the service from being "boring." The worship, like so much else, must be fun. Can fun and solemnity really mix. I doubt it! The Danes have a good word for what is increasingly happening in our churches on a Sunday morning. That word is "pjat" which may best be rendered as nonsense or silliness.

So much for some things which trouble me. Perhaps it's my age perhaps it's a critical attitude. I suspect I'm in a minority, but, come to think of it, that's nothing new for me.

Volume 50 number 7, July 2001

Early in June Johanne and I traveled to Troy, New York and the area in which I grew up. Since I no longer have any living relatives in that area, the journey was purely nostalgic. Some of the sites were quite familiar, others had changed to the extent that they were almost unrecognizable and some were gone completely. One could hardly expect that it would be otherwise after sixty years. We had been there ten years ago, but this time the changes were even more pronounced.

We traveled by Amtrak, with a rental car being our means of transportation in New York state. Traveling by train is comfortable and one can enjoy the countryside as one travels. The cost compares favorably with the airlines, especially if one takes into consideration the discounts available and the reduced cost for a second and third passenger in the same group. Amtrak does have its downside, however, largely because Congress consistently refuses adequate funding. Our closest station is some 50 miles from here and, more seriously, the trains are almost always hours late. Yet the trains are always full and there were hundreds of people boarding trains in Chicago. But, Congress would rather subsidize other things and engage in corporate welfare than help Amtrak.

In Chicago we met one of our daughters, Barbara, who came by Amtrak from Ft. Worth. The three of us then took off for Albany. It was afternoon of the next day when we arrived at our destination, picked up our rental car and located our motel. I once was as familiar with this area as with the back of my hand, but I soon realized this was no longer the case. The capitol city of Albany is now a maze the overhead highways, one way streets and heavy traffic and it was only after a few wrong turns that we found our motel.

The following day we began exploring Troy by visits to the two cemeteries in which my parents and ancestors are buried. These were both disappointing sights in that neither appeared to have been mowed yet this year and the ravages of time had not been adequately dealt with. The one very large cemetery provides a high promontory from which one can look out over the city and indeed the whole Hudson Valley. This promontory is one that I found most delightful in my youth.

The greatest shock was seeing the interior of the former Danish Church where I had spent many an hour in Sunday School, Saturday School and Vacation school. It has changed hands twice since the Danes sold it, and is now owned by Negro Baptists. I wish we had not gone in. During my childhood it was a relatively new church, somewhat like Luther Memorial. Today it has been completely changed — and I'm tempted to say wrecked.

Whoever did it lacked any sense of aesthetics. The balcony had been

213

greatly enlarged with a stairway on each side of the sanctuary. The pulpit had been removed from the side and placed in the center. The altar and communion rail were completely gone and drums, as well as other band instruments, littered the front of the church. Well, it's their church and I guess they can do what they want with it, but to one who could recall its former beauty and sanctity it was indeed a sorry sight.

The school buildings I attended are still standing, though some have long since become apartment houses. Lansingburgh High School has become an office building for the school district and a new high school has been built next to a junior high that was built as a public works project during the depression.

Not all was change and not all was decay. Using our rental car, and with our daughter Barbara driving, we headed north for the Adirondack Mountains. For me, no trip to the East would be complete without a visit to the Adirondacks. We spent a pleasant hour at beautiful Lake George before going still farther north. Then we crossed over into Vermont where we spent the night and enjoyed a broad view of the mountains in both states. The next day it rained, but we drove back to New York State and to Lake Placid where the winter Olympics have been held. In spite of the rain we enjoyed our ride through the mountains. My only regret is that I am no longer physically able to backpack in them as I once did.

Back in Troy, we spent some time trying to get information on Diamond Rock, a Lansingburgh landmark. It was a large rock formation covering a couple of acres and being at least 50 feet high. Though I knew where it should be, we simply could not find it. We did find some new buildings called Diamond Rock Apartments. No one, including some in the newspaper office, knew much about it except that it was gone. In any case, unbelievable as it seems, the large outcropping of rock has given way to more apartments -though there was plenty of land.

We spent the last day sightseeing in the Capitol District, returned the rental car, and boarded the train for the trip home. Some 28 hours later we arrived at Osceola, Iowa where another daughter met us. So ended a trip, the intent of which was to refresh old memories, but in reality it became a collection of new experiences, not all of which were pleasant.

Volume 50 number 10, October 2001

When we have been out on the highway and once again return safely, I often say to my wife, "Made it again." Few would disagree that, no matter how cautious one may be, the public highway is filled with threats to one's feeling of security. From mechanical failure to human failure, the threats are many and real. But these are threats we have learned to accept and to deal with. Almost all of them are accidental; very few are intentional. They are the price we must pay for our mobility.

The threat to our security that has come with the destruction of the World Trade Center and the devastation in Washington was intentional. It has shocked and brought us up short. Suddenly we realize that though this country is a world super power, even that power can be brought to its knees by the actions of madmen. As a kingpin in a drug operation said a few years ago, "Terrorism is the atom bomb of the poor." "Poor" may not be the word that best describes those who resort to terror it might be better to say "the underdog." But poor or underdog, terrorists have long since discovered that our very freedom that makes us vulnerable and that real or imagined complaints can be addressed in this way. It is name calling with a vengeance.

Of course not all threats to our security have come from external sources. America has its share of homegrown "nuts." Remember the episode of a few years ago when some "nut" tampered with a Tylenol package making the contents lethal? It led to a complete revolution in the packaging of many products. We have learned to live with that and the threat, while not eliminated, has certainly been reduced.

The external terrorist threat is not so easily eliminated or even reduced. I have no doubt that the perpetrators of the September 11th disaster will be tracked down and properly dealt with. But, make no mistake, that will not end the matter.

Terrorism is a way of life for some and especially for those who have no appreciation for the value of human life.

There are those, even in America, who see human life as expendable. As always, there is in this tragedy those who are ready to place blame while pounding a lectern for their own pet and asinine projects. Jerry Falwell, the TV evangelist, suggested that God no longer protects the United States and let this disaster happen because America has not accepted Falwell's agenda. Yes, he later apologized, but one wonders if he really had second thoughts.

A lesson driven home in the wake of the death and destruction visited on America on September 11th is that there is no security in modern technology, no matter how sophisticated. I have previously expressed the belief that it is an exercise in futility to pin one's hope for security on Star Wars and similar anti-missile defense systems. If the events in New York City and Washington proved nothing else they did point up the fallacy of thinking that security lies in that direction. One can only hope that the tragedies of that day, in effect, said to the administration, "So much for a missile defense system so much for Star Wars."

This is not to say that we must not take precautions. Every possible avenue of terror should be explored and addressed. The most obvious is our transportation system. The airlines are the most vulnerable and have, for some time been seeking to promote security in flying. It would appear that security has become a bit relaxed. Airport security must be strengthened; whatever it takes to make all flights as secure as possible must be done. Attention must also be given to rail and bus transportation, as well as bridges, high-rise buildings, schools and, yes, even churches.

With the possible exception of the airliner that crashed into Long Island Sound a couple of years ago, most terrorism has manifested itself on other continents. We have come to feel relatively safe, sheltered as we are by two large oceans. The World Trade Center and the Pentagon are reminders that those oceans no longer shelter us.

All of this is going to change our way of life, not only in the immediate future, but for years to come. Insecurity will be our way of life for an indefinite future. We are not accustomed to this and it may cramp our style, but there is no real alternative. We may face delays, we may have to put up with inconveniences, we may even have to limit our travel in some cases, but when we are literally placing our lives in the hands of security experts we cannot afford to question their judgment.

When all is said and done, we must be aware that life is insecure. Perhaps at the end of each day we should be thankful that we have made it through the day again. And, be thankful also for what the terrorists and their possible successors cannot do. The spirit of our people has not been destroyed and they have driven us together as only a war can. Their senseless action has had an unintended consequence. In spite of our differences, we are "one nation under God, indivisible, with liberty and justice for all."

One final word: As Americans we need to do some introspection to see if we can discern why some hate America so much.

Volume 51 number 2, February 2002

It has been said many times that the events of September 11th mark a kind of turning point in American history. Certainly the destruction of the twin towers of the World Trade Center and the calamitous loss of life that resulted was a low blow that continues to have many consequences of which heightened airline security is only one. But to suggest that this is a decisive turning point for America is to place an undue emphasis on the present and to exhibit an ignorance of, or at least a lack of interest in the past. It is, for example, to forget that foreign invaders deliberately burned public buildings, including the White House, in a second war with the British begun in 1812 and lasting until 1815. It is to forget that the America which emerged from the Civil War was decidedly different. It is, in effect, to say that anything that happened prior to yesterday is not at all important. It represents what has been called "the parochialism of the present."

It may be true that in the areas of science and technology we are ever standing on the threshold of something new, something glorious or inglorious, as the case may be. Though, even there, present innovations are built on past advances. However, our major concern here is in the field of human relations. We are what we are because of what we, or those who have gone before us, have been. This is true on both the personal and the collective levels. Few would question the fact that our nation was completely changed by the effects that the Second World War has had upon American society. Those effects are by no means limited to the war itself.

A concrete example may serve to clarify this. One of the consequences of that war was the GI Bill which made it possible for thousands of veterans to earn college degrees and even attend graduate schools and earn advanced degrees. The impact that this has had upon our nation is incalculable. Not only has the educational level been raised, but we have enjoyed the benefits brought by the work of thousands of engineers and scientists whom we would otherwise not have had. The GI Bill is a part of our history and, though we may seldom think of it as such, it is a prime example of how the past has had an effect upon us and our nation. Through this "first" America has irrevocably been changed for the better.

History is sometimes thought to be a study of a succession of wars, of names and of dates. As such it can be boring and appear to have no immediate value, especially if one thinks of monetary values. Unfortunately, many students do think only in those terms and parents, and even colleges, often encourage that sort of thing. On learning that 1 planned to attend college, someone said to me, 'That's fine if you can get a good job out of it." Education is more than a means to a good job; it is more than a means to a monetary end.

I seldom do more than scan George Will's newspaper column. His philosophical position is not exactly "my cup of tea." I did, however, give more than passing attention to one of his recent columns. He wrote of the ignorance of history on the part of many college students today. Only 22% of college seniors, he reported, knew that the noted words, "the government of the people, by the people and for the people," are a part of Lincoln's Gettysburg Address. Worse yet, students may graduate from many an American college without taking a single history course. This is the "parochialism of the present" carried to an extreme. It has long-term implications for American democracy. Unless we have at least a smattering of information about the past we can hardly act wisely in the present. Unless we can know something of the mistakes that have been made we are doomed to repeat them.

History is the chronological record of events that have had an influence or produced an alteration in the status of an individual, a nation, or the world. It is a record of that which has made us what we are today, whether we think in terms of individuals, a people, or humanity. The American Civil War, which was fought to preserve the Union, has had profound implications for all of us, whether we are aware of them or not. Henry Ford once said, "History is more or less bunk." Many have said that and would today say essentially the same. Yet the fact is, we ignore history at our peril. As Shakespeare has written, "What's past is prologue." The ancient Greek, Thucydides, comes at the matter from a somewhat different view. Writing of history? he said, "It is philosophy learned from example."

Rather than marking a turning point in the story of our nation, September 11th marks a learning point in the march of American Democracy. We have already learned much from that disaster and the more we learn the less chance there is of such a disaster being repeated.

Volume 51 number 4, April 2002

All new, all new, all new! This is the message the television networks leave with us every time they announce a different show. The viewer is enticed to the program by the fact that it is not a rerun, but an entirely new show. Meanwhile, the networks continue to offer the same tired, old recipe of malice, mayhem and murder, interspersed by comedies that are more silly than funny and news programs that contain a little news and a great deal of advertising.

The networks are hardly novices in the field of advertising. They have long known of our penchant for that which is new. Cereals that have for years been a staple of the breakfast diet suddenly appear in a different box and are touted as being new. Laundry and other soaps that have been used by the housewife for generations appear on the shelves of the marketplace as now being '"new and improved." This, incidentally, raises the question as to how good earlier versions were. One can only improve that which needs improving. Some things of course are really improved or at least are changed by the addition of various features. Automobiles and computers, to name but two items, regularly change, but whether one really needs all the gadgets, gimmicks, power and speed of the new models is debatable. Be that as it may, what is new sells and the old is left behind.

It is a fact of life that most of us are fascinated by that which is new. This has its bright side in that modern society is a reflection of this. There was a time, not so long ago, when one could hardly drive 50 miles without a flat tire or other repair. New and improved vehicles make it possible to drive thousands of miles without any repair. New computer software makes it possible to do many things in half the time. New appliances of one kind or another make possible the saving of time while doing a better job. Improved soaps make it possible to get clothes cleaner while new cereals make for more healthy living. This emphasis on the new does have a decidedly beneficial impact on society.

Competition plays a major role in presenting the new. Those who are behind the many products offered, be they corporations, small businesses or individuals, are anxious to alert the buying public to their product. To do so they stress that their product is either new or improved or perhaps both and better than that of their competitors.. The price of an item may also be reduced through competition

There is also, however, a downside in this fascination with the new and an addiction to it by the consumer. Not all things that are new are better, but because there is a propensity to think so, landfills are rapidly becoming repositories for everything from toasters to tea kettles and from furniture to television sets. If archeologists a thousand years from now were to examine our landfills they could hardly conclude other than that we were a profligate people.

From childhood on we have heard the doctrine of competition and the free market preached. There is a good deal of truth in this. Whether that doctrine has all the virtues claimed for it, however, is an open question. There is, without question, a good deal of waste related to competition. Ours is, in effect, a throw-away society. Have you, for example, tried to have a pair of shoes repaired recently? It has been my experience that there are almost no shoe repair establishments left. The same might be said of watch and clock repair. Further, even perfectly good and relatively new buildings are consigned to the wrecking ball and hauled off to the landfill.

This fascination with the new has spilled over into the church. Fortunately, the Gospel itself is not new, but the manner in which it is presented is constantly being revised. The Sunday bulletin should perhaps more correctly be called the program for the service because one does not always know what is to happen next. There was a time, within even a short memories, when the service was the same from Sunday to Sunday and no one stayed home because he was bored. But then came television with its ever-new entertainment and some began to believe that if the church was to compete it would have to adapt. The worship service must embrace new elements. Some hymns were shortened, sometimes the men would sing one verse and the next would be sung by the women. Modem hymns were introduced, especially those with a snappy refrain. (Refrain may also mean to "hold oneself from doing something" — and this would often fit well.) The degree of change varies from place to place, but those services I have attended have all had elements of the new. In short, the service has become different and new, but whether or not it has been improved would depend upon who was asked.

One should not oppose the new just because it is new, but neither should one blindly embrace it. The critical question is whether it is better. A little verse, the source of which is unknown, comes to mind as a cautionary approach to the new.

Be not the first by whom the new is tried,
Nor yet the last to lay the old aside.

Volume 51 number 8, August 2002

It is ironic that what has long been known as the Holy Land should now be anything but holy. It is an indication that when humans come into conflict over the holy the fury of hell is not far to seek. Palestine has been regarded as Holy by Arab, Christian and Jew as their place of origin and the home of sacred places of their religion. Both Arab and Jew have laid claim to the land or at least parts of it. The Jews claim that the land was given to them by God, though they did have to dislodge others in order to occupy the area. Then, in 68 A.D., the Roman Empire destroyed such independence as the Jews had long known. The diaspora, the settlement of Jews in many places outside of Palestine, became a fact of history. Some never forgot, however, and the idea of a Jewish homeland in Palestine continued to smolder through the centuries.

Jerusalem, the holy city, changed hands again and again during the Christian crusades from the eleventh to the thirteenth centuries. Eventually the land was held by the Turks until after the First World War when the British established control over the area. Meanwhile, Arabs and Jews lived together or in their own settlements in the leading cities of Palestine. Zionism, the name given to the idea of reestablishing a Jewish state in the Holy Land, led to friction between the groups. At an international meeting in 1897 a Zionist group was organized for this purpose. The Turkish government was far from enthused over this development. However, with the defeat of Turkey, the British took this matter under advisement. Even before the war was over the British adopted the Balfour Declaration in 1917, which brought support for a Zionist movement. The support for a Jewish state was conditioned on the thought "that nothing shall be done which may prejudice the civil and religious rights of existing non Jewish communities in Palestine." There the matter of a Jewish state rested until 1947.

During the intervening years, though the Jewish state did not materialize, there began to be conflict between the Arab and the Jew. The Hebrew language was revived and a Hebrew University was begun in 1925. Modem agricultural machinery was brought in and the Arabs began to fear that a western state would result. They raised objection to these developments and demanded that immigration of Jews to Palestine be ended. It was not ended and, with the advent of the Nazi regime in Germany, Jews migrated to Palestine in ever greater numbers. The Arabs responded with a resort to terrorism and the Jews responded with similar violent activity. This led to a British Commission proposal to settle the dispute in 1936. It was proposed that the area should be divided into three parts, one for the Arabs, one for the Jews and one for the British. Neither the Arabs nor the Jews were willing to accept this plan and both groups denounced it with equal vigor.

Then, under the authority of the United Nations, a Jewish State was established in 1947 and a division of the land between the Jews and the Arabs was effected. This did not yield a peaceful solution. When the Jews declared their independence the next year they were immediately faced with an attack by the Arabs, a war which the Arabs lost. Since then there have been a series of wars with a net increase in the territory of the Jews. These have given reason for hatred and violence on the part of both the Arabs and the Jews; a hatred and a violence that persists to this day. Each day brings a new headline born of violence in the Middle East.

A part of the difficulty is that there is not one entity called the Arabs and another called the Jews. Each group is made up of many factions. There are extremists and radicals in both groups. Those who would be inclined to make peace must share in the consequences of the behavior of the extremists. Another factor that makes a solution so difficult is that many see the problem as one of survival. Extremists on both sides make it plain that they will be satisfied by nothing less than the complete elimination of all rival claims. Finally, the factor of religion comes into play, making it a heady mix indeed.

Both the Arabs and the Jews continue to seek a solution and end to the problem — albeit a solution and an end that will favor their side and never mind its correctness or fairness. But, the deaths and the devastation go on and even become steadily worse. One would think that both the Arabs and the Jews could see this, but they appear to be so blinded by their own desires that reason is cast aside. Meanwhile, sympathy and support from outsiders, not least from the United States, complicates the problem.

The prognosis? Don't look for an end any time soon. Unless and until calmer heads and new leadership are forthcoming on both sides there is not likely to be any end to the mutual slaughter. What has long been known as the Holy Land has become a living example of hell.

Volume 52 number 4, April 2003

There has been a visible and significantly increased rise in patriotic fervor since the destruction of the twin towers of the World Trade Center. Flags have been retrieved from a moth ball existence the sale of flags has vastly increased. Flags are everywhere, from lapel pins and clothing to flagstaffs and are even flown from moving vehicles. One would certainly expect this display of patriotism in the wake of the dastardly acts 9/11. Patriotism of this kind is both noticeable and inexpensive. However, one may be pardoned for wondering to what extent patriotism manifested itself on April 15th.

The deadline for filing of income taxes on that day makes a different kind of patriotic demand, one that is more meaningful and one that could be more costly. Judging by the information available there will not be a very patriotic response. Ads, leaflets and brochures urge the individual to let the experts file for you and thus reduce the government's take. Even the Pension Board of the ELCA gets into the act with trying to save one from taxes. Everywhere the emphasis seems to be the same, "'Here are some tricks that will enable you to pay as little as possible."

It seems safe to say that no one, including this writer, likes to pay taxes. President Bush, along with most politicians of either party, has long since discovered that lowering taxes and providing rebates is much more to the liking of the electorate. Then, too, there are program cuts at every level of government. Federal, state and local officials opt for cutting programs of one kind or another. Schools go begging, homelessness increases, welfare recipients are neglected, potholes remain unfilled, and in general, we can no longer take pride in our infrastructure. Horrendous deficits for years to come are contemplated, even without adding in the cost of a war; war upon which the administration seems determined. In the long run, our children and our grandchildren will suffer for this official parsimony. Borrowing funds, going into ever more debt, is another way to avoid raising taxes but, here again, this is passing the burden to future generations.

Fund raisers for the church are fond of citing the words of Jesus which they believe will enable the church to be entrusted with more money. Jesus said, "Render to Caesar the things that are Caesar's and to God the things that are God's." As often as it is cited, that statement no longer applies, particularly in this country. Neither does it apply to giving money to the church and assuming that one is thereby giving to God. "The things that are God's," are not to be measured in dollars and cents.

The concern here, however, is with the phrase, "Render to Caesar." This implies supporting a dictatorship which is not the system of government that exists here. Ours is a Democracy and when we pay taxes here we are, in effect, pooling our funds with those of our neighbor to do those things together that we cannot do alone. We cannot alone, for example, provide for defense, we cannot construct highways, we cannot provide schools, we cannot maintain, much less rebuild, our nation's infrastructure. When a young law student once complained to Justice Oliver Wendell Holmes about the taxes he had to pay. Justice Holmes replied simply, "With taxes I buy civilization." In a nutshell, that's it; that is precisely what we are doing.

To be sure, tax dollars are not always spent as you or I might prefer, but the answer to that problem is not to withhold taxes but, at the next election, hope that some- one whose interests are like yours, is elected.

Probably the most equitable way to raise tax dollars is through the graduated income tax where people are taxed on the basis of their income. Until the passage of the Sixteenth Amendment the income tax had a checkered history. Such a tax was used briefly during the Civil War. In 1894 Congress established an income tax. That tax was mild in that it provided for a tax of two percent on incomes of more than $4,000 per year. Then, the next year, the U. S. Supreme Court ruled that it was a direct tax, subject to apportionment among the states on the basis of population and therefore contrary to the Constitution. The passage of the Sixteenth Amendment in 1913 obviated this difficulty. Most states also have some form of income tax.

Equitable or not, taxes are not pleasant. Most would rather be free to spend their money as they see fit. But in a democracy we owe it to our fellow citizens to, as it were, chip in and do our fair share toward providing for the needs of all. We can find all kinds of excuses for not providing our fair share, but even if we are not subjected to an IRS audit, and even if we are never caught, we do have to live with ourselves and that is the bottom line. Flying a flag is one form of patriotism, a form through which we make our neighbor aware of our feelings for our country. More important is the honest and fair payment of taxes, which is personal and reveals to the individual himself what he thinks of his country.

Volume 52 number 9, September 2003

The name preferred by its devotees is gaming but, it is still gambling. Gambling has long fascinated men and women and for just as long has robbed the many for the benefit of the few.

There is archeological evidence that bones were used as dice as long as forty thousand years ago. There is also evidence that some were "loaded dice," that is, dice weighted to fall a certain way. Trickery is hardly a new method of bilking your neighbor. Archeologists can also point to facts showing that gambling casinos existed in ancient Egypt. In the Roman world, when soldiers were stationed in all parts of the Roman Empire, they often saw little action. To relieve his boredom, the soldier might risk his money, and even his life, at gambling.

I have no specific information on gambling or games of chance during the Middle Ages. However, given human nature, we may be quite sure such practices flourished at that time. The peasantry, with their limited means, may have gambled infrequently, if at all but, the nobility and the clergy had ample time and means to take risks in the interests of increasing their share of the world's goods.

It was undoubtedly the Puritan influence which kept America free of lotteries and gambling for so long. There still is no national lottery as there is in some countries. Denmark, for example, has long had a national lottery. But though it was not sanctioned by the state, gambling and games of chance flourished in America. In many cases games of chance were utilized by the church as a way of raising funds. The chief promoter of this was the Roman Catholic Church though the practice was not confined exclusively to that body.

In my younger days I worked for six years in a woolen mill. There were many Roman Catholics who also worked there and there was hardly a week when they did not sell tickets for this or that raffle sponsored by their church. Raffles and other games of chance, which are essentially gambling, have been going on in America for many decades. Though outright gambling was not approved by the state, it, too, flourished during the first half of the Twentieth Century. In the mill, as in most work- places, there were those who represented the so-called "numbers racket." Those who were so inclined could place a bet on a specific three digit number for ten cents. If that number, which was based on the daily receipts at a designated race track, was the lucky one for that day the one who chose to bet on it would receive a payoff.

In this connection I want to digress a bit to present an interesting and amusing example of human gullibility. Choosing the winning number was of course basic and there were so-called "Dream Books" to help with this. The idea was that if one had had a dream during the night, a number associated with that type of dream could be found in the book. This would supposedly be the lucky number. To my knowledge the only one who ever profited by this was the publisher of the "Dream Book."

If I am not mistaken, the move toward legalized gambling began with Bingo. Bingo was and is widely used in the Roman church in particular to bring funds to the coffers of that body. Mewing this, politic leaders said, in effect, "'If Bingo can raise funds for the church, just think what a lottery could do for the state." So the lottery was born in America, gambling legalized and from there it was but a short step to the casino. Today America has become a gamblers paradise. Not so many years ago Las Vegas was the gambling capital of America. Because of its many casinos and its notoriety it may still hold that title, but today it has many rivals.

There is still no national lottery in this country, but the states have long since seized upon this as a way to replenish diminishing treasuries. Some states have banded together in an attempt to make the prize, the jackpot, ever larger and thus attract more buyers of lottery tickets. When the jackpot gets high, running into the hundreds of millions of dollars, the excitement among the gamblers is at fever pitch and there is a mad rush to buy lottery tickets. The newspapers have a field day when the winner is finally announced. All kinds of questions are asked of the winner not least of which are what will be done with the winnings. The winner, incidentally, suddenly finds all kinds of friends he never knew he had.

In this day, when taxes are being reduced and every imaginable service is being cut, lawmakers may soon find themselves turning to bake sales to balance city and state budgets. Increasingly they must rely on the revenues from lotteries and casinos to keep the state functioning. They have long since learned that the electorate would rather gamble than pay taxes.

Twelve good rules are ascribed to Charles I of England, the last of which is "lay no wagers." He lost his head to the executioner in 1649, but it was not for this reason. Indeed this remains a good rule to follow because, in spite of their popularity lotteries and casinos have been a pitfall for many an unsuspecting gambler who thought he was just gaming.

Volume 52 number 10, October 2003

The word diversity is becoming more and more prominent in our vocabulary. It is used to describe the kind of population we increasingly have in all parts of the United States. For decades America has been thought of as the great melting pot in which people of many different backgrounds are melted together, as it were, to form one American people. The Germans, the Irish, the Italians, the Danes and other European Caucasian immigrants, regardless of background, all became Americans. Oh, it took a while for them to learn the language and, in many cases they sought to preserve their heritage but, by and large, this was now their home and they took pride in it.

There has long been another way of looking at America. Some would insist it is not a melting pot, but a salad bowl: a salad bowl in which the various ingredients each lend their particular flavor to the salad. This would certainly be the preferred description of America today. Schools, churches and other social institutions seek a measure of diversity in order to grow and not be viewed as discriminatory.

It is not strange that diversity is the preferred word in describing the American population today. This country is becoming increasingly diverse to the extent that within the lifetimes of our grandchildren the white Caucasian immigrants will be in a minority and there will be no group numbering fifty percent. At the present rate of growth it would appear that the Hispanic population will exceed others. Immigrants from the Pacific Rim countries, Japan, China, Vietnam, Cambodia, and Korea, who are already numerous on the west coast, will continue to come and will become a significant factor in the population of this country. Muslims from the mideast, in spite of the present antipathy toward them, will make further inroads in the United States. Blacks, who have been here for more than a century, will see their numbers augmented by refugees and others from Africa.

Diversity becomes increasingly obvious as an election period approaches. Then we have candidates and office holders appealing to various components of the salad bowl, often using the immigrant's native language to show unity with them. Diversity will increasingly be seen and felt in matters of religion. The recent flap over installing a copy of the Ten Commandments in a court house in Alabama points up this problem. Food patterns have also changed drastically within the past fifty years. Pizza, pasta and tacos have come to the fore in that time and have become favorite of many in the younger generations.

One can see some strange things growing out of increasing diversity. In Solvang, noted for its authentic Danish food, one finds this served by a

Mexican waitress. In old people's homes, whose residents are of European extraction, Mexican foods sometimes become a part of the diet. In the Des Moines phone book, for instance, ads for Chinese, Japanese, Vietnamese, Mexican and Italian appear to far outnumber those for restaurants serving traditional foods. New England roast beef, Boston baked beans, Southern fried chicken, Midwestern steaks and the many other regional favorites are rapidly giving way to ethnic favorites.

We are, as John F. Kennedy once wrote, "A nation of immigrants." Well aware of this, we accept and even welcome new immigrants. But, if the truth were known, we are not nearly as enthused about diversity as our utterances indicate. The truth of the matter is we prefer to associate with those of a similar background. We prefer them as neighbors, as fellow church members, as our elected representatives. Yes, we know we shouldn't, but we do.

We who are of Danish background give ample evidence of this. Visitors travel hundreds and even thousands of miles to meet at Danebod, Solvang and Menucha to share a few days with those of a similar background and like minds. At home we tend to single out those with whom we have a good deal in common. We do not consciously exclude others, but it is something that happens in the natural course of events. They, by the same token, exclude us. Blacks, Muslims, Mexicans, and others, tend to settle in enclaves where they can share similarities with others of like mind. And, as might be expected, there are mutual complaints and recriminations.

A diverse population means that we are a country of Asian-Americans, African-Americans, Mexican-Americans, Danish-Americans — and one could go on. All too often the first half of the description takes precedence and, as long as it does, America will be a land of great diversity. There is really no such thing as a hyphenated America. One cannot be both African and American or Danish and America. One can be of African or Danish background, but that is not the same thing. As long as the salad bowl continues to grow and does not become a melting pot, just so long will we have diversity and the many problems attendant upon it.

There is a tendency for the press and the electronic media to speak of diversity as if it were a good thing in itself. It is good as far as it goes. It is a fact of American life and most of us are quite willing to accept it, but, rightly or wrongly, it has been my observation that most Americans, of whatever background, do not embrace it. Diversity is a necessary step, but let us not mistake it for the goal.

Volume 52 number 12, December 2003

It is commonplace in many quarters to bemoan the fact that the real meaning and the significance of Christmas celebration has become obscured by the commercialization of the holiday. Not only so, but the shopping period seems to become longer each year. Merchants, by one means or another, tend to foster the period and take full advantage of it. Before condemning the merchant too harshly, however, we must realize that this is a vital part of their livelihood and, to a very large extent the success or failure of their business depends on the Christmas shopping season. We must also reflect on our own role in what may be called the Christmas rush.

Implicit in such criticism of the modem Christmas is the notion that in the so-called old days Christmas was observed with a large measure of decorum and the religious message was in the foreground. In some cases it was, but on the whole, nothing could be farther from the truth. From time immemorial, Christmas has been the basis for celebrations of one kind or another, and some of them have been riotous indeed.

Leaving aside the fact that the exact day or even the month and year of the birth of Jesus is not known, in the early Christian era the Church fathers were opposed to any such celebration. As one of them is reported to have said, it was sinful to observe Christ's birthday "As though He were a King Pharaoh." Nevertheless, as time went on and Christianity became established as the official religion of the Roman Empire, pagan customs and rituals came to be associated with the birth of the Master. Eventually, the date was set at December 25th because this coincided with pagan festivals and the Jewish Feast of Dedication of the Temple.

As the Roman Empire faded from the scene, the holiday did not. Secular elements were added to the festival as it was observed in northern Europe. In England the day was observed with a variety of practices. A bounteous meal appears to have been a consistent part of the observance. Sometimes the guests were entertained by wandering minstrels who sang of the deeds of the national heroes. Hunting, jousting, and gambling of one kind or another became a traditional part of the celebration. Alfred the Great set aside 12 days for the Christmas festival during the ninth century. Following the Norman Conquest in 1066, many great castles were built and the feudal system, with its division of people into classes, was adopted. Christmas became more pronounced as a great festival with food and drink being plentiful and music, games, dancing and caroling being taken in to the observance. The result was that, contrary to the Church fathers, Christmas became the most popular holiday in England during the Middle Ages.

When the Puritans came to power under Oliver Cromwell, all religious festivals were forbidden, but Christmas customs were revived after the Restoration of the monarchy in 1660. Some of the nobles provided lavish Christmas dinner for people of other classes. Some of the earlier excesses were abolished and card playing became favorite holiday pursuit.

The Puritans brought their opposition to holiday customs with them to America, while in other parts of the new world, the descendants of the Cavaliers, in other colonies, continued such practices as had accrued to the holiday in England. This was generally true in the South, with such things as the use of fireworks being added. In the Southwest the Spanish influence made itself felt in still other customs.

In Massachusetts, under Puritan rule, Christmas continued for a time to be a sedate and pious affair with no outward display. By contrast, the Dutch in New York were enamored of Christmas festivities and feasting, coupled with merriment was the order of the day. During the American Revolution, General Washington took advantage of the holiday to cross the Delaware River and attacked the German troops who suffered from too much Christmas food and drink.

Gradually, as immigration shaped the United States, old customs were observed and new ones added until today Christmas is celebrated in a variety of ways. It is marked however, by the prominence of feasting and shopping. The latter has become so pervasive that if one were to characterize Christmas in our time we would have to call it the age of the commercialization of Christmas.

The burden of all this is that it is not just in the present time but that throughout the centuries the Christmas holiday has been celebrated in such manner that Christ has often been lost in the shuffle. Other than rail against the common practice, there is not much, if anything, one can do to, as some would say, "'put Christ back in Christmas.'

In any event, what happens in the world around us is not the determining factor for the individual. We have no right to suggest that their observance of the holiday is any less important because of the traditions and customs others may follow. In the final analysis, the observance of Christmas is an individual matter to the extent that even the most zealous shopper may be more aware of the coming of Christ than the most sedate and pious churchgoer.

Volume 53 number 2, February 2004

The television commercials preceding or during a broadcast are often more amusing and informative than the program for which they provide sponsorship. Automotive commercials have become especially plentiful during the past year or so. I find particular amusement in the many commercials for cars and trucks. What in an earlier day would be referred to as a pickup is now called a truck. Presumably it is more manly to drive a truck than a mere pickup. It should be noted, incidentally, that one rarely sees any evidence of items being hauled in the bed of the truck. Someone once told me that to be a man in a certain state, one must have a truck with the gun rack and a dog. Have truck makers missed the boat by not having a built-in gun rack in their trucks?

Truck commercials generally provide the greatest amusement.

Often they are shown slogging across or through a stream and up a steep and rough mountain trail. Mud is much in evidence, especially on the truck, but regardless of it and any other obstacles the truck pushes steadily on — thus apparently proving how powerful it is. Of course the fact that it should not be there in the first place is not even alluded to. The fact that trucks, mountain bikes and snowmobiles are a serious threat to the environment makes no difference to their devotees. They want to have fun regardless of the cost to nature and the rest of humanity.

In the commercials for automobiles the emphasis is generally on the latest gadgets and upon the power and the luxury that can be the owners. Sport utility vehicles (SUV's) are generally present in greater number, partly because that is what the buyer has to be convinced he wants and both the dealer and the maker can reap greater profits from the sale of such. I have heard various reasons for having an SUV but they are questionable to say the least.

One thing which one seldom hears about these days is mileage ratings. There was a time, after the 1973 oil crisis, that cars became smaller, the weight was reduced and the mileage improved. Some cars could even get 40 miles or more per gallon of fuel. Those days are gone! Today cars are bigger, loaded with gadgets and luxury is in. Mileage has decreased considerably. These days a rating of 30 or more miles per gallon for highway driving is considered very good. Seldom does one see a commercial in which mileage is emphasized, or even mentioned.

If many commercials strike me as humorous, there are some that decidedly do not. I refer to those commercials in which power and speed are emphasized. There is still some question as to whether and to what extent television influences human behavior. Be that as it may, it is not difficult to see a relationship between the emphasis on power and speed in the commercials and behavior on the streets of the city and the open highway. It is ironic that in a time when we can go so far in so little time that so many are in such a hurry. Slow down and live should be more than an empty slogan.

Incidentally, where are the hard times if a man wants a truck or a family wants an SUV. One can't laugh that off.

At long last the Iowa caucuses are over. For months they have dragged on and the last few weeks have been especially intense. Mail boxes have been full, the telephone rings several times a day, polls are taken almost daily and the newspaper has been full of it.

I can see some values in the Iowa caucuses — especially for the hotels, restaurants, car rental agencies, bus companies and merchants generally. My major complaint however, is that the election process has been stretched out to the point where it is almost ridiculous. I suppose it is only natural that as soon as one election is over thoughts should turn to the next one. However, to actually begin to campaign two and even three years before a presidential election is to distort the whole process. It means that there are men and women, including the president, running around the country raising funds and insuring votes. It further means that they neglect the offices they were elected to fill — and for which they are being paid.

Fund raising by candidates is a necessity and long campaigns make it even more necessary. The candidates spent millions of dollars in Iowa alone and this will be duplicated in all states having caucuses or primaries. All this is to say nothing of the spending for the general election in which more millions will be spent. It would seem there are no hard times when an election is at stake.

Fun is the "'in'" thing these days. Caucuses and elections can be fun and more often provide humor, but they better be more than humorous and fun or democracy will go down the drain.

Volume 53 number 3, March 2004

The four hundred year period which roughly began with the end of the fourteenth century is sometimes referred to as the age of the commercial revolution. It was centered to a great extent in and around the Mediterranean Sea. In the fifteenth and the sixteenth centuries this commercialization was given new impetus by the many voyages of discovery and explorations that took place in that 200 year period.

Belief that the world was flat and that those who ventured out could sail off the edge of the world had long deterred exploration. However, by the twelfth century educated Europeans generally accepted the idea that the earth is a sphere. Further, invention of new tools for reckoning positions at sea also made it possible to venture out beyond the known into the unknown. The reasons for wanting to venture out are not far to seek. Trade with the Orient was a monopoly of the Italian cities and the Spanish and Portuguese were anxious to find a route to the Far East that would enable them share in the luxuries that could be imported from the Far East without having to pay tribute to the Italians in the form of high prices. Another reason was the religious zeal of the Spanish. A missionary fervor to convert the heathen contributed greatly to the voyages of discovery and exploration undertaken by the Spanish. Norse sailors had long since sailed to the shores of America, but for some obscure reason this did not become general knowledge at that time. It fell to the Portuguese to become the pioneers in exploring the unknown. Not all of the early explorers were Portuguese of course. Columbus, for example, was rebuffed by them and turned to the Spanish for support. The English, the French and the Dutch also became active in promoting voyages of discovery and exploration.

The result of all this was that the commercial revolution became one of the most important developments in the European world. The power of money became obvious and the age of discovery contributed to the growth of the capitalistic system. Today all parts of the world are known and have been explored, and in many cases settled. By and large, there are no new frontiers on earth. But if there are no frontiers on earth there are plenty of frontiers for further exploration and science has already begun to give attention to these.

The frontiers today are extra-terrestrial and modern science is already busily at work seeking to learn about them and from them. The moon landing in 1969 was a major milestone in the exploration of outer space. The moon was chosen for early exploration because of its proximity to the earth. Now, some 35 years later, the emphasis is upon Mars, millions of miles farther out. Peering intently through their telescopes, scientists have not been able to detect any sign of life on the planet and therefore Mars has long been regarded as a dead planet. The emphasis today is not on finding life but upon learning whether water, a necessary ingredient of life, has ever existed on Mars. The findings of science in this matter will shed light on whether there ever has been life on Mars and, if so, on what happened to it. Further, their findings may help to explain the origins of the universe and of human life.

It is often said that in our sophisticated time we have lost any sense of awe and wonder. So many things that to earlier generations might seem miraculous are taken in stride by we who live at this particular time. Yet the very accomplishment of the many feats of modern science are in themselves ample cause for awe and wonder. Just imagine, from a laboratory in Pasadena, California scientists could choose a spot for landing on Mars, millions of miles away and known only through a telescope. Just think of the fact that they were able to construct, package and send a small vehicle that would be capable of roving and reporting on the landscape. Just imagine that despite the many hazards involved, that the vehicle can be sent to Mars and begin to function. Most of us can just stand in awe and wonder at what the human mind can accomplish.

Now the president has called for further exploration of the universe. This would be a costly venture, especially at this time when there is so little money for so many necessary projects. He has also called for manned space flights to Mars. This would be even more costly, dangerous and, given the present status of the project, even unnecessary. There is so much to be learned from such exploration, not least knowledge about the origins of the universe and of life, giving modern exploration a religious dimension just as the earlier voyages of discovery had. Yes, there should be further exploration of the universe, but not in these times of massive deficits and then only with unmanned space flights.

The voyages of discovery of the 15th and 16th centuries waited on the advances in scientific and navigational fields. Voyages of discovery in the 21st century should proceed no less slowly, securely and safely. A disaster of one kind or another could set back the exploration of outer space for generations. It is better to stand in awe and wonder than in regret and recrimination.

Volume 54 number 9, September 2004

Someone has given me a bumper sticker which at once appeals to my sense of humor and to my position with regard to the forthcoming election.

However, I do not intend to put this on my bumper. One reason is that I do not decorate my car with signs, humorous or otherwise. More importantly, I do not view this election, or any election, as being a bumper sticker election. Neither is it a 15 or 30 second commercial election, nor yet a talk show election. I have no hesitation in saying that those who base their position on such should really not be voting. Such things as bumper stickers and TV spot commercials do not contribute to an informed electorate as is presupposed by a democracy. There are serious and even divisive issues in this election; more so than is generally the case. None of us, of course, is fully informed nor even as informed as we might like to be, but at least we have gotten beyond the bumper sticker and the TV spot commercial phase.

Unless one is completely blinded by partisanship, the view that one gets of the world, and more particularly, of this country is far from reassuring. The founding fathers, men like Washington, Adams and Jefferson, men who willingly pledged their lives and their sacred honor in behalf of the future of this country, would be appalled at the present state of affairs. With the country embroiled in a war with those who hate America dedicated to holding the country hostage to terror; while at home the "haves" are constantly arrayed against the "have nots," our problems are many. Unemployment is rampant; millions cannot afford the medical attention they desperately need and finally, the environment grows more sick by the day and no one seems to care. Coming closer to our own time, one does not need to wonder long how men like Alfred Jensen, Johannes Knudsen or Alfred C. Nielsen would have reacted to the state of our nation today.

Both political parties offer solutions for our present problems. One candidate offers what is essentially more of the same in the expectation that this is the only way to a better nation and world. His opponent offers answers that may sound good but that are predicated on the cooperation of a like-minded Congress. Meanwhile both candidates are engaged in a battle about irrelevancies of the past, when they should be giving more attention to the future. The media, both electronic and print, are at least partly responsible for this state of affairs. It is to their advantage to stir up a good fight.

I make no secret of my own position. I am a good deal less than enthused about the present administration. The secrecy that has surrounded it from the beginning is not conducive of good government. I am unalterably opposed to tax breaks and refunds for those who quite obviously do not need them. The whole concept of preemptive war is anathema to me. The reasons for such a strike should be indelibly fixed in the minds of all, both at home and abroad. History is cluttered with the wreckage of nations that began what they could not complete.

The earth sustains and preserves us; it cannot long continue to be abused and misused for present profit. Global warming is not a problem for tomorrow; it needs attention today. I strongly object to reckless spending and leaving the bill for our children, grandchildren and great grandchildren. I could go on citing things to which I object, but above all, I object to the arrogance with which America confronts the United Nations, born in San Francisco, incidentally. Neither can we casually ignore the rest of the world. Our leaders do not have all the answers and it often appears they do not even know the right questions.

Are we presently more secure? For all of our much heralded efforts, fear is abroad in our land as never before. Periodic, so-called terror alerts, which bear the marks of political motivation, are based on evidence whose age is measured, not in days, or even weeks, but in years. How long must we live as if there is a terrorist hiding behind every light pole?

We, in America have consistently refused to come to grips with the root of the problem - i.e. the reason, the motive, for terrorism. This may show determination and consistency, but in the words of Emerson, "A foolish consistency is the hobgoblin of little minds." Certainly the fault is not all on our side, but we are not completely blameless. No matter how unpleasant it may be, we must begin to give some attention to the motive. Instead, the powers that be have us removing our shoes in airports, which most of us would gladly do if we thought the terror would then go away.

I am well aware that I am taking advantage of my position in writing these lines. Frankly, however, I am not at all sure that the opposition ticket in this election has the right answers, but at least it is an alternative. Personally, I would have preferred to see the bottom half of that ticket at the top. Be that as it may, as a democracy we have started down a slippery slope that can only result in the American dream becoming a nightmare.

Volume 54 number 12, December 2004

On a December night in 1818, Joseph Mohr, the assistant parish priest in the little Austrian village of Obemdorph, was returning home. He had just seen a simple performance of the Christmas story and had enjoyed the hospitality of one of his parishioners. So pleased was he, and so beautiful was the night that instead of going directly home he climbed a small peak near the village and let the beauty of the night speak to him.

Taken together, the events of the evening so inspired him that when he did return home he sat down at once to put some of his thoughts into words. The next morning he took what he had written to an organist friend, Franz Grubber, and asked him to set it to music. By evening the work was finished and thus was created one of the best known and most loved of all Christmas carols, "Silent Night."

When we hear "Silent Night," we know almost instinctively that it must have been born out of a quiet contemplation of the wonders of God. The hustle and bustle that marks so much of everyday life is strangely out of place when the carol is heard. It is, for example, an affront to human sensitivities when "Silent Night" comes blaring out of a loudspeaker at a crowd of Christmas shoppers.

Intense activity is necessarily a part of the Christmas season. A worthy celebration of the festival does require planning and preparation. But, it must not be forgotten that the preparation is not the festival and it must not be allowed to shut out the real meaning of the event.

Somewhere in the Christmas season there must be time to sit back and let the wonder and joy of the event speak to us. One could hardly imagine Joseph Mohr being inspired to write "Silent Night" as he hurried down the street with his arms full of packages.

Christmas is not something that we can absorb "on the run". There is a need to pause and to contemplate the wonders and beauties of God's world. There is a need to ponder the message which came to the world with the Christ child.

Preparations are good and they are necessary but let us always be aware that the real joy of the festival lies not in how well these are attended to. It grows out of the fact and the implications of the birth of Christ.

Bells have long been associated with religion. Even in the pre-Christian era, bells were important factors in religion. In ancient Egypt, bells were rung at the feast of the heathen god Osiris. Jewish priests adorned their robes with bells and they used hand bells in some ceremonies. The priests at Athens used bells. The emperor Augustus decreed that a bell was to be hung in front of the Temple of Jupiter.

So far as is known, bells were first used by the early Christians to call people to worship. "A Saxon king, Egbert, is reported to have decreed that all church services be announced by ringing bells."[1] The ringing of the church bell on a Sunday morning has long been recognized as a call to worship. I have seen Sunday bulletins in which the service for the day was preceded by announcing "the ringing of the Bell." How much better, and more correct to say, "Call to worship."

Bells have often announced sad events also. Deaths have often been, and still are, announced that way. I can recall that in my first parish I often tolled the church bell to announce a death, tolling it once for each year of the person's age.

But, it is with the Christmas connection to the bell that I am here concerned. Though it was not so at the beginning, through the centuries bells have become inseparably related to that particular festal day, to the extent that Christmas would not seem the same without bells. So many hymns refer to bells in many different languages. In the English language one of outstanding hymns is Longfellow's "I Heard the Bells on Christmas Day." In the Danish language it is perhaps Grundtvig's "Kimer, I Klokker!"

Jacob Riis, the noted Danish immigrant of a century ago, tells that in his native town of Ribe, the town band would ascend the tower of the church. Here they then played four hymns, one in each direction. Then the big bells of the church would sound out and Christmas would be at hand.

Puritans, of course, objected to the sounding of church bells and any other indication that Christmas was near. Instead of ringing church bells, a town crier went around town with a strange sounding hand bell reminding people that they were not to celebrate the day. After the restoration and Charles the Second's ascent to the throne, bells again came into use and happily rang out the good news of the birth of Jesus.

In addition to its use in the church and to references to it in hymnology, bells are an important part of the Christmas celebration in other ways. In artwork of all kinds, from the Christmas greeting card to the merchandise displays, bells are an integral part of Christmas.

[1] Krythe, Maymie R., *All About Christmas*, Harper, New York, 1954, p. 125.

Volume 55 number 3, March 2005

Parents often name babies and forget that one day that baby is going to be an 80 or 90 year old person. Imagine a scene in a nursing home where a ninety year old is a newcomer with an odd-ball, cute baby name. Can't you hear the other residents saying, "who." Then, too, some names are dated. One can often tell by a name of a person who was the favorite movie star or football hero of the parents many years ago.

Naming a child is one of the most important and lasting things parents will ever do. A poorly chosen name may well plague the child into adulthood and old age. What parents thought was cute may not seem nearly so cute fifty years down the road. There is an ample supply of both boys and girls names so there is no real need to invent new ones. An invented name tells more about the parents than about the child who must bear it.

In America, nevertheless, we have freedom; freedom among other things to give a name of the parent's choosing a child. To the parents that name might be cute but, as the child gets older, he or she might have other and less kind words for it. Unless certain legal steps are taken, the person is now stuck with that name for life. Freedom implies responsibility and the freedom to name implies a responsibility to look ahead to the adulthood of that child.

In Denmark, the Scandinavian countries, and some others, like France, the naming of a child is a more serious matter. Of the countries named, Denmark is the most strict. The purpose of Denmark's Law on Personal Names is to protect the innocent; innocent children who would otherwise have to go through life burdened by ridiculous or even silly names. Those expecting a child can choose from among 7,000 West European names; 3,000 boy's names and 4,000 girl's names, with the addition of some ethnic names for those from the Middle East. If parents do not choose an approved name they may appeal to their local parish. The final authority rests with the Ministry of Ecclesiastical Affairs. The law applies only if one of the parents is Danish.

In general, the law provides that boys and girls cannot have the same name, the first names may not be last names and that bizarre names may be used only if they are common. Parents may seek to be creative by using unorthodox spellings. Such strange spellings are usually rejected.

An old law, which aimed at bringing order to surnames, had existed for a century or more. The catalyst for change was the furor that attended the use of Tessa for a girl's first name. Tessa is much like "tisse," which in Danish means to urinate.

We will continue to have strange and even silly names in America as long as we have freedom. Freedom is a precious commodity which must be used wisely because there is a price. In this case it is the children who will have to pay the price for their parents' abuse of freedom.

The section on names in Denmark is based on an article in the International Herald Tribune which has come through the courtesy of Carl F. Nielsen.

We are becoming a people addicted to drugs. I refer to those legal drugs which can be purchased in any drug store or even a supermarket; drugs that may, in some cases, be just as harmful. There are also those for which a prescription is required. The drug companies urge us to "ask your doctor" about some drugs. Then usually comes a long list of possible side effects which are often more serious than the ailment that the drug is to treat.

There are drugs on the market that have great value; drugs that may even be life-saving, but there are also drugs of questionable value. The countless TV drug commercials are fast making us a pill popping public who readily diagnose our own real or imagined ailments. "Ask your doctor" is a code word for "tell your doctor." Tell the doctor what you want and, if the doctor is as malleable as the drug companies hope, he or she will accede to your wishes.

Incidentally, the pharmaceutical industry would have us believe that the high cost of drugs is due to the costs incurred in research and development. It is true enough that research and development is costly, but those who have studied the matter tell us that the industry spends much more on advertising. Have you watched TV at news time lately? The ever-present commercials present one new drug after another for your consideration. The pharmaceutical industry hopes that you will conclude that is just the drug you need.

The pharmaceutical industry strives to make us addicted to legal drugs which can cost countless lives and untold dollars. Drug companies, whose bottom line is enhanced by the number of pill-poppers they can snare, are playing fast and loose with the health and finances of the public.

Volume 55 number 11, November 2005

Beauty around us, glory above us,
Lovely is earth and the smiling skies,
Singing we pass along Pilgrims upon our way
Thro' these fair lands to paradise!

In some songbooks and hymnals this song is grouped with Christmas hymns, probably because of the last stanza which refers to the Christmas miracle. It occurs to me, however that it could as well be a thanksgiving hymn. Certainly, if one takes an unbiased look at the world around us one would have to agree that there is beauty around us and that we are greatly privileged to live in "these fair lands." The natural heritage which is ours exceeds any expectations we could have. When contemplated, the wonders of the natural world are indeed cause for thanksgiving. The vastness of our land, its variety and its wonders are ample causes for thanksgiving. There is no need to search for the fabled Garden of Eden we live in it. There is no need to dream of a paradise we have it all around us. Our natural heritage provides us with much for which to be thankful.

Like so many other things that confront us on a daily basis, we tend to take our natural heritage for granted. Not only do we take it for granted, but we often mistreat it. In the human concern with expansion and development, the earth, the good earth, as Pearl Buck called it, is not given much, if any, consideration. Good farmland is often taken for development purposes and houses and highways replace the crops that could be raised, crops that could feed man and beast, crops that could be used for fuel and crops that could provide an income for someone. Streams, rivers and lakes are often polluted to such an extent that they can no longer be enjoyed by the public. The life sustaining air surrounding many of our cities is so polluted as to make it unfit for many who suffer definite ailments. Not only so, but science tells us that this same pollution is contributing to global warming, a warming which will have disastrous consequences for the earth and its inhabitants. In a word, the earth, which provides so much for human care, does not receive much, if any, care in return.

The good earth does get plenty of attention at times of natural disaster. Hurricanes, floods, tsunamis, forest fires, earthquakes and other natural disasters call attention to the earth. Some would even explain these things by calling them "acts of God" - a favorite line of the insurance industry. Whether or not God had anything to do with such disasters is a moot question. From my perspective such an explanation is a simplification which will not bear examination.

The harvest festival was another way of recognizing the good earth. I well remember the harvest festivals which were so prominent in the congregations of the old Danish Church a couple of generations ago. These were especially common in rural congregations. There was generally decorating with com shocks, pumpkins and gaily colored leaves. A festive pot luck meal, followed by an out-of-town speaker, rounded out the program for the day. The purpose was to recognize and to give thanks for the harvest, whether such had been bountiful or not. There is a similarity between the harvest festival and Thanksgiving except that the latter is of a more general nature.

Therefore, be it Thanksgiving or harvest festival, included in the list of things for which you are thankful, should be the good earth, "these fair lands," which are ours to enjoy and to care for.

A word that appears with ever more frequency in the newspapers and in advertisements of many different kinds is that little word FUN. Whatever it is you should have fun doing it, using it and even eating it. Do you seek the necessary credits to earn a college degree of one kind or another? Many colleges now tell you that earning those credits will be fun. Never mind the fact that there will be much hard work involved.

Looking for a new means of transportation. Many a television commercial will tell you how much fun it is to drive a particular model. Sure, driving might be fun, but if that is all, you are headed for trouble. It may be fun to eat pizza, but paying for it may take some of the fun out of it. The item that really caught my attention was the church that advertised its services as fun. Well, maybe, but I can't quite imagine going to a church service to have fun.

I must confess that I get a bit concerned that everything has to be fun. Fun is amusement, sport. Fun is good and is necessary, but life is, as the saying goes, not all fun and games.

Volume 61 number 10, October 2011

The Job Search

There are few things worse for a family than having the breadwinner lose his or her job. Unemployment insurance may tide the family over for a time but it is hardly a long-term solution to the problem. So, the search for a job goes on as the unemployed walk the streets, entering one door after another, seeking the ever-elusive opportunity to earn a living.

Because in these times the situation has become so critical throughout the country, attention has come to be focused on the president. Some of the members of the Congress, who should know better, call upon the president to create millions of jobs.

Yet the fact is that a great percentage of those jobs have been irretrievably lost, thanks to technological advances, advances that have made it possible to eliminate a large number of those jobs. This is true of the sanitation department, a department responsible for garbage collection in Des Moines, Iowa, a city with which I am most familiar.

Prior to the recent change there were three men on each truck, the driver in the cab up front, and two men on a platform at the rear. These men would retrieve the garbage cans or other containers from each side of the street and empty them into a bin from which a mechanical device would sweep them into the main body of the truck. Now the jobs held by the two men on the platform have been eliminated and the driver can do it all.

He drives the truck and operates a mechanical device, powered by the truck's engine, via a power take-off and hydraulics, that enables him to mechanically pick up a plastic container and empty it into the truck. Thus two jobs are eliminated. Multiply that by the number of garbage routes in the city and the saving is great enough to persuade a city council to buy into the change.

Of course the conversion cost is sizeable, but since it is a one-time-only cost it does not figure so prominently. Advances in technology have caused many a similar job loss - jobs that are gone forever. This is not to take a Luddite position, but to suggest that progress has consequences.

The Second Amendment

A great deal has been said and written about the Second Amendment especially by some of those who are hopeful of becoming president. For most part it reveals a frightening ignorance of American history on the part of those who seek a major role in making that history.

For some it appears to be enough to say, "I'm pro Second Amendment."

What is meant by this generally refers to that portion of the amendment which guarantees the right "to keep and bear arms." That phrase is, of course, taken out of context and made to stand alone, thus altering completely the meaning intended.

The entire amendment became a part of the Constitution in 1791 and has nothing to do with America in the twenty-first century.

The reference to a "well regulated militia" is basic to a correct understanding the amendment. In the early 18th and part of the 19th centuries, there was no standing army, though there was an embryo navy. There was no war department or department of defense to supply them with weapons of every kind. They were responsible for bringing their own weapons, which were usually rifles used for game hunting.

This is why the second amendment specifically states that "the right of the people to keep and bear arms, shall not be infringed." As the nation grew and a war department, later called the department of defense was added, the second amendment became largely irrelevant except, it may be argued, people may keep and bear rifles used for hunting game. It does not permit the keeping and bearing of hand guns, AK 47's, and other death dealing weapons. It does not lend support to those who would have this country become an armed camp where every difference of opinion may be settled by a bullet.

Supporters of hand guns and other assorted weapons are fond of saying they are needed for self defense. What they do not say is that carrying such a weapon is the most certain way to be killed. A criminal is not about to give time for another to bring forth a gun.